THE FLIGHT OF THE MEW GULL

BY THE SAME AUTHOR

Sigh for a Merlin

THE FLIGHT
OF THE
MEW GULL

ALEX HENSHAW

JOHN MURRAY · LONDON

First published 1980
by John Murray (Publishers) Ltd
50 Albemarle Street, London WIX 4BD

Printed in Great Britain by
Latimer Trend & Company Ltd Plymouth

British Library Cataloguing in Publication Data

Henshaw, Alex
    The flight of the Mew Gull.
    1. Mew Gull (Racing plane)
    2. Airplanes—Test flying
    I. Title
    629.134'53'0924   TL685.6

ISBN 0-7195-3740-1

30 01

✳ Contents

✳ *Author's Note*

The following account was first written in draft for my family shortly after the Cape record flight, but World War II prevented my adapting it to a larger audience. The detail is exactly as I recorded it at the time.

I am grateful to Dennis Baker for the maps; to Mrs Phyllis McDougall for the index; to *Aeroplane Monthly* for permission to reproduce the technical drawings between pages 302 and 303, and F.D. Bradbrooke's account of flying G-AEXF; to Michael Turner for his magnificent jacket picture; and to all those at my publishers who have contributed so much to the final results.

I would also like to acknowledge the following picture sources: plates 16 and 17, *The Aeroplane* from P.H.T. Green Collection; plate 32, Abelard Photography.

A.H.

❋ Illustrations

To the memory of
MY FATHER
to whom I owe everything

PART ONE: Age of Innocence

1 ✳ *First wings*

I MUST HAVE CAUSED my parents a great deal of worry. The earliest recollection I have of shock was on my mother's face when a policeman came to the door with a summons for Alexander Adolphus Dumfries Henshaw. I think I was nine at the time. I was petrified and immediately thought of my poaching efforts on the railway cutting with my double-barrelled ·410, but from the injured and ashamed look on my mother's face, I guessed it must be something more serious. I had forgotten that two weeks before I had cycled to the cinema in Lincoln, and when I came to ride home in the dark, my lights failed. As it was five miles or more, I couldn't walk, so I took a chance. Unfortunately for me, just when I thought I was in the clear an enormous figure loomed out of the night and grabbed my handlebars, and although I explained to the policeman that my dynamo had failed, he said I ought to know better and wrote things down in a little book. I now looked at this very official document with my name in clear print and wondered what my father would say. In fact he said very little, although he was not at all pleased. 'You want to learn the eleventh commandment,' he said. 'It's one of my own: Thou shalt not get caught.'

I suffered days of anguish whilst my parents discussed who was to take me to court. Then quite suddenly the position came to me very clearly: no one was going to take me; I had got myself into this mess and I would get myself out of it. My mother would not hear of it, but my father, who I think really appreciated my stand, said 'OK, if that's how you feel about it.' I knew the ancient Roman Stonebow very well, but I had not known it was also a Magistrates Court. I sneaked in and hid behind a chair.

Then suddenly huge lumbering policemen seemed to be every-where and they were calling 'Henshaw, Henshaw'. When I moved out of my hiding place, a policeman nearly fell over me and said, 'What are you doing there, sonny? This is no place for you.' 'My name is Henshaw,' I said. The Magistrates were somewhat non-plussed and in reply to their query as to who was defending me, I said I didn't understand what they meant. Then one of the elderly gentlemen on the bench asked me if I had any money. When I said I hadn't, he asked, with a loud guffaw, if I knew the prison sentence for non-payment of fines. Before I could reply, a lady magistrate spoke up sharply and rebuked him for frightening the child. There was a hushed conversation between the Chairman, the Clerk, the policeman who booked me and a senior police officer. I guessed the police were getting it in the neck for having brought me there, as the constable, to my glee, back-tracked from the bench, very red in the face, and the lady magistrate said in a very kindly voice, 'If you promise never to do it again, you can go.'

A few years later my mother looked out of the window, ex-claimed and said, 'There's a policeman coming up the drive!' I couldn't think of anything really bad I had done recently, so I was not unduly worried, but when he said in a loud voice he had a document for Alexander Adolphus Dumfries Henshaw I wanted to die. If only the floor would open up and swallow me. I was so shaken that I did not hear my mother's gasp of joy, or the policeman saying what pleasure it gave him to request, on behalf of the Lincoln County Magistrates, if I could attend an official ceremony to be presented with the Royal Humane Society's award for saving a boy's life in the River Witham the summer before. I remembered the incident well, but was em-barrassed to read the citation and the press reports, and thought they grossly exaggerated the true situation. Inwardly I wanted to say it was not strictly true and there were others involved as well as myself, but I hadn't the courage. The press reports said I dived fully clothed into the river and saved the boy as he was going down for the third time. The true story is that I heard the boy yell whilst I was dressing on the bank. I rushed on to the wooden ferry moored near the edge of the water, and paused to take off my trousers and shoes as they were new, and mother had said she would tan me if I messed them up. When I dived in the boy had panicked and I had a job to hold him up, but did so as I trod water frantically; whilst I was working slowly towards the bank, other boys rushed in and grabbed us both. The most gratifying part of the whole incident to me was when I went again to the Lincoln Magistrates Court and heard, not 'Henshaw' called, but, 'Would Master Henshaw kindly step forward, please?'

During that period of my life, water and I seemed to go together, for the next summer I was at Trusthorpe, on the East Coast, when someone rushed up to me one evening and said, 'There's a dog in the Grift Drain, drowning.' I ran on to the beach right away, and saw a small crowd watching a little Yorkshire terrier being swept back and forth as the tide surged up and down the Grift sea defence drain-run, really a large wooden open-faced tunnel on the seaward side, disappearing into the sandhills as a tunnel to link up with the land on the other side, from which it drained all the water. I knew the tunnel well, for in my more daring moments, and when the tide was going out, I had paddled a canvas canoe down it and out to sea. I realised at once that unless the dog was brought out it would be plunged into the tunnel with a large wave and that would be the end. Everyone was making suggestions how to reach the dog, but no one was doing anything, and the old lady who owned it was crying bitterly. I stood it so long, and then without really being able to help myself I slipped off my shirt and boots before anyone could stop me and jumped into the racing drain. I grabbed the small dog in my hands, waited for a wave to surge me upwards and as I did so held the dog up so that those on the side could reach it. Now I was in trouble, but whereas no one had been doing anything for the dog, several men rushed into action when they saw me in difficulties. By this time I was too near the tunnel entrance for comfort and I was a very relieved boy when two men were able to lean over the drain wall and grab me before another wave surged me under. My father played hell over this incident when he heard, but I could see he didn't mean a word of it, and in any case the pathetic little letter I received from the old lady made it all worthwhile.

My father was a great adventurer. He was one of a very large family, and at the age of sixteen ran away to America, landing with thirty shillings in his pocket. The first winter he spent in a lumber camp, but as the company owning the camp went bankrupt and the weather was bitterly cold, he had to stay there living on bad flour, bilberries and pork. It was not often he spoke of his early days, but when he did I hung on to every word. He trekked off into the Hudson Bay territory and at one time was alone on snowshoes with only a rifle and a little food, and the nearest white man was nearly a hundred miles away. Once he had a huge Scandinavian draw a knife on him, and as he lunged with the knife, my father hit him with all his strength, knocking him out; he took the knife from the inert body and kept it as a souvenir. After a long and often distressing period in which my father said he had never suffered or worked so hard in all his life he met, by chance, an old prospector, who took a liking to him. They had the unbelievable luck to discover a silver mine which enlarged considerably the original thirty shillings he had landed with in America, enabling him to return to England a richer and more experienced man.

I loved to get into an escapade with my father, who sometimes had bright ideas which went wrong. He once thought that a fleet of barges would solve some of the transport problems in his business, so he hired a sea captain to tow three barges on to the Frieston Marshes near Boston. The calibre of the sea captain may be judged by the fact that with a heavy-gauge hemp rope he tied one of the barges tight up to the Boston wharf at high tide and left it; when the tide dropped at least fifteen feet the barge dangled from the wharf with one end under the water like a black sausage on a butcher's hook. We eventually started down the River Witham in the tug, towing all the barges in a string aiming to reach the marshes at high tide, where the tug would run the barges as near to the shoreline as possible; then we would return with the tug to Boston. Unfortunately it didn't work out that way. We got rid of one of the barges, but then as we were going full blast with the next one the tug gave a sudden lurch which flung all of us on the deck into a heap, and we came to a sudden but definite stop. We were aground and there was nothing we could do about it until the next tide. We all went below, but as the boat was at an acute angle the quarters were very uncomfortable; the fire also smoked badly and we began to feel rather like badly packed kippers. My father suggested that we try to walk over the marshes and reach Frieston on foot, but the tug captain said it would be dangerous and wellnigh impossible. We stuck it out for an hour or so, but I could see my father was getting restless and working up to something. Finally he said, 'You stay here, Alex, I'll see if we can reach the shore on foot.' I said I could swim and jump, and where he went I would go. I shall never forget that walk over the marshes, with the tide running out of the almost full creeks and each of us walking over the samphire in the dim light, searching for a firm spot where we hoped we could jump across. If one of us had fallen in I don't know what would have happened, as the creek water was surging out really fast. However, eventually we saw the Frieston bank loom out of the darkness, and with a little more probing we found the local pub and soon had some transport to take us in a very bedraggled state to Boston.

Somewhere between the age of ten and twelve I was burning to do something, and finally persuaded my parents to allow me to take a canvas canoe, with a friend of my own age, from Lincoln to Boston for a week's camping along the River Witham. We couldn't afford a real tent but took along a sheet of canvas, which we aimed to prop up on sticks. We had a sail but found that every time we put it up we capsized. We had enough food on board for a week, supplemented by helping ourselves to the odd meal of potatoes growing in the fields near the river, and I had my faithful ·410 for rabbits and ducks.

The first day was wonderful. The river was like a black mirror, the only ripples were those made by our paddles and the canoe. The only sounds, a skylark high in the sky, or the occasional waterhen disturbed in the reeds as we went silently by.

The first night was fun and we enjoyed our meal, even if we did forget to salt the potatoes. The ground was not as soft as our comfortable beds at home and I do not think either of us slept very much.

The next day dawned fine and warm, but later on an ominous change took place and the blue sky suddenly developed dark, heavy clouds. By the afternoon it had started to rain, so we looked for a suitable place to erect our tent. We found a good spot underneath a large overhanging hedge: at first we were sheltered and no rain fell on to our makeshift tent, so we were quite happy; but as the rain continued it started dropping from the hedge on to our canvas and to our dismay leaked on to us and our blankets. Soon we were so wet that it did not matter whether we were inside the tent or outside in the pouring rain. We decided to strike camp and paddle down the river in the hope of finding a better shelter. As luck would have it, we came upon an old houseboat half submerged and heeling over at an alarming angle. Part of the roof was still on, and if we clung to the deck rail, we could lie on the wooden deck sheltered from most of the rain; but if we let go we fell into the river. Both of us were feeling very wretched, cold and miserable and only our pride kept us from striking for home. The night was for both of us the worst we had ever experienced. We couldn't sleep, and if we dozed off we slid into the water, which we did several times. It rained steadily all night and our canoe, tied up to the wreck of the boathouse, was well down in the water with our blankets gently floating in the bottom.

As dawn broke we were pretty demoralised. We couldn't talk for the wet and cold, we couldn't make a fire, and our food was ruined. Just when things seemed at their worst, the clouds suddenly started to break up, the rain stopped, and within an hour we were warming ourselves in glorious sunshine. From then on we organised ourselves somewhat better. We replenished our stocks at a nearby shop, dried out all our wet equipment, and then discovered that our canvas kept out the water if we did not touch it from the inside. We reached Boston and found a good spot to camp and prepare for our return. That night we made a

large bonfire, and we were enjoying the dying embers before
turning in when we heard movements in the tall grass some
distance away. As it was dark and we could not see, I whispered
to Eric, my friend, 'What shall we do?' I quickly loaded my
·410 and sat in the entrance of the tent with the gun covered by
a blanket. The rustling in the grass came nearer, and then
stopped. We shouted out, 'Who's there?' and out of the blackness
shuffled a tramp with long hair and a beard which covered his
whole face. I cocked the triggers of my ·410 and held it under the
blanket pointed towards him. After asking if we would heat some
water for him in his tin can, he warmed himself for a few moments in front of the dying fire and then went on his way. We
ourselves turned in, but I am afraid neither of us slept much
that night.

The time was approaching when I would soon have to make
up my mind what I was going to do with my life. I was no great
scholar. I hated school, but I loved the wide open spaces. My
headmaster's reports left me somewhat deflated when read by
my father; one of them said I was inclined to be pugnacious. I
thought at the time that this was a little unfair: I always felt that
I didn't go looking for trouble, but somehow it seemed to find me.
I was small for my age, and when an argument started I should
have backed down. Unfortunately, I never seemed to be able to
do this. As the other boys were almost always bigger than me, I
was fair game and I soon realised that unless I could win I was
on a hiding to nothing all the time. What I lacked in size I had
to make up in speed, agility and hitting power, and this I did.
Amongst boys that knew me I was soon treated with a respect un-
called for by a boy of my age and size, and I think we all got on
well together.

At heart I wanted to be an engineer; I always loved engines
and could strip an Austin 7, under my father's guidance, from
the age of ten. I also had a great feeling for the Services, but
doubted whether I was temperamentally suited for such a life.
This is not to say that I was unpatriotic, in fact all my life I have
felt intense emotions towards our Royal Family and the land of
my birth. I have never been able to analyse these emotions to any

real degree of satisfaction. It is true that both my father and my
mother were always loyal and patriotic, but certainly not in a
demonstrative way. It may well be that the seed was sown when
as a boy of seven or eight, I sat at the very desk and in the same
room that Shakespeare once used, and listened as the form-
master recounted details of our struggles in Flanders, the Somme
and elsewhere. When, from my father's shoulders, I saw the first
Lord Mayor's show after the 1914–18 war, it was a sight that was
to live in my memory for ever. To me it seemed that the Empire
of that day was a large family, with typical family troubles,
difficulties and quarrels; but like any good family, when a mem-
ber is in serious trouble everyone else rallies round. When I saw
the parade with the Australians, who did the impossible at St
Quentin; the New Zealanders, probably the best infantrymen in
two World Wars; the Canadians, who took Vimy Ridge at
enormous cost; and so many others from Gurkhas to Senegalese,
from submariners to airmen, all of whom came to our aid when
in dire need, it left me so filled with emotion I was unable to see
or talk.

My father was a businessman with an astute mind, and as such
he saw no great future in the professions, so my future hung in the
balance for a long time. Eventually it was agreed that I should be
an engineer. I was to be apprenticed to Rolls-Royce at Derby and
would try to take a degree at Loughborough University. I was
now at an age when life was a great adventure, full of enormous
expectations. I had no real responsibilities, I loved sport and was
naïve enough to think all my heroes were made of carat gold and
that in the world there were only two types of people, the good
and the bad. My great loves at this time were my labrador dog,
Jock, and my gun, and I would march or sit for hours in any
weather after duck, geese, partridge and pheasant. When I was
told there was a waiting list of two years at Rolls-Royce, I was
not unduly disturbed. I don't think that my father thought the
same way. He had varied business interests in those days, so that
I did the rounds to determine if I showed any particular aptitude.
First I went into his radio business, which was booming with
crystal sets being made and sold in large numbers. I didn't like

that and have never really understood the mysteries of what was then a comparatively new science. I then went into my father's new garage enterprise. This I liked, but as a future business career it did not appeal.

I then moved over to the coast, where my father had a small holiday building concern. I liked this because it gave me a wide variety of practical experience, I wasn't covered with oil and grease all the time, and I had ample opportunity to shoot the moment the season opened. There was one big snag, however. I didn't earn much money. I did not expect my father to give me more than he would other boys of my age, but my expenses were rising, so were my day-to-day requirements. I decided to open up a small business of my own, making concrete slabs, posts, etc. As I stubbornly insisted upon putting in my normal working hours for my father, it meant getting up early in the morning, sometimes at four o'clock, and working late in the evening. I made some money, but it was terribly hard work. My father soon got upset at this way of life and suggested for my last year before going to Rolls, that I should go on to the sales department of his fertiliser business. The area chosen was Wisbech, and my father generously gave me one of the recently designed little two-seater MGs to send me on my way very proudly, with Jock in the passenger seat. I liked the work at once. I met nice people, made good friends and could indulge in my favourite pastime, shooting.

The only part that marred those early days was the depression in agriculture. It saddened me beyond words to see how honest, hardworking people could fail and lose their farms through no fault of their own. At the same time it did a great deal to toughen me up from the business point of view. My job was to sell, but at the same time to get paid for what we had sold the year before. In a depressed market that is not always easy to do. About that time one of my father's chief salesmen got himself into trouble and did a moonlight flit. I asked if I could take over his job on the same terms given to him and my father agreed to this arrangement as a temporary measure until I went away to Rolls-Royce. The new arrangement stirred me into action. I think I had always pulled my weight, and in any case I loved the job, but now I had the smell of success in my nostrils and a responsibility to which I had never before been accustomed. I also had other plans of my own.

Dad had taken me to the Isle of Man TT races for years, and among my heroes were Alex Bennett, Stanley Woods, Graham Walker, and Wal Handley. I admired Bennett's quiet, competent manner and the remarkable results he achieved, but I disliked the flamboyancy of some of the riders like Freddie Dixon. I longed to get my hands on a really fast motorcycle and find out what I could do. My father knew this, and argued strongly against it.

One morning I was taking Jock for a walk along the river bank. The day was perfect, not a breath of wind and not a cloud in the sky. From out of the blue I heard the sound of an aircraft, and then quite suddenly, and for no reason that I could guess other than the pilot being filled with the joys of spring, the aeroplane wheeled in the sky and dived down to the river, flattening out a few feet above the water. I think it was a Bristol Bulldog fighter. It looked marvellous as the slipstream disturbed the calm water of the river and then pulled up into a climbing turn to disappear into the sunshine. I sat down on the rough bank with Jock and began to think. I wondered if my father would let me fly.

Up until that moment I had not given flying any thought at all. Once during a visit to the Brooklands JCC race meeting, Dad had treated me to a joy flight, but this was of such short duration, so cold and windy and noisy that the impression was a poor one. I think it must have been a DH9 and the pilot may have been Captain Barnard. But on this beautiful summer morning as I watched, spellbound, the ripples made by the slipstream died away on the glassy surface of the water, and silence returned broken only by the shrill call of a high-flying lark, I felt a tight burning inside me. It precluded all thoughts of anything else. I must get into the clear blue sky above and explore those enormous white billowy clouds. I knew at that moment I had only one aim, only one desire: I just had to fly.

I had to be very careful in my approach to my father, who was unusually perceptive, so I said to him during my next week-end at home, 'Dad, I have saved up some money and would like to spend it either on a 350 TT motorcycle, or go somewhere and learn to fly.' He paused a moment, and then said, 'I wouldn't spend money on either, but if you must, you will probably find flying safer.' This was all I needed.

The following morning, Dad and I drove to Skegness, where I had seen a flying club advertised. We met M. D. L. Scott and Captain G. A. Pennington, the two principals of the club. Scott was a likeable personality who spent nearly all his time flying. Pennington as a pilot was a product of the tail-end of World War I. There always seemed to be girls about. I shudder to think what my own reactions would have been if my son had suggested he went to such a 'school', but astonishingly my father did not put his foot down to stop me. Basically, it was organised for joy-riding. Tim Scott did much of the instructing, but this was of a most elementary nature, and beyond the solo stage there was nothing very encouraging. A boy could, however, learn many things, if he stayed there, quite unconnected with flying. As there were continual financial crises there was always plenty of excitement around, especially when someone from London was sent up to collect a machine for arrears of hire-purchase monies. However this was the nearest and in fact the only flying club I knew, and I dearly wanted to fly. Rather than pay for my instruction by the hour, I suggested I pay them a lump sum for my flying licence. This rather shook them, but after a trial lesson they were so keen to do business that it was agreed that I should be taught to A-licence standards for £35. The machine was a Gipsy I wooden Moth, G-AAKM, and I started right away. After six hours I was pronounced ready for solo, due, I think, more to the economics of the deal than to my proficiency as a pilot.

As Skegness was not licensed for first solo flights, we had to fly over to be approved by Captain H. Love at Heddon, near Hull. We chose a suitable day and went over in convoy with the other club Moth and another local soloist, Eric Longstaff. Dad had gone over by car and was already celebrating with Captain Norman Blackburn, from the nearby Blackburn aircraft factory, when we arrived. The oral examination prior to solo was always a bit of a joke among pilots at that time, so it presented no difficulty. Eric Longstaff went off solo first and made a nice landing. I followed, but in the meantime the wind had increased and I had to work hard to get in my figure-of-eights over the aerodrome, doing steep turns to keep inside the boundaries. The result was that Captain Love said I was OK, but, in his opinion, overconfident. I didn't want to argue, but I felt far from that.

Before we returned, a disturbing thing happened. While we were all in the clubhouse, a National Flying School black and yellow Moth landed. Love and Blackburn knew the pilot, who had a passenger with him. They were on a day's pleasure-flying in the hired machine and they took off to return to London minutes before us. After we had crossed the Humber, I looked down at the outskirts of Grimsby and noticed masses of people moving like ants to some objective. I pointed this out to Scott over the intercom and after a brief pause I heard him say, 'My God, it's the N.F.S. machine.' I looked again, and what I had taken to be a fairground was the scattered remains of the Moth with hundreds of people milling around it. Apparently, an inter-plane strut had broken, and the aircraft had disintegrated in the air, to fall near what is now Waltham aerodrome.

Tim Scott turned in the cockpit to look at me with a grim face. I felt sick in the stomach and wondered if this flying lark was such a good idea after all. When everyone had returned to the little semi-detached on the Roman Bank that served us as a club-house, the accident which had shaken everyone was pushed to one side. As the two solos were celebrated, mine in tomato juice, and most of the others in something stronger, Pennington said to my father, 'You ought to buy your boy a Moth.' To my astonish-ment my father said, 'Yes, I think you're right.' In less than half an hour Scott rang a friend he knew, who had a Gipsy I Moth for sale, and he said he would bring it up the next day for us to inspect. The outcome of that conversation was that the owner came up and went back with my father's cheque for £300—an enormous amount to me in those days—and I was to collect the machine from Hanworth at the week-end.

I shall never forget the day we went down to Hanworth for the first time. I picked Pennington up at Skegness at six in the morning and we rushed down by road. Hanworth was a beautiful spot in the spring sunshine. It had the unusual feature of having the club and living quarters placed in the middle of the airfield, and set out in lovely surroundings of shrubs and flowers. It was a thriving centre of the aviation social life of the southern counties. Pennington navigated, and, as the proud owner of G-AALN, I flew back to Skegness.

I spent a great deal of time at the aerodrome, in fact every moment I could spare. Several pupils came to take their commercial licences, and I felt rather sorry for them with the limited facilities and the restricted atmosphere that prevailed. Scott and Pennington would do the most outrageous acts. I remember when a man Scott knew came up to hire the club's recently acquired Puss Moth. He arrived in a shining sports-saloon Lagonda, but before flying off in the Puss Moth, he went to great pains to obtain an assurance that his car would be safe in the hangar, and he then carefully locked every door. When he had gone, the sight of the ignition key still in the dashboard of the sparkling Lagonda was too much for Scott and Pennington, so they set about finding out how to open it up. Eventually they were able to ease open one of the windows, and, by manipulating with a piece of wire, release the inside door catch. They then disconnected the speedometer, and were soon on the road to show off their new acquisition to some promising girlfriends. They used the car for three days and then carefully cleaned it up and put it back in its original position. The owner arrived back in the Puss Moth and collected his car, oblivious that it had been put to good use during his absence.

Several of the pupils left before they reached the B-licence stage. One however, whom I shall call Harry, persisted, although I think everyone had given him up as a 'no-hoper'. His grandmother was paying the fees, as his grandfather's dying wish was that Harry should become a commercial pilot. To say the least he did not impress. After solo at some indeterminate stage that was not discussed, his first adventure was to get lost and be

forced to land in a ploughed field a few miles inland. Why he
had not flown eastwards until he struck the coast was not explained. The next, but more serious incident, was to take up a
passenger and in turning over the sea at Skegness to dig in a
wingtip, killing the passenger and writing off the aircraft. There
were many other escapades, but as we moved from Skegness
about that period I lost touch with him. The greatest surprise of
all was to come many years later in World War II, when a friend
of mine said, 'Do you remember Harry? I met him the other
day; he is a group captain and in Bennett's Pathfinder Group.'

I wanted to learn aerobatics, but, other than the loop and
spins, neither Pennington nor Scott could help. I also wanted to
become proficient at navigation, but again, other than a map,
compass and the triangle of velocities, my knowledge was nil. I
think Scott and Pennington must have got browned off with me,
as Pennington told me one day that I should gain experience at
high altitudes, and suggested I should see how high I could get.
I see in my log-book that I made 15,500 ft. To be fair to Scott,
he was furious when he heard what Pennington had foolishly
told a novice pilot to do.

Whilst I was struggling to coax a few more feet out of the
Moth, unbeknown to me Scott and Lewis Tindall, an instructor
at the club, were fighting for their lives on a sandbank in the
Wash. Apparently, Scott was in the habit of flying off with a
passenger to a lonely sandbank or beach on the Norfolk side,
but this time Tindall and Scott said they were looking for seals.
Anyhow, the unexpected happened to their Gipsy engine when
it exploded with a con rod through the side. As the sun was going
down they could see the lights of Skegness but thought they
would have a better chance of force-landing on a dry sandbank,
which appeared to be very near the Skegness foreshore. They
landed safely and waited expectantly for someone to come out in
a boat. When no one did so and as the town seemed close, they
took off their clothes and started to swim for the shore. After
nearly an hour they looked back and saw that instead of reaching
Skegness they were still no distance at all from the Puss Moth
and were being carried southwards by the tide. They struggled

back to the sandbank to find their clothes had been washed away, and that the sea was gradually creeping towards the aircraft. In desperation, they had to act quickly and decided to set the machine on fire to attract attention. As their clothes had gone, and also their cigarettes and matches, they dipped a rag in the petrol tank, and, disconnecting a plug lead, tried to set fire to the rag by turning over the airscrew and shorting the lead to ignite it. They did this until the water was up to their waists and they were both exhausted, with raw and bleeding hands. Then, just when they were about to give up, the rag fired and they flung it into the opened petrol tank. The resulting blaze lit up the sky, and, as luck would have it, a trawler, the *Lizzie Anne*, was operating nearby. Those on board saw the flames and in the nick of time picked up both the pilots, now extremely the worse for wear and nearly dead from exposure.

Although I did not appreciate it at the time, I was becoming bored with the limited type of flying I was able to do. One wet and dreary day I landed on the airfield and the engine of the Moth stopped as I came to a standstill. I knew full well that I should not attempt to start it unless someone was handling the throttle, or I had chocks under the wheels, but as I saw no one was coming out to me, and it was a long wet walk to the hangar, I decided to swing the engine myself. I swung the prop, and the engine started and then stopped. I went back to the cockpit and eased the throttle open a little, then gave it another swing and it stopped again. More throttle. This time as I swung the engine burst into life and the aircraft started to move rapidly forward. I leapt to one side, stumbling on the wet grass, as the whirling blades whistled over my head. I clutched at the leading edge of the port wing as it passed over me, but my hands were wet and muddy from my fall so that I could not get a good hold and it slipped from my grasp. I thought I had lost it altogether, but made a desperate grab at the tailplane and got a more secure hold. I think, but for the wet state of the field, which was covered with pools of water, and the very heavy, now saturated leather coat, I could have hung on until the boy who was now picking his way from the hangar arrived to my rescue. It was not to be, however. As we careered round the field I was almost drowned as we plunged through pool after pool of water, my hands becoming frozen with the cold, and I was mortified to feel myself slowly slipping from the tailplane. The Moth surged away from me in a particularly bad patch of water, when at the same time out of the corner of my eye I could see the boy had missed clutching the starboard wing by seconds. I watched the machine gather speed and to my speechless astonishment it hit a patch of water, turned completely round, and then hurtled back towards us. The boy started to run away, but I got ready to tackle it, rather like a matador crouching for a charging bull. Just when I was poised for my leap to clutch at anything I could hold, the aircraft again struck a puddle of water and veered off at right angles. To onlookers, it must have been like a panto-mime. Each time the machine struck water it would turn. One minute I would be crouched to leap and the next I would be chasing and slithering over the mud to intercept it. The bizarre comedy came to an abrupt finish when the aircraft weather-cocked into wind, ready I thought for the take-off, and then ran into the dyke at the northern boundary of the airfield with a resounding crunch. I was wet, cold and thoroughly dejected and also filled with remorse.

Many times I have looked back at this incident, and although at the time I thought it was the end of the world, I have since felt it was the best lesson I have ever learnt. I do not think I have ever been casual about flying since that day. I learnt to ap-preciate my good luck in those few moments of torture, and from then on my one aim was to strive for perfection in whatever I was doing. In spite of any shortcomings the Skegness Aero Club may have had—and at the time there were probably many other clubs as casual—I am quite sure my basic training was as sound as could be obtained at that time.

Dad was very good when he saw what had happened. Scott and Pennington thought it was a huge joke, but quickly got Blackburns to collect the Moth for repairs, and Lewis Tindall, who had his own Spartan three-seater, said I could fly with him any time. Lewis, in fact, did a great deal to help my remorse. He insisted he wanted someone to help him find a suitable place to establish an aero club at Grimsby, so I spent many hours flying with him over various sites, until we found what is now Waltham aerodrome.

It was some time before my machine was ready to collect, but on 17 July 1932 Lewis landed me at Brough to the sound of sirens and fire-engine bells as a Bluebird spun into one of the Blackburn hangars. I felt sick as we watched the bodies being taken away. Lewis said, 'Just like a bloody Bluebird; a brick would fly better.' Not a statement to inspire confidence in a young pilot. Naturally, I was not allowed to take my Moth away until I had paid for the repairs. This came to £30 more than I had been quoted. I objected to Captain Norman Blackburn, one of the directors, and in his jovial, back-slapping Yorkshire way he asked why didn't I swop my machine for a brand-new Bluebird: and he wouldn't charge me a penny. I had enough humour left in me to say that I didn't think my father would like the funeral expenses. I was then taken to the main office to see Charles Blackburn, his brother, who appeared to be very upset at my dissatisfaction with the account. He said they had never had a disgruntled client before, and made quite a ceremony of recording my views in the company ledger. But I still had to pay the full amount. Lewis Tindall waited for me so that we could return in loose formation: he had asked me to tea, and I was to follow him into a field on the outskirts of Grimsby near his house. When he had landed I thought the field was too damned small, and it was next to a cemetery; as I touched down in what Lewis said was 'a spot-on landing', I thought what a hell of a day to start flying again.

2 ※ *Dad takes to the air*

THAT YEAR Scott and Pennington organised an air-display and race meeting. It was a great success and I saw for the first time some of the aviation personalities invited to attend. I also entered my first race. I was to take off at the same time as another Moth flown by Tommy Lipton. At the moment of take-off the wind changed to broadside and I saw Fred Rowarth, the starter and handicapper, looking a little apprehensive; but the race had started and he flagged us off. As I gathered speed I couldn't control the crosswind, the airfield was small, and I had the four-storey Royal Oak Hotel to climb over near the airfield boundary. The wind was forcing me to starboard, and as I glanced over my right shoulder I looked right into Tommy Lipton's cockpit: it was the first time I had ever been able to read the ASI of one machine whilst flying in another. (Unbeknown to me, Lipton had done about the same amount of flying as I had, and when we discussed the incident years later it was to find that he had cursed me just as I had him.) I came last in the race and my engine was losing power. The next day the ground engineer spent hours on checking it over, but could find nothing wrong. It so happened that the club had recently engaged Jack Humphreys, a well-known ground engineer, who had flown with Amy Johnson on her flight to Japan, and he arrived as I was pondering what to do about my engine. Jack and I got on well from the very start. He quickly checked things over, ran the engine on full throttle, and said, 'Take the exhaust pipe off.' We did so, and found the muffler inside had corroded and collapsed, almost blocking the exhaust pipe itself. We cut the muffler out and from then on I had no more trouble with loss of power.

My father had by now become enthusiastic about flying and wanted to take instruction. It was agreed that I should give him primary dual instruction in our own machine, and then he would take a final course with the club. This worked out very well, but once nearly ended in disaster. Dad had got to the circuit and landing stage, and we had been using a long and narrow field near the aerodrome, because there was no traffic and it was dead into wind and the ground was a little smoother. One day we had carried out about four landings and take-offs with Dad in the pilot's cockpit and me in the front passenger seat with dual controls. Dad's flying had been all right until the last circuit, when he was yawing about all over the place. I said over the intercom, 'Keep the bloody thing straight.' He was about to reply when I glanced back and saw the sternpost and rudder leaning over at an alarming angle, and moving slightly as the rudder bar was used. Dry in the mouth, I said as quietly and as calmly as I could, 'I'll take over, Dad.' Dad thought I was fed up with his flying, and was blaming the machine. I said nothing, but concentrated on going down as evenly and smoothly as I knew how without turning. Fortunately the air was calm and I went in to land from where we were, down wind, switching off the engine as the wheels touched ground. 'What the hell did you want to do that for?' my father shouted. I said, 'Take a look behind you.' The rudder had collapsed at the longeron supports, and the only thing that kept it from leaving the machine altogether were the steel control cables to the rudder bar. My father looked at the crumpled tail and then at me, and after a pause said, 'My God.' It was late in the summer, when the clay soil of Lincolnshire was badly cracked and as hard as concrete, and we had a tail skid on the Moth as opposed to the tail wheel. The combination of all these factors must have contributed to the structural failure.

Dad was forty-five when he went solo, and it was a very good effort on his part as it was unusual for anyone of his age to learn to fly. He hated flying on a compass course, particularly on a sluggish northerly bearing. Even years later he found difficulty, as I well remember from a flight back from Heston. Dad had wanted to take the controls of the Leopard Moth, so I sat in the back seat and read a book. When I saw Ely Cathedral go past on the starboard side I knew we were nearly home, and closed my eyes for a nap. About twenty minutes later I opened them again to see if our airfield was in sight. I could recognise nothing, and as it was near dusk and getting a little hazy I thought we might have flown west of course over country with which I was not familiar. To my astonishment, the next moment I saw Ely Cathedral being passed on the port side. I tapped Dad on the shoulder and said, 'Why are you going back to Heston?' He replied, 'Don't talk so bloody silly; I'm dead on course. There's Ely cathedral.' I leaned forward, tapped the compass, and said, 'You're on a direct reciprocal.' He said, 'It's this bloody compass. It never was any good.' Dad's memory and knowledge of the British Isles was really fantastic. Many times, particularly in bad weather, when we would be groping our way to some aerodrome or other, and I would be uncertain of my exact position, he would lean over and say 'You're all right, son, I know that pub down there. If you turn right at the next crossroads, that will bring you right on to the aerodrome.'

I still had my hankering for a fast motorcycle. I borrowed one of Tyrell-Smith's old TT bikes from a local amateur TT rider, Austin Monks, and during the summer used it to get out at dawn and chase all over the countryside at racing speeds. In those days it was rare to see anyone on the road at that hour in the morning: I used to hide the bike in our stables, and push it away from the house for starting, so that my father would not hear. I was caught out, however, when going down Keal hill at well over 100 mph; the engine seized up and I was lucky to grab the clutch in split seconds to save me from a nasty spill. Even so, we left a deep black tyre-mark 40 yards long down the middle of the road before I was able to throw it out of gear. As I was now stranded, I had to ring up my father to collect me. Needless to say he was not very pleased.

I was now working hard and achieving such results that neither Dad nor I mentioned the Rolls apprenticeship. I had gone cold on it because I was now earning more in a month than

I would in years at Derby or Loughborough, I was also ambitious and flying was expensive.

At the Skegness race meeting I had met Nick Comper,* managing director of the Comper Aircraft Company, and admired his little single-seater Comper Swift. I suggested to my father that I could put some money towards one if he would loan me the balance. To my surprise he willingly agreed and I went down to Heston to see Eady, the sales director, and place the order in time for the 1933 King's Cup Air Race. The basic price was £550, but I had the machine specially faired and cleaned up for racing so that it cost me a little more. The idea was that Dad should use the Moth now he had gone solo, whilst I flew the Swift in various races. It did not however work out quite like that.

I took delivery of my Swift, G-ACGL, on 6 June 1933, the day of the Hendon Air Display. It rained solidly all day with low cloud and bad visibility. I was anxious to get home in my bright new red machine, and get in some flying practice. I was able to do this only much later in the day, but not before nearly flying into Harrow church as I groped through the murk. I loved the Swift: it was like putting a pair of wings on to your back. The only doubtful part was the Pobjoy 75 'R' engine, a beautifully designed and constructed piece of machinery, but a little fragile in the sense that it was not always reliable, as I soon found out. After familiarising myself thoroughly with the flying characteristics of the Swift I flew over the whole length of the King's Cup course, noting points for navigation. My engine had started to use oil and was smoking badly, so I went back to the Comper works at Heston. They were not very helpful: other than changing the oil pump, which did nothing to cure the trouble, they said I would have to leave the machine with them for a few days. As

---

* Nick Comper was a quietly spoken, gentlemanly ex-RAF officer with a flair for aircraft design as well as being a first-class pilot. The most famous of his designs was the Pobjoy Swift, and from that he went on to design and produce the Mouse, the Streak and the Kite before his company closed down in 1934. I always thought that Nick would have a tremendous future in aviation, as certainly the little Swift was one of the most delightful aircraft I have ever flown. Inconceivably, however, Nick died at the early age of forty-two in June 1939 as the result of a tragic misfortune.

the King's Cup race was only two days away, I was dejected and demoralised. Nick Comper was sympathetic and sorry about the engine, but blamed Pobjoy's, and it was obvious that as I was a nonentity it was no great loss if I did not fly in the race. He did however ring Pobjoy's Hooton works and they said they were sending their chief engineer down to Hatfield the next day especially for the race.

I flew from Heston to Hatfield in a cloud of smoke, oil streaming down my beautifully polished fuselage. When Jack Knowles, the chief engineer of Pobjoy's, arrived from Hooton he swung the engine over and said laconically, 'Scraper rings and we can't strip and assemble in time for the race.' My father, who was standing by, said, 'There's no such word as can't,' and started to galvanise people into action. De Havillands let us use their workshops; I rushed off in the Moth for spare parts; and Knowles and his mechanics worked through the night to dismantle the engine. Early the following morning the Swift was pushed out for an engine run; it gave full power without a trace of smoke, but Knowles was not too happy. 'They smother these engines with inhibitor all over the place when they pack them in crates and I shall also have to check the valves after every lap,' he said. I was happier—the Swift was at least on the starting line—and I spent every minute I had to spare cleaning the machine so that it sparkled like the jewel I thought it was.

In those days it was a little unusual for a race pilot to work on his own machine, and as I was taken for a mechanic I overheard many snatches of conversation, not all of them complimentary. The most biting were from the schoolboys: 'Look at this smashing Swift,' I heard a group shout. 'Number 6,' another one said, 'Henshaw. Never heard of him, he's no good. Let's find Wally Hope's machine: that's the one that's going to win.'

As I polished the chromium exhausts with a mixture of chalk and liquid ammonia, an elderly gentleman was peering closely into my cockpit, and I asked what he wanted to know. He said he did not know much about aircraft, but he was having to learn. I asked him why, and he replied, 'I have just entered three Tomtits in today's race; do you think they will do any good?' I

said, 'You must be Sir William Morris. I am afraid this is my
first big race, so I am not the best person to ask.'

At that time I was confused and bewildered by all the tremendous activity around me. I was unknown, so that although I
was not involved in social commitments, I was terrified of making
a fool of myself and putting up a bad show in the race ahead. I

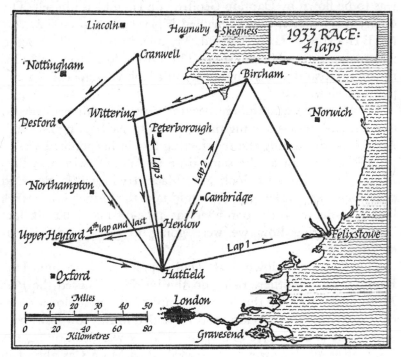

King's Cup 1933: total 830·80 miles,
4th lap was two circuits

concerned myself with the pilots against whom I had to compete
and who had great reputations. I watched in particular Flight-
Lieutenant E. C. T. Edwards, who had a similar Swift to my
own, but who had several minutes start on me in handicap because of my machine being specially cleaned up and faired for
racing. Both the Edwards boys, Spinks and Jumbo, were excellent pilots, and in later years I was to race against them many,
many times. I often think back to them now, especially as I

C

watch Jumbo Edwards train the Oxford Boat Race crew on the Thames. W. L. Hope was also to be watched, having won the race more times than anyone. It was rumoured that De Havilland could pull something off as they had two new designs in the race. The Leopard, a replacement for the Puss Moth, which had had a very good record but which was structurally a little unsound, was to be flown by Captain Geoffrey de Havilland himself. The other, the Dragon, a twin-engined biplane, was to be flown by the DH test pilot Hubert Broad. My own instructor, Tim Scott, was racing the club Puss Moth. There were in fact seven Swifts in the race, so that my chances didn't look very good from any point of view.

Suddenly the atmosphere became feverish with excitement, and I found myself taxying the Swift on to the starting line with Mr Reynolds holding the red starting flag in his hands. I was to go off on this lap at the same time as Angus Irwin in a Puss Moth. Seeing the tense look on my face, Irwin had kindly, and probably wisely, asked me if I would take the inside position: we had a 90-degree turn soon after the take-off and I had in fact been wondering how we were going to get round without colliding.

The flag went down with Dad on one wingtip and Jack Knowles on the other. Being on the inside, I ignored the Puss Moth as we rose for the turn and pushed the nose down on to course. With a slight beam wind I decided to stay low down and aim at the church spire of a village I knew was dead on course. I was distracted, however, as Irwin's Puss Moth was almost in formation with me on the starboard side, and his passenger kept up a running commentary with his hands and face, which I found most disconcerting. I knew I must not rely on the Puss Moth's navigation, and it needed iron discipline to ignore it completely. Also, we were so close I had to keep an eye open all the time in case we collided. The strange thing is that we held this position all the way to Felixstowe. Then my plan was to climb to 1000 ft to take advantage of the slight tail wind, I did this on a fairly sharp turn and suddenly found myself on my own. Irwin was just as puzzled as I was when I discussed this with him later. As he said, 'Nothing altered in my machine, but from the turn onwards you slowly but surely pulled away from me.'

I saw no one else on the run to Bircham Newton, and, as I pushed the nose down into the upwind leg back to Hatfield, I saw away in the distance the Dragon with Broad and eight passengers on board. It seemed an age before I caught up with him, but having Ely Cathedral as an excellent course marker I really got down to some low, concentrated flying. The excitement was great in the Dragon as I came alongside almost underneath the cumbersome twin. Again I forced myself not to look at the passengers gesticulating to me, and slowly pulled ahead as Hatfield began to draw near. Dad and Knowles and a few others who had taken a mild interest in me were elated when I landed: I was fourth in my heat, but there was still a long way to go. One of the Swifts, ACBY, flown by Johnnie Walker, had already crashed without serious injury to the pilot, but according to the experts on the ground the race was still open. My next heat went without incident, except that I was nearly misled by another Swift. I saw this machine miles ahead, but some distance off my own course. I was convinced it was Edwards, and, knowing how much better pilot and navigator he was than I, nearly convinced myself that I was off track and should follow him. Fortunately, I had followed the route almost field for field and hesitated as I did so, and then I suddenly saw the other Swift turn and come back to the course on which I was flying. As I passed him easily I saw it was ABJR, flown by Bannister, who later that year was to be lost in the Channel in a DH Dragon. This time, when I landed at Hatfield, I had a job to get out of the machine for the people crowding around me. It was rumoured that I was going to be up with the winners and there was wild betting on the next heat prior to the final. Tim Scott had run out of petrol and had landed near the Clock Hotel; I mildly wondered who the pretty barmaid was.

The next heat was the eliminator for the final and I was tensed up. Again, on this heat, I saw and passed another Swift. I noticed it as we approached Desford and had a few jittery moments when I realised that unless I reduced speed we were

going to hit the turn together. As reducing speed was quite un-
thinkable, I came beneath the other Swift and inside. I looked
up to see it was ABWE flown by Neville Stack. I never saw him
again, but Stack complained to Nick Comper later on that I had
left him standing. I really got down to it on the way back, and
with my wheels touching the leaves on some tall trees near
Northampton I gave myself a lecture for being so stupid. When
I landed, however, there was jubilation; I was first in the heat,
a certain for the final, and a possibility as a new King's Cup
winner.

Waiting for the final was excruciating. I only wanted to think
about my engine and my navigation, but I couldn't get a moment
to myself. People I had never seen before came up as old friends,
pressmen and photographers were all over me, and of course
Dad was having a ball. Everyone was asking him where I had
come from, and where I had been trained. Dad loved to tell one
story of a pilot who said, 'I don't care where he comes from, but
the b . . . passed me as if he was on rails.' When I did find time
to work things out, I reckoned the only way I could win was if
one or two of the others got lost or had engine trouble, and as
there were seven left, this was unlikely.

And so it turned out. The finish was close, but it was a clear-
cut victory for Geoffrey de Havilland in the Leopard Moth. I
had, however, won the coveted Siddeley Trophy, having covered
830·8 miles at a speed of 127·78 mph, some ten miles or so
slower than the winner. It was an overwhelming day for me. I
couldn't get away from the press people and the photographers.
C. G. Grey, the king of the aviation press in those days, and also
Editor of the *Aeroplane*, was very kind. He said, 'You are the
youngest pilot ever to win the Siddeley Trophy. We have never
heard of you, and it is not often we see a King's Cup pilot
working on and cleaning his own machine.' C. G. Grey was to
give me a great deal more moral support over the many years
until his death in the 1950s.

Nick Comper came up to me breathless saying, 'Magnificent,
a really splendid show.' All his indifference had disappeared, and
as an older pilot he knew that my Swift had been so near winning

the race that a little more effort on his part, a little more assistance on such things as airscrews, spinners, or even a different
tailskid or tyres could have won the day.

My name was called over the aerodrome loudspeakers to come
to the rostrum for the presentation. I squeezed my way over,
through the milling crowd, but the police, seeing a boy in over-
alls, not too clean, would not let me through. Commander
Harold Perrin, the Royal Aero Club secretary, saw me and
barked at the police to stand aside. I was then greeted by Sir
Francis MacLean, Lord Gorell, Captain Geoffrey de Havilland
and Bill Styran, runner-up in the race. From the comments one
would have thought I had won the King's Cup, and not Captain
de Havilland. It was all very heady stuff for a young boy, and
perhaps I may be forgiven if I became a little drunk on it.

I never forgot the friends I made on that day, however. Joe
Scholes, the National Benzole aviation manager, was the only
petrol rep to have bothered with me before the race, and I
never used any other petrol until 1938, when I had to go to a
higher-octane fuel which National Benzole were unable to produce. The same applied to Leonard Morgan, the KLG plug
manager: I never used any other brand of sparking plug. A
gratifying side issue of the race, but important, quite apart from
the huge trophy, was the prize money and various perks from
advertising which I turned over to my father, and I was soon well
on the way to clearing my debt. I could now think of nothing
else but racing.

To my surprise I had in some small way become a local ex-
hibit, and all sorts of people looked me up as if they had known
me all my life. I was working on both the Swift and the Moth at
Skegness one afternoon, when one of the mechanics brought
around a motorcycle to show me. 'Timed at over 100 mph at
Brooklands,' he said. 'The Ariel has never been made that could
do a hundred,' I retorted. 'I'll bet you a pound it will. Try it,'
the mechanic replied. I took the motorcycle on to the Roman
Bank road, a straight run which went beside the airfield, and to
my surprise on the first run I nearly touched the hundred before
I had to brake for a corner. I made the return run, this time

accelerating more fiercely, and was just building up to maximum speed without a soul on the road except a car coming towards me on the correct side—one second I had a clear run, the next I was horrified to see the car turn broadside on the road, completely blocking my path.

There was one terrifying moment before I could even touch a brake or swerve, then I hit the car amidships. I have a hazy recollection of trying to crawl up off the tarmac road with one arm limp, which I thought at the time was broken, to hear in a misty background Lewis Tindall fighting with the man who had been driving the car. Apparently, he had not seen me, and I had knocked his car off the road some thirty feet or so into the adjoining gardens. The motorcycle, a tangled mass of metal, could easily have been placed inside a small dustbin. One of the club members took me along to the hospital and a nurse patched me up at various places from top to toe, but as no bones appeared to be broken I refused to stay. I was very angry with myself, and was determined to make light of the matter. Friends helped me to put the machine away in the hangar and I then insisted on driving myself home alone. I shall never forget that drive; it was only fifteen miles but I had to hang on with everything I had; I never knew until then why people ask for water. Near the village of Mumby I knew I was going to pass out unless I had a cold drink. I lurched to a stop, staggered up to a cottage and sank on to the doorstep until a kind old lady brought me a glass of water. Revived a little, I crawled back the last few miles in the car to my father, who had been told over the telephone and was waiting for me with the doctor.

For the remainder of the summer there was a race meeting at some place or other each week-end. I entered for every race and my luck continued. Life had become very pleasant, and Dad and I enjoyed the new environment in which we found ourselves. As a newcomer, and only a boy, the reputation I had suddenly inherited as a result of the King's Cup race was constantly on trial, although it did pave the way for us very smoothly. I found myself among good friends most of the time, but became conscious there were others waiting the opportunity to crack me down.

Aviation attracts a wider and more varied cross-section of humanity than any other sport in which I had yet participated. I think I know, or have known, some of the finest and most remarkable personalities it is possible to meet, and yet at the same time there have been others who could only be described as the dregs of humanity. I found that at each meeting those with mutual interests soon established a common bond and drifted into small groups, because they genuinely liked one another or were interested in what they had to say or do. I was no exception, and even after forty years those who are still alive are my firm friends.

My next big race was the London to Cardiff, and I was pipped at the post by Bill Styran in his Leopard Moth, the same machine that he had used in the King's Cup. I was learning many tricks of the trade, but at times was over-keen. I won the Round the Ridings race, only to be told I was disqualified for missing a turn. I certainly had not missed the turn, which was the centre of Brough aerodrome, but I did admit that my wing might have been in the centre of the turning circle and not on the outside rim. It was a bitter and expensive lesson, but I learned it well.

The next day was the Round the Houses race, a short triangular circuit with church spires as the turning points. In the heat I came second, and had adopted an Immelmann type of turn as the circuit was so short and this meant approaching the turns at a low level, pulling up into a vertical climb, and then peeling off to rocket down on to course. It was exciting and one had to be alert as there were five other competitors, and on the final lap we were all bunched up together so that it was every man for himself.

I was on the starting line for the final when Fred Rowarth, the official starter and handicapper, came over to me and said in a fatherly manner, 'Alex, I shouldn't go in for those turns if I were you; we tried them out very thoroughly for the last Schneider Trophy race, and we found they were slower than the orthodox turn.' I thanked him and followed his advice. I thought I couldn't possibly win anyway, as a Miles Hawk, which had beaten me in the heat, was now in the final without any change of handicap. To my surprise, when we bunched on the final turn, I was a few yards ahead of the Hawk and was almost line abreast with two Moths in an exciting last-minute mêlée as the airfield came in sight. I crossed the finishing line first, but with only yards to spare. Elated, I landed and taxied over to Dad, who had a box of cleaning materials I'd given him to take care of. I then set about polishing the Swift, with my father helping, in time to enter the machine for the *Concours d'Elegance*. The Swift won second prize, so that all in all Dad and I could say we had had a very good week-end.

As race after race continued throughout the summer, all at full throttle and maximum revs, I was very happy with my little Pobjoy 'R' engine and began to be a little sceptical about all the doubting Thomases who had offered so much free advice and warnings. My complacency was shattered during the London to Newcastle race. I had been flagged off from Brooklands aerodrome into a head-wind to Newcastle, the weather was good, and I was clipping across the downs near Dunstable when it happened: the engine with many protesting bangs and explosions lapsed into a rather frightening silence. I had never done a dead-stick landing over strange country before, and I frantically twisted around in the cockpit looking for the most likely place to put down. I had little choice and less time as I glided towards what appeared to be a level piece of grass on a hillside. My approach speed was normal but I had not calculated for the gradient. I judged the approach all right but when I flattened out without any power there was insufficient speed to lift the nose up the hillside. The result was a fairly heavy landing and an abrupt stop. Fortunately, the only damage was to one of the balsawood axle fairings. After a long walk to a post office near Tring, I was able to telephone Brooklands Aviation, and they promised to send someone out right away. Not long after I had returned to the machine I heard the sound of a Moth and it landed fairly close to where I had been standing waving my arms to indicate the best spot. The pilot was Bill Thorne, and the ground engineer Chris Bancroft. Thorne had to use a lot of engine to put his machine down and still had to keep the power

on to stop running backwards down the hill until he had taxied
to a more level spot near my Swift. Bancroft knew his stuff on
the Pobjoy: the ignition timing had slipped, and it was not long
before he had the engine running and I was able to do a somewhat unorthodox downwind, downhill take-off.

As the summer came to an end; so did the various race meet-
ings. I had had a wonderful run, far beyond my greatest expectations, but it had created one big problem. My father was
not really able to join in most of the time, as he came by car and
left the Moth in the hangar. We both thought the answer was a
fast two- to four-seater of some sort, with an eye to the racing
side, but at the same time suitable for travel abroad.

I was very keen to get overseas experience. I had made only
one trip abroad, in April before taking delivery of the Swift. It
had been a short, sharp experience, but well worthwhile. I had
made Lyon in the first day, which was considered quite good in
a Gipsy I Moth, but was dismayed to find out how quickly my
money was evaporating on fuel, food and incidentals. In fact,
although I had intended to go as far as Milan, I soon realised
that unless I returned without any more night stops, I should be
out of money. The weather was wonderful, with the freshness of
spring in the air—that is, until I reached the English Channel,
when it turned out to be cold and foggy. I made two attempts to
reach Lympne but in the end was forced to turn and land at St
Inglevert. I was now in an embarrassing situation; I had only
ten shillings left in my wallet. St Inglevert was cold, lonely, and
just a large grass field, a relic of World War I days. The most I
could get out of the solitary attendant was that Calais was
20 km away, and that there was a small hotel down the lane
from the aerodrome, at the point where it joined the main road.
A smart walk down the country lane soon brought me to a
decrepit-looking building and I hesitated before going inside.
The feel of my thin wallet however made up my mind for me. I
entered and faced a well-built man talking to a filthy-looking
peasant, and I couldn't decide if it was the cow-dung on his
rubber boots or the man himself who exuded such an unpleasant
odour. In my schoolboy French I asked if there was accommoda-

tion available, and out of the corner of his mouth the man said to the peasant, 'Le petit Parisien.' I didn't like the jibe, but let it pass, and then to my astonishment he said, 'Well, cock, what can I do for you?' I told him my difficulties and rather lamely said, 'I can only give you ten shillings in English money.' As it turned out, I had the best meal since I had left home, a clean and comfortable bed and a firm handshake when I left, with the words, 'Pedlar Palmer will always welcome a Britisher. You come and see me next time you are this way, you'll always be welcome.' When I got home and described the man and the incident, Dad said, 'Well I'm damned. That must be Pedlar Palmer, the boxer. He killed a man in a contest and left the country.'

3 ✳ *Friday flight*

AS THE AUTUMN approached, flying began to ease off, mostly owing to the weather and the cold. I was delighted therefore to read about the proposed Oasis Race in the desert near Cairo, to be held at Christmas. I persuaded my father to let me enter the Swift, and he arranged to go out by steamer. I soon started to make preparations, the first of which was to fly over to Hooton and have the engine top-overhauled by Pobjoys. This seemed to start a run of misfortunes for me. On the way to Hooton I noticed that the starboard tyre looked an odd shape, and peering at it more closely, I decided that it must be punctured. As the tyre was of the doughnut type, and the wheel itself exceedingly small, I was not happy with the prospect of landing. When I arrived at Hooton I circled several times to make them aware something was wrong, and then decided to land crosswind on a slight turn so that the weight of the machine would be thrown on to the sound wheel and tyre. It was as well I did, for when the full weight of the machine finally settled on both wheels the punctured tyre was torn off and the small sharp hub dug into the soft grass. The Swift lurched to one side, started to go over on its nose, and finally settled back with a heavy bump on to the tailskid.

I stayed until the engine was overhauled and then took the machine up for a test flight. I have always made a practice of using as much of an aerodrome for take-off as possible, no matter how large. It was fortunate in this case that I did so. The Swift, with the freshly tuned engine, took off well and I was airborne before the middle of the aerodrome, but when I was about fifty feet up, the engine cut dead. In those days, polo was played on a section of Hooton aerodrome and, as this was beautifully kept, aircraft normally avoided the area. I did not have sufficient room to continue straight on as it would have put me into some trees, but by turning slightly I was able to land on the polo ground without damage. Pobjoy and Knowles, who had been watching me, rushed over by car and there was an uncomfortable silence while the trouble was diagnosed and put right.

The range on the Swift was between 350 and 400 miles, so that when all the formalities had been cleared and the maps prepared, I decided to go via Sicily and the North African coast and to leave in plenty of time. Learning from my previous experience, I carried a fuel carnet and traveller's cheques so that I was not likely to be bothered by financial problems. My date of departure was Friday the 13th of December 1933, at first light on a cold, windy day from Heston. Dad strapped me into the cockpit, we agreed to meet at Shepheard's Hotel, Cairo, and off I flew full of confidence. My first stop was at Lympne, and, although I am not superstitious I began to wonder about this Friday the 13th business. It was cold, the flight was unpleasant, and the wind had increased to such an extent that I was glad to land behind the shelter of the tall trees as I dropped into the customs area at Lympne.

By the time I had crossed the Channel the wind had increased to gale force. I was being thrown about all over the place, and, although I told myself it was my imagination, I thought I detected a change in the note of the engine. I also found that my navigation left a great deal to be desired. I had prided myself that I could fly a course spot-on, but I soon realised that it is one thing to have a large-scale map, good weather and calm conditions, and another to have maps without much detail, small in scale, and the machine bucking like a bronco in a rodeo, with the compass needle swinging wildly from one side to the other. In fact it got so bad that the maps shot off my lap, fell on to the cockpit floor, and with each violent bump shot into the air with me making frantic grabs to stop the slipstream sucking them overboard. It was becoming colder, I was tired of fighting with the machine to keep it straight, and after an hour's flying I had no idea where I was. I tried hard to pick out any good landmark on my map, but it was almost impossible for me to focus, and without shoulder harness I could not possibly have held on.

It became clear that not only should I soon need some petrol, but I was completely lost, and in this gale I was going to have difficulty in getting down. I gritted my teeth, cursed myself for navigating badly, and pushed on hoping something would turn up to indicate my position. I was out of luck; my petrol gauge was reading low and I had to find a place to land. I needed somewhere near a garage for petrol, near a post office to send my father a cable, and, most of all, I must land without damage. All this seemed a tall order at the time, but I spotted a small town where on the outskirts there were woodlands with grazing fields in between. I chose what I thought the best of these fields, and hoped the trees would provide some shelter.

The Swift came in rather like a falling leaf, but the moment the wheels touched I taxied quickly up to the trees where it was comparatively calm. A passing motorist had seen me land, and, with a mixture of French, English and sign language, I was soon on my way to the local post office and garage. All this took time, and although my father received my telegram and was assured that I was OK, someone reported me going down in the Channel; I was overdue at Le Bourget, and the English press had published in the late editions that I was missing. When I did arrive at Le Bourget later that day, the wind had calmed down a little and I was greeted by several English pilots, who had stayed all day on the airport because of the atrocious weather.

The forecast for the following day was worse and Jock Cameron, who was flying Lady Margaret Drummond-Hay and an American friend, a former Airship Commander, out to Cairo, warned me that I should have a very nasty flight in a machine like the Swift, and calculated what he thought would be my best course: 'I think you will find the trip tomorrow a wee bit rough, laddie, and if I were you I would follow the railway to Dijon. Ye canna mistake it, as it is the only line with electric cables running along it to the south of France.'

In the morning it was bitterly cold, the wind was just short of gale force and it was beginning to snow. None of the pilots going to Cairo were happy with conditions and some chose to spend another day in Paris. Agar and Guy Robson, both in Napier Gulls, decided to go, but neither could get their engines started because of the extreme temperatures. I was elated, as, after ten minutes swinging, the propeller of my little Pobjoy burst into life.

Following railway lines was beneath my dignity, and I set course for Dijon with an allowance of twenty degrees for drift. I was soon in trouble again. My hands were so cold I could hardly hold the controls or the maps. The machine was again bucking so violently that the compass was all over the place, and, leaving the congested suburbs of Paris behind, I could not recognise a thing. Just when I was beginning to despair I spotted a railway line and at the same time saw the electric cables Jock had told me about. Without hesitation I pushed my pride to one side and dived on to the newfound friend. Although it weaved about a bit and occasionally disappeared into a short tunnel, the line took me all the way to Dijon, where I arrived to land in six inches of virgin snow.

The wind by this time had abated, and when I set course for Lyon I found to my relief that in spite of the snow obliterating the countryside I was navigating a better course. In fact, I had made such good time that I decided to push on to Marseilles and be the first of the British contingent to arrive there. I was frozen refuelling in the snow at Lyon and felt numb to the bone, but hoped that I would soon be running into better and warmer weather. I had been flying ten minutes or so when the light began to fail, and as it was still early in the day I could not understand what was happening. I rubbed the goggles over with my leather glove and was shocked to find my hand greasy with oil and the visibility good without them.

I immediately thought the oil filler cap had been left off at Lyon, as oil was being sprayed out along the fuselage. I spun round rapidly and returned, but on landing my spirits sank as inspection showed the oil tank had split and the contents were oozing out, trickling down the undercarriage and creating a black patch on the frozen snow. Luckily there was a good mechanic at the airfield, and without hesitation he pushed the machine into the hangar and began stripping the cowlings off. He worked so well that I thought I should still have time to reach Marseilles, but when he ran the engine up my joy was shortlived; the tank burst at the weld seam and oil again poured out.

We started work all over again, but this time the bright mechanic used a different welding process and late that night announced he would be ready for an engine test in the morning. I was so frozen pushing the machine through the snow for an engine run at first light that I made a promise to myself that I would never have another open-cockpit aeroplane. This time the mechanic wisely insisted on filling up with hot oil, the test seemed to be OK, and off I set once again for Marseilles. To my surprise, when I landed I saw that most of the other competitors had arrived, but had not left for the next stage. I decided to waste no time and to set off as soon as I could get refuelled.

I was always careful to run the petrol through a chamois filter and when the tanker arrived with an elaborate gauze filter I protested mildly, but permitted them to carry on filling up my tank. I reckoned at this rate I should easily reach La Spezia or Rome that day. The weather was much better, but cold, as I swung the Swift into wind for the take-off. I was away and the prospects ahead looked good: suddenly the engine spluttered and stopped. Thankful of my golden rule for a long take-off and a large aerodrome, I was able with a little hectic manoeuvring to land and come to a standstill just short of the aerodrome boundary. Mechanics and onlookers rushed out to me. As the engine had been running well before refuelling, I immediately suspected the petrol, so the first thing to do was examine the filter. This was found to be half-full of water, and we replaced it after cleaning and started the engine. It burst into life, ran for a few minutes, and then spluttered and finally stopped. Further examination showed the filter half-full of water again. There was nothing for it but to empty the main petrol tank.

I was not alone with my troubles: Guy Robson could not get his engine started. It was one of the new Napier six-cylinder models, which had recently been introduced; they gave the Percival Gull a fair performance, but at the time little was known about them and they proved to be unreliable. Guy was one of the 1930s jet-set, and always seemed to have an exotic female with him. On this occasion he was travelling with another pilot, which was just as well, because the next day his engine failed over the Mediterranean and he was extremely lucky to force-land near Ajaccio in Corsica. Lady Margaret Drummond-Hay had decided the weather was not good enough and Jock Cameron was having the Stinson serviced while they waited. The Earl of Ronaldshay's party were flying in an Airspeed Courier, piloted by an American. They were not to race in Egypt, but were going out to India on business. They were unhappy because although they had a faster machine than my Swift, they had been behind me the whole way across France. Apparently their pilot liked flying down valleys, but it nearly always turned out to be the wrong valley and they had to keep back-tracking. They had been nearly frozen and were not enjoying the trip.

I worked with the mechanics on my machine, but it was late in the afternoon before we had drained off the petrol tank and feed lines, and flushed everything out thoroughly. It was dark as we did an engine test, and, as I was anxious to leave early in the morning, I decided to carry out a test flight. Although it was dark, the snow reflected a great deal of light, and with the large hangar doors open I could use them as a beacon to keep me from getting lost. The engine appeared to sound OK and I landed hoping I would have a clear run the next day.

It was still bitterly cold in the morning and I left the others trying to start their engines, and set off for Cannes. Once over the mountains the weather changed and I landed on the small grass airfield at Cannes to find most of the snow had disappeared. The wonderful balmy atmosphere filled me with relaxation, but I was unable to clear Customs at Cannes and had to fly a little further down the coast to Nice. I didn't think much of this, as Nice airfield was just a small strip of scrub and sand running down to the sea with a tin shed that served as a hangar. A boy was in attendance, who did not seem to be very helpful, but a passing motorist stopped, asked me in English if he could help, and said he would fetch a Customs officer from the seaport of Nice just down the road. I did not particularly like the look of my new French friend in the first instance, but he was so kind and helpful that it was almost impossible to keep him at arm's length. He said his name was Jean S., and before I left he made me promise to look him up on my return flight.

I felt the remainder of my trip was going to be easier. The weather was wonderful, and of course the scenery magnificent. I landed at La Spezia amid pools of water, but the sun still shone; here the aerodrome officials would not let me charge the landing fees on to my fuel carnet account as was customary, nor would they change my traveller's cheques, so I had to hire a car and go to the bank in the town before I was able to leave. This made me rather late, but as the weather was marvellous I did not worry too much and thought I should reach Rome before sunset. I quickly realised, when I had been flying for about an hour, that I had no idea of the time of sunset or sunrise in this part of the world, and I cursed my casualness once again when I found that the compass was difficult to see inside the cockpit without lights. The awesome-looking snowcap mountains had by this time taken on a purple hue as the sun sank lower and lower and I was still a long way from my destination. Working out roughly how far there was to go, it became obvious that I was going to be searching for the aerodrome in the dark. Never having been to Rome before, the prospect gave me some sobering thoughts as to what I should and should not have done. I could not go back to La Spezia, and there was no aerodrome nearer— or was there?

In the failing light I pulled the map nearer to my face and noticed a military zone, almost on my route about sixty miles north-west of Rome, with an airfield. It also came home to me with a shock that because of the Abyssinian war we were almost enemies of Italy. I had been instructed on no account to land at a military base, as, in retaliation for imposing sanctions against them, the Italians would most probably put British pilots under

D

arrest and impound their machines. I decided to try and reach Rome. The sun had now disappeared and it was getting really dark. I could see the coastline and could just make out blurred buildings below, and I knew that in a very short while it would be impossible for me to land without lights. Military base or not, if I could find that airfield I was going to land before it was too late. Fortunately, it was near the sea, and as I circled low I could make out the dim outline of a concrete apron and some large hangars. Losing no time, I decided to use the grey concrete as a guide and felt for the ground with an engine approach which would bring me parallel to the hangars and near the grey concrete of the apron.

I cut the engine as my wheels touched and waited in the dark silence that prevailed. Suddenly there were shouts, orders and the rattle of rifles. As I climbed from the machine it was to be greeted by an armed guard of a dozen men and an officer, who might just have stepped out of a part in a Gilbert and Sullivan opera. No one could speak English so I was marched off at a smart pace to the guardroom and, I suspected, prison. Another officer had arrived and asked me in English who I was and what I was doing there. He then said, with a degree of awe, that the commandant wished to see me. He disappeared with most of the guard, but two soldiers with fixed bayonets marched on either side of me. When we arrived at the commandant's headquarters, all hell seemed to be let loose, and, although I could not understand a word, it was obvious that the commandant stamping up and down was tearing everyone present into little pieces. When he finally paused I said to the officer with me, 'What is going on? I am not a spy.' He replied, 'The Commandant is furious that we did not put the boundary lights on for you, and he says you might have been hurt. He is very sorry, and asked if you would take dinner with him in the officers' mess.'

At first it was all very formal, and then I think because of my youth they thawed out, were good fun and extremely kind. I was given a clean, compact little bedroom from where I could hear the roar of the sea, and in the morning I found my machine sparkling like new and the oil and petrol tanks filled to the brim.

When I finally took my leave, it was to a mixture of heel-clicking, snappy salutes amidst all the comic opera uniforms, and embraces for someone who might have been a long-lost friend.

I was glad when I saw Rome that I had not tried to find it in the dark. It was a poor aerodrome in a built-up area, surrounded by a racetrack, and there were many obstructions to catch the unwary. On arrival I was greeted by Ronaldshay, who was leaving for Naples, where he proposed spending the night. He knew about my escapade the previous evening, as, expecting to meet me at Rome, he started inquiries when I did not arrive and found out what had happened.

The indescribably beautiful sight of Naples in the sunshine was marred for me by the now unmistakable sound coming from my engine. It was a louder version of what I thought I had heard on leaving England. I investigated on landing and found there was very little compression on No. 5 cylinder. The nearest spare parts were at Heston, and I was not sure of the qualifications of the Italian ground engineer. I decided to sleep on the problem and went into Naples with Ronaldshay. We had great fun arguing with the Italians over prices and rooms. Lord Ronaldshay was only a few years older than I, and now that we were in a sunnier climate, with his pilot only having to follow the coastline of Italy, he was much happier.

In the morning I was far from happy: I had desperately wanted to arrive in Cairo before my father and welcome him off the steamer. Even if everything worked out to perfection, and the spares arrived, and the Italian ground engineer could do the repairs, it would take several days. If I carried on there was a high risk involved: I had a long sea crossing; if I broke down in the desert I might lose the machine, if not my life. In Paris I had been the guest of Jean Lacombe, the very experienced Comper Aircraft Company representative. He said I was going to be very tight on fuel on some of my sections along the North African coast, but there was nothing I could do about it as there were no other landing places in between. Now, with my engine down on power my range would be even less than before.

On reflection, I think it was at this stage in my life that I began to calculate and reason things out for myself. Today, I say to my son when he has a tricky problem, make out a profit and loss account, that will give you the answer. This is what I started to do then, and what I have done ever since. I put down all the points in detail: those that are good go into the credit side, and those that are bad on to the debit. I carefully add up the result, and there is the answer.

At Naples I was frustrated, uncertain and torn with various emotions, and not able to make a firm decision. As I mulled my formula over in my mind, however, the position began to clarify itself, and I was surprised to find the confusion disappearing and calm resolution taking its place. I was going to return home at once. If the engine kept going, well and good; if it failed, I hoped it would be on or near a good aerodrome and at least nearer to England than I was at the present moment.

When I went to clear aerodrome control I had another piece of bad news: there was a gale blowing in the sector between Naples and Rome and it was unsafe to fly. I argued with the aerodrome control officer, a young lieutenant, that if the gale was not actually blowing at Rome I should be all right. He replied that I could suffer a severe structural failure to my machine in the turbulence coming off the mountains. I had a lot of faith in the strength of the Swift, particularly in the wings, and argued that my aircraft had a very high structural safety factor. I was somewhat deflated when, instead of arguing, the young lieutenant said in broken English, 'You sign this documento, you go.' It was a typewritten form absolving the Italian Air Force from any responsibility in the event of my death as a result of the weather conditions *en route*. The die was cast and I took off. For the first fifty miles or so flying conditions were perfect, but then ahead I saw a dramatic change in the pattern of the surface of the sea, and I guessed this was where I would have to brace myself.

The gale hit me like an express train, and for the next hour it was not flying, but a matter of keeping the machine in the air. I was petrified as I was taken down what could have been an enormous never-ending lift, the next minute to be flung with my head between my knees. If anyone had told me I would be torn and flung about the sky, one second right side up, the next second inverted, or one moment at 1500 ft and the next in danger of hitting the rocks below, I would not have believed them. I wished I had not been so blasé in signing the lieutenant's indemnity form and had followed his advice. Just when I thought either the engine, the airframe or I should have to give up the struggle, the wind abated and I saw the outskirts of Rome in the distance.

There another blow of a different kind awaited me. I was told when clearing the control at Rome for take-off that both Pisa and La Spezia were flooded and likely to be so for several days. I plotted my course very carefully and calculated that a direct flight from Rome to Nice was the limit of my range. If I reduced power a little I might improve upon this, but then I had to contend with the loss of compression in No. 5 cylinder, which I suspected to be due to a faulty valve.

My state of despair overruled my common sense; I was tired, dirty and fed up. All I wanted to do now was get home. I was lucky in so far as the weather was now perfect, with little or no wind. I kept a careful check on my fuel consumption as far as I was able, because gauges then were notoriously inaccurate. I had nothing to worry about until the point of no return, and at that stage I thought I had enough fuel to reach Nice without undue worry. Across the bay of Genoa, however, I was not so sure. The gauge looked ominously low, and by the time I was level with San Remo there was nothing on it at all. I pondered whether to make for the shoreline, so that if the motor stopped I should be on or near land; or whether to keep an accurate course and reduce the distance as much as possible. I decided that the coast was so rough and rocky, the mountainous terrain impossible for landing, and that I had better stay where I was.

I thought the Swift would turn over if it hit the water, so I undid my Sutton harness and unbuttoned my heavy leather coat in readiness. My mouth was so dry I could scarcely breathe. The visibility was good and I could see Nice miles before I reached it: my suspense was indescribable. I went in to land without even a circuit, pulled up near the tin hangar and switched off the engine. When I had recovered my breath, I opened up the petrol tank and peered in; by gently rocking the machine I could see the bottom of the tank dry with only a pint or so of petrol in the base of the sump.

I was not in any mood to look up Jean S. the Frenchman, but I had hardly dismissed the thought from my mind before there was a loud hail from the road and there he was, complete with customs officer. From the port he had seen me cross the bay and, as it was evening, knew I would be staying overnight. It is impossible to remain depressed on the Riviera for long and after I had had a hot bath and a meal I felt on top of the world again. Jean introduced me to the realm of high-grade photography: he had a Leica with every conceivable type of lens and attachment, and told me he earned his living by selling photographs. This I learned later was true, but not in the manner he had implied.

I left early the next morning for Marseilles, Lyon and Dijon. The start was perfect but it was not long before I ran into the cold blustery wind of northern Europe again. My engine was still running, albeit roughly, as I struggled into Dijon, the sun down on the horizon. I crossed my fingers and hoped one more day would see me across the Channel. Next morning the snow had almost disappeared, but although it was fine I was told that Paris was under a blanket of fog and I had to hang around all morning. Eventually I was told that the weather over Le Bourget was beginning to improve with the fog now only in patches, so I decided to take off. Navigation in the calm air was fairly easy, and when I struck the fog it was in thin patches so I did not worry unduly. As I approached Paris, however, the fog thickened and I found myself overflying areas for some time before I spotted a clear patch where I could see the ground. I was so near Le Bourget that I felt sure if I had any luck at all I should be able to see it in a clearing through the fog. I did not have any luck.

When I was sure there was no clearing over where the aerodrome should have been, I decided to fly back and land in one of the clear spaces I had previously been flying over. To my horror, when I turned back there were no clear spaces. As the sun began to go down, so the fog had filled in. I now felt sick in the stomach and it needed all my determination to keep from panicking. I decided to return on my reciprocal track for a while, and then, if I did not find a clearing, I had no alternative than to crashland through the fog. I failed to find any clear patches at all. I could see only the tops of trees making a smudgy outline in the fog. If there were trees, I reasoned, then I was over open country and not the built-up suburbs of Paris or a town. I eased the throttle and started to glide down beside the trees. As I entered the cold dark mass of swirling fog, I held my hand on the throttle in readiness. For a moment I saw nothing, and then suddenly I spotted the gleam of water and long grass. I slammed the throttle open and shot up above the fog into the weak winter sunshine once again.

I was resigned to crashing now, but whereas at first I had nearly panicked with fright, I was now so angry with my own stupidity, the anguish I was going to cause my family, that I was coldly and calmly calculating what was likely to happen to me. My thoughts in this direction did nothing to reassure me, however. I chose another clump of trees and started on my next, and, I dumbly realised, my final attempt.

This time I disappeared into the murk so close to the trees that it seemed almost dark after the clear sky above. I had a glimpse of brown earth below, snapped off the engine switches and put my right arm in front of my face. The machine touched down roughly and pulled up quickly: I had landed on a ploughed field which had been harrowed and was now frozen. In my ecstatic elation at having been saved from what I had made sure was my last flight, I jumped out of the Swift, ran a few yards expecting to see something, and then when I turned, was unable to find the machine. I blundered this way and that and eventually came upon the edge of the field and the clump of trees I had seen from the air; using this as a rough guide after a few attempts I found the Swift and decided to cover the engine and peg it down for the night.

I was rather surprised that no one had appeared whilst I was

trying to make the Swift secure for the night. I could not twist
the steel screw pegging irons into the frozen ground but was not
worried as there was not a breath of wind. I then took my overnight case out of the machine and walked into the fog. I came
upon some farm buildings, and hearing something shouted, 'Is
anyone there?' The noise stopped immediately and out of the
gloom came a farm labourer carrying a lantern. I don't think
either of us understood a word the other was saying, but he
beckoned me to follow him. We walked what seemed an awful
long way, until we came to a village, where with difficulty I was
able to make myself understood. They were all very helpful and
kind and fixed me up with a meal and bed at the one and only
tavern nearby.

In the morning I peered out anxiously, and was relieved to
find the sun shining with a very sharp hoar-frost, making everything sparkle in the bright light. All the villagers came out to see
me off, and I was glad that I had put covers over the engine and
cockpit, for the engine started without much trouble. I was very
lucky that the ground had been frozen: the soil looked heavy and
wet, and I dared not think what either landing or take-off would
have been like had the weather been warmer.

I was so near Paris that I was sure I should have sunshine all
the way, but my spirits sank again when only a few miles from Le
Bourget I again encountered the fog of the previous night. I
circled overhead, but again there were no gaps; I had no
alternative other than to turn back. I realised that I should have
to take on more fuel before I made another attempt, and turning
on to a reciprocal course, decided to land in a suitable field near
a village with a garage as soon as I ran out of the fog. I chose a
long, narrow stubble field running beside some houses, with a
small garage on a main road nearby. In no time at all the local
gendarme came out to me on his cycle and we went to his office
to telephone the airport. The news there was good as they expected the fog to clear within an hour. I put 20 litres of best
French petrol on board from some tins, and as I did so a lady
with an English voice begged me to come across to her house and
have a cup of coffee. When I tried to refuse, the lady said she had

left England during the Great War as a nurse and had never had the opportunity to return; she was married to a Frenchman but longed to speak to someone English. Surely I could not refuse her on Christmas Eve? I had lost all count of time and this information came as rather a shock, so I walked over to her house and spent a pleasant hour drinking hot coffee and eating delicious mincepies.

This time when I took off all went well. I landed at Le Bourget, quickly refuelled, and set off for Croydon. My luck was still out. Near Beauvais the engine, which had slowly been getting rougher and noisier, began to misfire badly, and, as I had Beauvais airfield in view, I landed without hesitation. I cleaned the sparking plugs and checked the magnetos and filters and started the engine. Apart from the accustomed roughness and low revs it ran all right, so I decided to push on. I reached the Channel in the afternoon and knew I did not have a great deal of time to reach Croydon before dark, but after my past experience, to be flying once again over my home soil inspired me to do almost anything.

The lights of Croydon lit up the winter sky as I landed: the Christmas decorations were abundant, and Customs and Immigration officers were in a festive mood. I was still very anxious to get home, and when I found the Comper Aircraft factory was closed over Christmas for several days I decided to fly on to Skegness. The weather was bad all the way. Near Spalding I realised I was going to be in a similar predicament to that of the previous day and decided to land in a large grass field before the fog closed in completely. I stayed the night with some kind farm people in a very rural atmosphere. As I landed at Skegness the next morning Leslie Honour, the ground engineer, came across to welcome me back and made a grimace when he heard my engine tick over. I had left on Friday the 13th and had been away almost exactly thirteen days. I reckoned there must be something in this superstition business.

4 ✳ *Flying a spy*

WHEN DAD RETURNED from Cairo, we both agreed that we must change the Swift and the Moth for something more suitable, and after a few trials in other machines we decided to purchase a new Leopard Moth from Henleys of Heston. I parted with my little Swift on 7 March 1934, and we agreed to deliver the Moth with a new C of A when the Leopard Moth was ready to collect at the end of the month.

Of all the machines we have owned, I look back on the Leopard Moth as giving us the most comfortable, the most carefree, and, in many ways, the most enjoyable flying we ever had. It had no intricate instrument panel, no complicated retractable undercarriage, and no temperamental variable-pitch airscrew. It was safe, easy and a gentleman's machine, with a performance to match, and we had many happy hours in it. At the time we were flying mostly over civilised countries, and I suppose much of the enjoyment was to be derived from the fact that there were no heavy responsibilities entailed in planning long flights over sea, desert or jungle, with all the various formalities that are often required flying through strange and remote lands. The seating also suited us. A pilot's seat in front, with two comfortable side-by-side seats in the back, and enough room for Dad and me to change places at the pilot's seat when we wished, and adequate luggage accommodation. The difference between a closed machine and an open cockpit is beyond comparison, and, in my opinion, no one who has flown both would ever go back to the noise and the continuous wind buffeting for any serious form of travel. I was also able to carry out all the maintenance work, on both airframe and engine, throughout the time we had the machine, and when finally we parted with it I was proud that it looked almost as new.

All that winter I had frequent correspondence with Jean S. He would write almost weekly, usually sending some quite remarkable photographs taken with his Leica equipment. He suggested that we should visit him in France and make a special trip to photograph Mont Blanc. Dad thought this would be fun, so I made the arrangements. It was during the month of May, with the weather most of the time perfect, and visually navigation was easy in the closed machine.

On leaving Dijon for Chamonix we encountered a good deal of cloud and were almost in sight of Mont Blanc when the weather worsened. Jean said he knew the valley to Chamonix well, and told me to follow his instructions. Mindful of past adventures of this kind, I was certainly not taking any chances with my father on board, and told him to sit back and mind his own business, as we were returning to Dijon. Jean was not very pleased with me, but I knew that less than a year before he had flown with an English pilot called Bill Lyons, and, due mainly to Jean's navigation, they had followed a valley which led them into high mountains. With the weather deteriorating they had to crash the machine into a hillside, and although they were not hurt, Lyons had an expensive bill to meet.

The next day we set off again and Jean started to take shots from every angle. We were able to get close in to the summit of Mont Blanc and in the brilliant light it was an exhilarating and fascinating sight. Jean was not content with the mountains themselves, but was photographing all the frontier areas, and asked me to fly further over the Italian border so that he could get a better shot. We stayed above the Alps until the cloud began to thicken, and then turned due west to drop down into the valley of the Rhône for lunch at Lyon.

Lyon was both military and civil in those days, and when I saw a new type of Breguet aeroplane on the opposite side of the airfield to the civilian part, I asked if we could have a look at it. Jean said at once he would take us over. As we were looking at the machine a French Air Force officer came over: he said civilians were not allowed on that part of the aerodrome, and started to create a fuss. Jean whispered something in the officer's ear, showed him a card, and to our surprise the officer saluted, apologised and walked away. On our way to Nice that afternoon I started to make detours to avoid the prohibited area around Toulon, but Jean said it would be all right: if we were reported, all I had to do was give his name.

On our return home, sure enough, there was a letter from the Department of Civil Aviation enclosing a copy of a complaint from the French Air Ministry, concerning British aircraft G-ACLO over Toulon. I wrote with my tongue in my cheek, saying the matter should be referred to Jean, and to my surprise I heard nothing further concerning the incident. It gave Dad and me food for thought.

We were now really making use of the Leopard Moth, particularly for events like the Isle of Man TT races, where we could leave home, fly direct over the sea to a field behind the pits, see the race and be home again the same day in time for tea. Having the airfield near home now also helped a great deal, as we were not too happy at Skegness for various reasons. When Eric West, a farmer friend, said he had a field like a billiard table at Bar Fen which we could use as we liked, Dad had the hangar dismantled and re-erected there, some five miles from where we lived. I raced the Leopard Moth in 1934 with moderate success, but had no luck in the King's Cup. It was again run in a series of eliminating heats and I was knocked out by one place in the first lap to Heyford, Old Sarum, Whitchurch and Hatfield.

In one race at Sherburn-in-Elmet later in the year, I lost by the narrowest margin through an incident which might have had a more dramatic end. It was a very short circuit, clear of buildings, and we made our turns round bell tents that had been set up in grass fields.

The last stretch to the finishing line was over rough scrub ground, with trees dotted here and there. I was bunched up with several machines as I banked vertically on the sharp final turn and with a quick glance around calculated that but for the Hendy 302 I should make the finishing line first. The Hendy,

flown by Carol Napier, was streaking in, clipping the trees, and
would be across the line in seconds. I was right alongside and
overtaking, struggling to get the last ounce out of my machine,
and in my desperation getting lower and lower. Just when I had
the race in the bag, I felt the aircraft lunge and sink almost on to
the ground, which was only a few feet below. There was a sharp
twang, the Leopard shot forward again, and at the same time
there was a rough buffeting as the air brakes were pulled on. I
quickly snatched them off and the next second we were across
the finishing line, but I was only level with the Hendy's tail and
Napier won by about four to five yards. I had hit a steel control
wire that had been slung between the trees. My metal airscrew
had fortunately cut the cable, but, as it dragged away it had torn
my starboard brake cable from the undercarriage and at the
same time twisted the airbrakes into the on position. Apart from
a nick in the airscrew and a slight cut in the starboard tyre,
there was no other damage.

Whilst the Leopard was an excellent machine for Dad and me
to wander about Europe, I was always looking for something
which had a better performance. I think my stock in the British
aviation world was such that I had no difficulty in flying almost
everything available; the trouble was, of course, the limited
number of suitable aircraft. I was asked to race a Comper Swift,
fitted with a special Gipsy high-compression racing engine, in the
Cinque Ports trophy at Lympne. It was probably one of the
fastest private machines in the country at that time, but it had
limited uses, and, like my own Swift, had an open cockpit and
was a single-seater. It was considered a hot rod at the time and,
although I did not have any success in the race, I enjoyed the
fun of being scratchman and chasing the slower machines.
Several well-known pilots were preparing for the Australia race
later in the year. I would have liked to compete, but did not
mention it to my father as inwardly I did not think I was
sufficiently qualified by experience or competence. It was rumoured that De Havillands were designing a very fast twin-
engined machine, especially for the race, and several pilots
backed by sponsors had placed orders.

Almost the last race for me in the Leopard that year was the London to Newcastle on the same route on which I had come to grief the year before. This time I was lined up to go off with Sid Sparks in an identical type of machine. Sparks was an ex-TT rider and would give nothing away. He was also a very experienced pilot. This time on take-off we had to fly up to a flag on the Brooklands embankment before turning right about 100 degrees on to track. As we waited for the starter's flag to go down, I sensed that as the race had not attracted a very exciting entry, several of my friends and some other pilots were betting on which was going to be the first Leopard Moth to reach Newcastle, and that put both Sparks and myself on our mettle. I had the disadvantage of being on the outside of the turn, and I was scheming as I opened up the engine as to how I could possibly reach the turning point before Sparks. We both released our brakes as the flag went down and the machines shot forward. We lifted off the ground at about the same time, and Sparks climbed slightly to prepare for the turn about 50 feet up on the top of the racetrack embankment. I kept my machine right down, clipping the grass and edged slightly to starboard, so that I was literally sliding underneath Sparks's machine. I held this position right up to the embankment and it gave me about half a machine's length in front as I pulled up the concrete banking for the turn. As I was now on the inside of the turn I had the advantage, and Sparks had to give way as we banked vertically on to course. Having now got in front I concentrated on the job in hand, and, although I was only fourth in the race, I did finish nearly two miles an hour faster than the other Leopard Moth.

The Australia race was due to start at Mildenhall at first light on 20 October 1935. As we wanted to see the machines away, we had to leave well before it was light if we were to land at Mildenhall without complaints. We apparently caused some slight disturbance on this particular morning as we flew over the Wash near Sutton Bridge, for suddenly all the lights of this Royal Air Force aerodrome there were switched on.

It was a tremendous thrill seeing all the aircraft take off from Mildenhall, and I have often thought that sometimes the friends and relatives on the ground got a greater thrill at such events than the pilots who were actually competing. I knew nearly all the competitors, and as I saw them disappearing with their exhausts glowing in the dim morning light, I felt a pang of envy and was determined to gain enough experience so that I, too, might one day be able to take part in such an historic race.

Dad was very good about it all and helped me in everything. For hours we would fly in cloud, or, if I plotted a long triangular course and the cloud was not thick enough, I would cover my head and the instrument panel with a blanket so that I could see nothing other than the instruments and Dad would sit in the back and say very little unless we were approaching another aircraft.

Jean continued his plethora of correspondence and magnificent supply of photographs, and suggested we toured Germany, where he had obtained an invitation for me to visit the Bucher works and fly their different types of machines. I wanted no second invitation as I would have loved to own a Bucher Jungmeister, which I then considered one of the best small aerobatic machines in the world.

Travelling in Germany for British aircraft owners in those days was a happy and satisfying experience. In the main we got on well with the Germans and they made us welcome wherever we went. At the same time, the Deutschmark was in such a state that, owing to the special currency rate that prevailed for sterling, we could have a holiday for almost nothing. In fact, providing they could substantiate the amounts they required to spend, some pilots would cash large sums of sterling, smuggle the marks out of Germany at the high rate of exchange and finish up, if they were not found out, with a handsome profit. It was a risky business if you owned your aircraft, however, as you faced conviction and confiscation of the machine if caught. There was no love lost between the Germans and the French, but Jean was accepted because he was with us. I made a great many friends, flew many aircraft and was impressed with their glider movement, which was growing enormously. Fräulein Lisle Bach, one of Germany's leading glider pilots, was most hospitable and helpful in showing us around. Jean again persuaded me to fly to various points for what he termed special photography, and neither Dad nor I were too happy about it. But he was very helpful in many ways, a good conversationalist, intelligent, and, as he spoke five languages fluently, we could fly almost anywhere in Europe without difficulty.

Before we left Jean in Paris on our previous visit, Dad had asked him if there was anything he would like us to bring, the next time we came over. He said he would like an English camel-hair coat, so Dad promised him he should have it. On my return, I enthused to Dad about the fantastic control I had had when flying the German Bucher, and said I wished I could have flown as well as the German test pilot who demonstrated it. Dad said, 'You were OK. All you need is practice. Why don't you get something suitable?'

In March 1935, Jean wrote suggesting a big tour of Europe. As Dad had just bought him a magnificent camel-hair overcoat he said, 'We might as well go and give him the coat, before the warm weather starts.' Again Jean laid on an extensive tour of Germany as a start, so, having picked him up at Brussels, we made for Berlin. The weather was good, but very cold for the time of year. As we were to travel mostly in southern Europe, Dad had with him only a Burberry raincoat, so he asked Jean if he would mind him wearing the camel-hair coat he had brought and which he so lovingly admired.

Having spent all the time Jean seemed to need in Germany, we were due to leave Nuremberg for Venice. On the morning of departure at our hotel I wanted to check a point on the maps with Jean, and, now knowing him so well, I gave a sharp tap on his door and marched in. He was bending over his case of Leica attachments and he quickly covered the case and turned towards me. Something about his attitude made me say to him, 'What have you got there, Jean?' He replied, 'It is nothing; I was getting some films ready.' I walked past him and looked at the large Leica case. There was a long telephoto lens that I thought I had seen Jean put down as I entered. I picked it up, and before Jean could stop me, unscrewed the dust cap at one

1   Dad as a young man in North America
2   Dad and A.H. with DH Gipsy I Moth, Skegness, April 1932
3   Accepting the Siddeley Trophy from Lord Gorell, 1933: Geoffrey de
    Havilland with King's Cup; Bill Styran on left

4   Happy days in the DH Leopard Moth, Stag Lane 1934
5   Top secret Breguet at Lyon-Brun, 1934

end. The lens was crammed tight with high-denomination mark notes.

For a moment I looked at Jean, speechless. I then said, very quietly, 'Jean, you were going to smuggle this out of Germany, without my knowing anything about it, weren't you. You also know that if you were caught, I should be involved as pilot and owner of the aircraft. We would never dream of treating our friends in this way.' He replied with a great deal of agitation, 'It is only a little bullion deal I do. The Germans will never find out. I will share the profit I make with you.' When I exploded at this Jean tried to stand on what dignity he could muster, and said he didn't see what I was getting so excited about. I stormed out, went over to my father's room and said, 'Let's get out of here Dad, I've just had a hell of a row with Jean.' I then told him what had happened. We left Nuremberg and as we cleared the surrounding hills the sun came out: it was suddenly springtime and warm. Dad started to take off his coat and then burst out laughing: 'I'd like to see the look on that Frenchman's face when he realises I've still got his camel-hair coat on.'

E

5 ✳ *Active aerobatics*

IT SO HAPPENED that an Arrow Active, which Flight-Lieutenant 'Curly' Leach had used to give aerobatic shows all over the country, was on offer for sale at Yeadon. I used to be thrilled with Leach's upward rolls as he flung the very manoeuvrable biplane around the sky, and I lost no time in flying to Yeadon to try it out. I loved it at once and arranged to collect the machine as soon as the C of A had been completed.

I learnt more about flying from the Arrow Active than from any other aircraft before or since. It was a strongly built metal biplane, with a Cirrus Hermes IIB engine, and the large open single-seater cockpit permitted the pilot a good view.* Although it took me some time, I think I made that machine do everything it was possible for a biplane to do. I practised all the normal aerobatic manoeuvres like loops, rolls, upward rolls and spins constantly, but it was on such things as flick rolls, inverted spins, inverted gliding and tail slides and 'bunts' that I found more difficulty and realised they had to be treated with respect.

That winter I spent a great deal of time and thought trying to improve the performance of the Active. It was tedious and exacting work, and not very rewarding. I did not feel the Leopard would do much good in the King's Cup and I hoped I could coax more out of the Active than the handicappers would expect. For days I would be covered in red or silver dope as I tried to smooth off the rather solid construction of the little metal biplane. I began to realise, however, that the task was not going to show the results I had expected, and that I would need a small army of ground engineers to carry out all that I wanted to do. At the

* There were actually only two machines built and one is still flying today.

end of a day's solid work I could see very little for my efforts, and, what was more important, I found it most difficult to assess exactly what I had really achieved. When you are searching for fractions of a mile an hour, not only is the work involved laborious but the means of proving your handicraft can be equally so. Things like position errors, instrument calibration and so on, were factors I could take into account, but as the tests were usually carried out at zero feet along the beautiful stretch of sea-washed sand between Sutton and Saltfleet, I had also to bear in mind ambient temperature and the effect on engine power, thermals rising up from the sand if the tide had been out some time, and then of course, human error.

The time I liked best was very early on a spring or summer morning, when everything was so calm, and before even the skylarks had risen. We had an unusual number of severe early morning frosts that year and it was a real hardship to rise from a warm bed, don some suitable flying gear, and drive down to Bar Fen as the first streaks of light glinted on the hoar-frosted hedges. My younger brothers, Leslie and Eric, helped me at times, because once when I was altering the flight line of the engine it necessitated lifting the engine up and down slightly in the airframe bearers, and then flight testing until I got the maximum performance possible at full throttle over my testing zone. Handling cold metal and spanners with frozen fingers so early in the morning did not improve one's temper, even if it did give you an appetite for breakfast.

I never had much success racing the Active: the one race I might have won—although I think at times that could be debatable—was the Birmingham Contact race. The course was from Castle Bromwich to Stoke-on Trent, Tollerton, Braunstone, Sywell and return, but at each aerodrome the pilot or passenger had to land, get out of his machine and sign the marshal's book. There were no rules for landing except that it should be into wind. The marshal was situated at a table and tent at the end of the normal landing run, and the pilot was then free to taxi at any speed by following flags on the track out to the perimeter take-off point. This was quite a good test of airmanship as it called for good judgement and flying ability, to approach the landing area at maximum speed and full throttle and then to have to suddenly snap the throttle closed, throw off your speed in a quick series of vertical high-'G' turns near the ground and land probably off a quite vicious side-slip. The greatest danger was if another machine was doing the same thing at the same time, and, of course, the poor marshal should have got danger money, as he was the target for everyone, quite literally.

I was in my element for this very unorthodox form of landing, but there my advantage finished. The Active did not have wheel brakes, and on the day of the race there was a high wind. I was very satisfied with my approaches, landings and the run-up to the marshal, but then I had to throw off my Sutton harness, jump out of the machine, sign the book, jump into the cockpit, fix my harness, which in these turbulent conditions I dared not leave unfastened, and taxi to the take-off point. Anyone who has taxied a biplane without brakes or helping hands in a high wind will understand my predicament: to turn I needed thrust; to obtain the thrust I needed speed or engine power; and when I got both, the machine did not always go in the direction I wanted it to. I think my careering round the aerodrome must have scared the marshals to death, because all I saw at odd times out of the corner of my eye was someone running like hell to duck out of the way of my wings, which threatened to cut them down like a scythe. I managed two landings in this manner and as far as I could see, in spite of my ground gyrations, I was well up in the lead, but then something happened which makes me blush even to this day.

Dad had taken it upon himself to prepare my racing maps, and very well done they were. This time, however, because of the open cockpit, he had cut them into strips which showed only the course in between the respective aerodromes, and did not show the whole route and in particular the difference in angle between one route and another. We both agreed this was unnecessary, as I was landing each time and could readjust the compass for my new course. Since I had partially closed in the cockpit of the Active the light over the compass was poor. Now,

at Braunstone I quickly altered the compass ring to my new
course the moment I landed. As pilots will know, the practice
was to fly what is known as red to red, that is the compass
needle pointing on to the red mark on the verge ring. A glance
on take-off gave me the angle of turn on to the new course and
within minutes I was settled down right on track. My compass
was lined up beautifully, except for the bucking about in the
high wind. Then I sensed something was wrong. Flying visually,
my first check did not turn up just off the aerodrome as it
should have done. I thought I must have misjudged the angle of
the turn and searched frantically for an obvious fix. I saw one
which was not on my map and the awful truth dawned, leaving
me limp with mortification. Staring at the compass, I found I
was flying red to black, in fact a true reciprocal of the course I
should have been on. There was nothing I could do; races were
won by seconds, and if I turned back on to my correct course
now I should be miles behind the last competitor. Mortified and
deflated, I eased back the throttle and returned to Castle
Bromwich.

I was just about to send the entrance forms through for the
King's Cup, when Carol Napier, Designer and Managing
Director of Cirrus Engines, rang me up and asked if Dad and I
would lunch with him at Brough. When we arrived we had a
long conversation with him and his Sales Director, Johnny Gadd,
and were shown round the elaborate new engine factory recently constructed on the aerodrome at Brough. They had just
designed a new, larger engine for the light-aircraft market, and
Napier wanted me to use one in the next King's Cup race. In
fact, he said he was going to try to get his 'best hopes'—David
Atcherley, Spinks Edwards and myself—to use the engines, in
which the Cirrus works had great faith. I was very keen, but said
to Napier that I did not think my chances with the Active would
be very good, and as they were providing the engine free and
putting so much into it, would it not be a better idea if I saw
Fred Miles and asked if he could build me a suitable airframe.
This we all agreed was an excellent idea. Dad and I then went
over to Reading, saw Tommy Rose, Blossom and Fred Miles and

agreed a single-seater specification, based on the Hawk Major.

As always there were delays, and the Hawk was not ready for test until the day before the race; in fact they were putting in the tank control-cock indicator plate as a finishing touch when I stepped into the cockpit for the first time. Noting that one tank gauge was reading low as I taxied out for the take-off, I switched the control-cock on to the full tank, opened the throttle and was very soon airborne. Just when I was over the top of the Miles factory, there was a cough from the engine and it stopped, the airscrew windmilling silently. I had no height in which to get back, so I did a sharp turn whilst I had some speed left, and, at the risk of colliding with machines taking off, put down cross wind in the middle of the aerodrome, where I waited for the Miles mechanics to drive up to me. The trouble was quickly found. Someone had put the fuel cock indicator in the wrong position. When I had turned it on to the full tank I had in fact turned the cock off.

Again the air was electric with excitement for the start of the Blue Riband. This year's King's Cup course was over England, Scotland, Ireland and Wales. My machine, after a few initial faults, was going well. As we pushed it out for the start I said to Napier, 'When are you going to get your chaps to check the engine over, and change the plugs?' 'It's running OK isn't it?' he asked, and I replied 'Yes, it's going fine.' 'Then leave well alone,' he said.

There was a crowd round the machine as I started the engine about ten minutes before the flag was due to go down. As I ran it up and tested both switches, the engine spluttered and shook in the airframe as I used the port ignition system. I immediately suspected a sparking plug, and Napier was calling out for his mechanics with their toolkit, but they were at the end of the starting line working on Atcherley's Swift. They rushed up to my aircraft and were about to take the cowlings off, when I shouted to Napier from the cockpit, 'Leave the machine alone! You should have thought of that earlier: it's too damn late now.'

Dad came up: 'What are you going to do, son? Don't forget that you have got the Irish Sea to cross.' 'I look at it this way,

Dad. It will take them at least ten minutes to find the trouble, which would lose me the race anyway. There is a chance that she will be OK on the starboard ignition, so I am going.'

Everyone had heard my engine misfiring and they were milling round watching what I was going to do. I was very angry with Carol Napier and rubbed it in as I kept testing the switches and making the engine misfire. Mr Reynolds was now holding the flag up as if to say, 'There is still time to change your mind.'

The weather was good and the machine went well. It was a wonderful feeling clipping across the Highlands of Scotland in the crisp September morning air, as the grouse scuttled to one side at my rapid approach. There was 1303 miles full-throttle racing to be done in the day and although my spirits had dropped at the start, the machine was going so well I began to think ahead a little. The news at Newcastle had been encouraging and even better when I landed at Renfrew. Crossing the Irish Sea with a slight headwind, I got down to zero feet and was surprised to find out how fast the Miles Hawk could go. On landing at Newtownards I was quickly surrounded by friends and onlookers. Wal Handley, of TT fame, came up and said, 'Good going, Alex; I've been working out the times and you've got it in the bag.' As I taxied out I saw Spinks Edwards swinging the prop on his Gull, and it was still lifeless as I became airborne.

I decided on a gradual climb to 1000 ft to take advantage of the slight tailwind, and set course across the sea, my mind full of exciting possibilities. All of a sudden there was an enormous crack and the engine revs shot right off the revolution counter and screamed like a wild humming top, with clouds of smoke pouring from the cowling. As I always raced with my hand hard against the throttle, I snapped it closed and there was a deathly silence.

I had a perfect view of the sea in front of me, unobstructed by the propeller, which had sheared off the crankshaft and was now, presumably, whirling its way down to the depths below. My first reaction was to look for a ship, and spotting a large one some distance away heading for Belfast, I wondered which was the best way to land in water with an aeroplane.

Dad had insisted that I took one of the rubber seats from the Leopard to act as a lifebuoy, if needed, and I felt it to see if it had plenty of air inside. I thought I mustn't get my legs trapped in the cockpit when the machine hit the water, so I pulled them up and sat in the cockpit in a crouched position. I only had a lap seatbelt for harness, and as it was too large I decided to tuck it under the seat and out of the way. As I did a gliding turn over the ship, I debated where to ditch: I must take care not to do so in front of the bows so that I was run down; on the other hand I must make sure they had seen me, as I was coming down in absolute silence. I also wondered about my shoes: maybe if at the last moment I stood on the seat I shouldn't get them wet. I came in on a final turn into wind, almost alongside the steamer, and at the last moment, when I felt the machine was near the stall, I pulled the stick back and we dropped heavily into the sea. I had imagined the lunge into the sea would have felt rather like a dinghy in a rough swell, and I was rudely shocked as the impact shot me out of the cockpit like a bullet from a gun. Although my face missed the instrument panel and windscreen, my knee carried them away as if they had been made of tissue paper. I was flung out about thirty feet in front of the nose of the aircraft, and when I spluttered to the surface it was to see the Leopard cushion bobbing up and down on the waves some few feet away from me and the ship steaming off at what seemed to be high speed. I swam first of all to the cushion, and, using it to keep afloat, I trod water up to the Hawk. It was in a very sorry state and I never realised until then how much damage a 'soft landing' in water could do. The steamer was still moving away and for a few moments I thought they had not seen me.

As I waited, hanging on to the wreck, I was surprised to see the Gull VH-UVH of Melrose, the young Australian, circle low over me and the pilot waving reassuringly. After two circuits the Gull set off in the direction of Newtownards, and I immediately thought what a sporting thing to do, to go back, forfeit the race, just to bring me help. Moments later, however, the Gull went overhead at full throttle and I realised, somewhat cynically, that Melrose must have gone back on a reciprocal course for a short while before he had realised that he was going in the wrong direction. In actual fact, he completed the race and on arrival at Hatfield called the press representatives together and told them he had a photograph of Henshaw in the Irish Sea and would sell it to the highest bidder. The *Daily Express* gave him £50.

Although it was a warm September, it was cold waiting on the half-submerged fuselage of the Hawk, and I was more than pleased when a boat was lowered from the steamer, which had now come to a standstill nearly a mile away, and was rowed at a spanking pace towards me. The steamer turned out to be the *Manx Queen* and I got Captain Holcomb to wireless a message to my father that I was OK. Crowds were waiting for me as we docked in Belfast, as the news had got around very quickly, most of it grossly exaggerated. All I wanted to do was to get back to Hatfield in time to see the finish of the race.

Tommy Rose won in a similar make of machine to the one I had lost in the Irish Sea. Every one of the special Cirrus engines, of which so much was expected, failed to complete the course: Spinks Edwards could not get his engine started at Newtownards owing to a faulty impulse magneto; David Atcherley had a valve rocker arm seize, and was lucky to land on the beach north of Blackpool.

The racing season was now nearly over and I concluded the season with the Folkestone Air Trophy. The Arrow Active was not running too well, and I decided to take it over to Brough and see if they could fit a new engine with an inverted fuel system. My treatment of the Cirrus had been a little harsh as I was becoming obsessed with aerobatics. I had mastered the inverted spins, which I found required a certain technique to get into at the first attempt, and I had to allow myself plenty of room to pull out as the Active spun so viciously. In the inverted position, I had to pull the Sutton harness straps down hard, otherwise I felt my arms and legs had no control; I also found the Active came out of an inverted spin better one way than the other, but I can't remember which way it was.

I was also addicted with the idea that I could make the Active complete an outside loop, in those days generally called a 'bunt'. This normally started by slowing the machine down to a stall, and pushing the control column firmly forward so that it went first into a dive, and then, as the pressure was kept up on the control column, the machine went over on to its back and into a vertical inverted climb. The usual practice at this stage was to ease the elevator control back so that the aircraft came back to normal flying position in a half-loop, or the pilot kicked hard on the rudder as the aircraft was in the vertical position and completed what could be called an inverted Immelmann turn. I now know that it was not possible for me to complete an inverted loop in the Active without power in the inverted position, but in those days I was convinced I could do it. The result was I would go into faster and faster inverted dives in an effort to gain enough speed to push me over the top; I think Dad began to get worried, particularly as one day I had practised from 10,000 ft downwards, and on the last attempt I rolled out a few feet over the beach, where I knew Dad would be watching. As a rule, the engine would splutter a few times and open up after a few bangs caused by misfiring. This time it did not respond, and as the tide was well up I got ready for another ducking. The propeller was windmilling without any power, and then, at the last moment, when I had flattened out to drop into the waves at the edge of the beach, it suddenly burst into life and I was able to breathe freely again.

Dad didn't like these antics of mine, although he did not say much, but on my birthday he presented me with an Irvin parachute, and made me promise to wear it whenever I flew the Active. I had never put a parachute on before and did not know what to do with all the straps. To placate Dad, however, I put it on and as the harness seemed to be much too large to go round me I wore it like a bandolier, across my shoulders and under my legs and round my neck.

Some time later I flew into Grimsby, where Captain Harstone was the instructor. He had been very good to me with help and criticism when I was flying, and as I climbed out of the Active he said, 'My God! What the hell do you think you've got on there?' I said sheepishly, 'It was a present from my father,' and he replied, 'Yes, I'm all for it; but if you jump out with the harness in that position, you'll not only decapitate yourself, but you won't do your matrimonial prospects any good either.' He then spent a good half-hour adjusting the harness at all points until it looked and felt OK.

I was busy most of the autumn and it was not until after Christmas that I had the time to arrange to fly over with the Active and see Johnny Gadd and Carol Napier about a new engine, which they had agreed on the phone was feasible. The 30th of December was a crisp, cold day, with a strong westerly wind blowing. I left Tony, my Labrador, in the hangar as I only expected to be away an hour or so, and, after filling the Active up with petrol, took off for Brough.

It was such a clear day with billowy white clouds that I could not resist the temptation to do aerobatics on the way over. I climbed to about 8000 ft and rolled the Active on to its back in the direction of Brough and put it into a steep inverted dive, determined if I could to complete the outside loop. I got it up to the vertical inverted position and just when I thought I could force it over, the machine hung for a moment in the air, stalled and then slid back rapidly on its tail. I opened the throttle and the engine backfired. The next moment there was an explosion inside the engine cowling and the petrol tank at my feet burst into flames. My first reaction was to uncouple my Sutton harness and draw my feet up away from the heat. By now the flames were streaking up from the bottom of the cockpit as the slipstream acted like bellows in a blacksmith's forge. I knew if the heat melted the flexible fuel lines the tank could explode in my face, and in any case it was already too damned hot for comfort. Luckily I had riding-boots on, and when I glanced at them through what was fast becoming an inferno I hesitated no longer. With one hefty kick, over the side I went. In my panic I could not at first find the ripcord handle. When I did, I gave it such a mighty tug that it pulled completely away from the parachute pack and for a terrifying moment I thought it had broken. The parachute opened with a snap which punched the breath out of my body, and I glanced up gratefully to see the white parasol of silk gently holding me in the sky in a silence that seemed uncanny. I had dropped below the Active and as I watched the long plume of smoke and flames gracefully circling over my head, I realised I was not by any means in every sense of the expression out of the fire yet. The Active had gone into a perfect left-hand gliding turn and it looked as if on the next circuit it would collide with me. I prayed fervently, and thanked God a few seconds later as I was able to look down into the blazing cockpit from a few feet away as it glided past. It silently plummeted down in a cascade of smoke and flame, to explode in a field near the village of Covenham.

My troubles were still not over. The wind was so strong that I thought for a while I was going to be blown out to sea, which in the clear light lay below me with several ships and other craft at anchor in the Humber, and Grimsby and Cleethorpes making a pretty border around them. At one stage I thought I should never reach the ground and then the next moment I knew I was going to hit it hard: I could see the trees bending to the force of the wind and my landing was going to be rough. If I was un-conscious the parachute could drag me for miles unless it was obstructed or fouled on a building or telephone wires, so I undid my harness and hung firmly by my hands as I floated down the last hundred feet or so. When I landed in a grass field and rolled over and over, it was to see the free parachute tearing off in the wind to be caught up in some high trees.

Someone came running over to me panting with excitement and I borrowed a bicycle to hurry over to Covenham village shop and put in a call to my father. He was not in the house and I told our housekeeper to tell him I had baled out and would wait at Covenham until he arrived to pick me up. The house-keeper found him in the garden, but it was such a shock that he sprained his ankle in his effort to get to the telephone quickly. After Dad had picked me up we went over to the Active, a crumpled mass of smoking, burnt-out wreckage, in no way resembling the snappy looking little biplane it had been minutes before.

I went back to our own airfield to pick up Tony. I had bred

him from Jock, the Labrador I had had since boyhood, and he was to prove the most intelligent dog I ever knew. In fact, years later I was sure I could practise telepathy with him, and without word or signal I would look hard and long into his eyes willing him to do something, such as climbing into a chair or fetching my shoes. Without a sound he would stand up, look brightly and intently into my eyes and carry out what I had willed him to do. Often when shooting on one of my farms nearby, I would kill a hare or partridge and would say to Tony, 'I'm going to cover this up and leave it here, and don't forget where it is, as I want you to come back for it later on.' We would then shoot for the remainder of the day, and return home, which was about a mile and a half to two miles away, and as I cleaned the guns I would say to Tony, 'Isn't it about time you went back for that hare?' Tony would then look up at me to make sure what I had said and rush out of the house to return later as pleased as punch with the game in his mouth.

He'd flown on my lap as a pup in the Leopard and loved it, just as he loved riding in a car. As I approached the hangar on foot I whistled to him and to my astonishment his bristles went up and he growled. 'What the hell's wrong with you, you old fool?' I shouted. He took a wide circuit round me, bristles still up, cautious and suspicious. It then dawned on me that I had told him to look after things as I flew off, and he had expected me to return the same way. When I did not do so he must have thought it was a trick in his master's absence. I grabbed him and gave him a big hug, and as soon as he finally made up his mind it really was me his joy knew no bounds and he chased around picking anything up he could find to show his pleasure.

My misfortune with the Active was not quite at an end. In reporting the accident I had to produce my licence, which had expired by a few weeks. The next thing I knew I was being prosecuted for flying an aircraft invalidly.

6 ✳ *A Leopard in Europe*

WHAT DAD AND I really needed was a single-engine machine with a speed of 180–200 mph, a range of 1000 miles, a well-equipped instrument panel and cabin with three or four comfortable seats. Most aerodromes in those days were grass-fields and very few had night landing facilities. We also required good take-off performance from relatively poor landing grounds and the machine must have navigational and landing lights. Radio was rarely used in private aircraft, but above all both the airframe and engine should be reliable and go long periods between overhauls. The capital cost was also important. The German Messerschmitt Taifun was a possibility. We tried the American Stinson but did not like it or its low speed. Miles Aircraft were producing interesting and excellent performance machines but somehow at that time they seemed to lack the quality and refinement in workmanship that one expected. Percival seemed the best bet, but as we heard he was designing an improvement on the three-seat Gull which was to be called the Vega we decided to wait and see.

The loss of the Active left a void which I felt deeply, as whilst the Leopard was a wonderful means of transport there was nothing exciting about it. I spent my time in keeping it in first-class condition. With a block and tackle I took the engine out of the frame and did a thorough top overhaul. I would have liked to have tuned it for greater power output, but felt that safety and reliability was more important. As winter turned to spring, and we could still find nothing which suited us better than the Leopard, I decided to get in as much dead reckoning navigation and blind flying as I could. We decided to do another lengthy tour of Europe. I had acquired a special course computer, and made a promise to myself that I would ignore visual navigation completely and rely upon dead reckoning and my wonderful new computer whenever the opportunity was available.

Our first leg on this tour was to Basle, and apart from a slight drift owing to an increase in the wind, my navigation was not too bad. Basle aerodrome was a small grass field in the mountains, and the wind was switching about all over the place; I had to make two approaches before I was happy to put down. After a pleasant relaxed lunch, I looked at the Gipsy Major I had overhauled, it was clean and free of oil and was running as smooth as a sewing machine. I plotted a course for Vienna which would put us there just before dark, but we soon encountered some severe storms over the Tyrol, and as we needed over 10,000 ft to clear I re-routed my course to intercept the Danube at a point avoiding the worst of the weather. This, with the stronger winds we encountered, made us later than intended, but with the Danube now below I was not unduly worried, as it would lead us into Vienna. As the lights of Vienna appeared, the storm, which we thought we had left behind, built up becoming ominously dark with vivid streaks of lightning brightening up the sky from time to time. Dad and I were very pleased to see the lights of the city below, and we flew in the direction of the aerodrome. All we could see was the dark patch where we guessed the airport should have been, but then, as the storm broke, the rain fell in such a deluge that we could only see the glow of the Vienna street lights below. I flew round several times and said, 'What do we do now, Dad?' 'I can't understand why they don't put the bloody lights on,' he replied. Just when things looked serious and we were having to think of drastic measures, there was a flash below and the black patch came to life like a Christmas tree at a children's party; within minutes we were down and running into the Control Office before we got drenched to the skin.

The Austrians were very upset, one of the officials had apparently taken the key of the control switchboard away with him, and in the end they had had to break it open.

We spent a few wonderful days in Vienna, gaily unaware of

the tragic events that were shortly to follow. We then flew on to Budapest, to me the most wonderful city in Europe. A German said to me recently, 'Of course, if you knew Budapest before World War II, then you should never go back.' How true! Of all the wonderful times I think about in my youth, none stand out so vividly as the time Dad and I spent in that May of 1936: the idyllic evenings on the banks of the Danube; the nightingales on St Margaret's Isle; the gipsy bands and some of the prettiest women in the world; to say nothing of the rides through the colourful woods above Pezt and the fascination of the Pushta and the cowboys. We were both quite sad to leave, as with some of the haunting music still in our ears we set course for Warsaw.

I now felt somewhat ambitious with my new course and distance calculator and said to Dad, 'I'm going to ignore maps and set a direct course over the Carpathians for Warsaw.' I worked my course out very carefully, having one fix only for windspeed and direction. The weather up to the mountains was fine but storms and heavy cloud formed over the peaks. I made sure we had gained plenty of height and with confidence in my Reid & Sigrist turn-and-bank indicator, we ploughed into the billowy masses of cloud. Apart from the extremely bumpy conditions to be expected, we were, I thought going quite well, when suddenly the engine started to run a little rough, something it had never done before. I immediately thought with apprehension of my handiwork during the top overhaul, but at the same time I saw ice on the screen and the leading edges of the wings and struts. I had not given ice a thought: it had been very hot in Budapest and ice was the last thing I expected to encounter. My time said we should be over the main Carpathian ridge and I decided to hold my altitude and, if the engine cut completely, to carry on gliding down to what I hoped would be the Polish side.

Just then Dad shouted that he had spotted a hole in the clouds and as I quickly glanced in the direction he was pointing I saw the cloud was breaking up. Below, in pouring rain was a town, which in the fleeting glance I was able to get I presumed to be Krakow. Now feeling safe and sure, I put the Leopard into a very shallow dive and as we slowly lost height the ice dis-

6   A.H. with Labrador Tony beside the Active, Bar Fen
7   The remains of the Active at Covenham, 1935

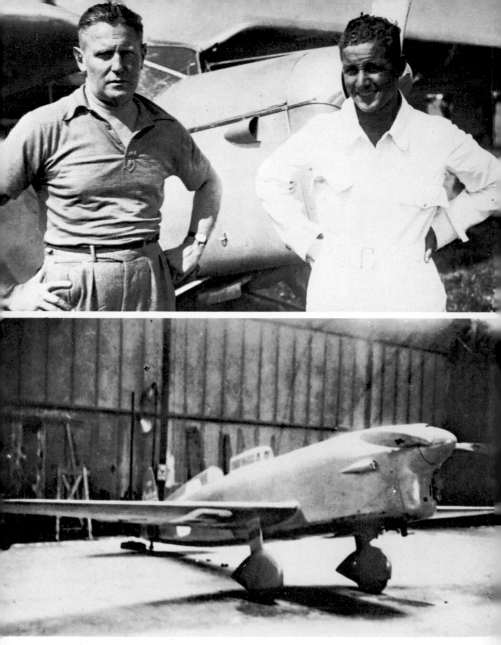

8   Bill Styran and A.H., London-Cardiff Race, 1933. Styran was killed
photographing the R101 memorial service at Beauvais
9   Coupe Deutsch Caudron, French favourite at Lympne, 1937

appeared, the engine regained its customary smoothness, and, as the clouds broke up, a vast expanse of open farmland heavily studded with belts of trees lay below us.

Determined to test out my dead reckoning I ignored maps until my watch said that Warsaw should be in sight. I hung on a little while with great expectancy, but then when I finally realised Warsaw was not going to show up I snatched at the maps and tried anxiously to find out where we were. The map showed dozens of main roads running in all directions and I was puzzled because all I could see below were dusty cart-tracks. I guessed that the wind had changed and I was to one side of my correct course. The trouble was I did not know which side. We had a large river in sight, and I said to Dad if we followed it I was sure it would bring us to Warsaw: on a blind guess I turned eastwards. What I did not know was that the town I took to be Krakow was in fact Tarnow, and I was already well to the east when we were over the mountains.

We followed the winding river as it snaked slowly through the countryside without a sign of a road or village. I knew now I had turned in the wrong direction and with petrol running low I could not change my mind. Dad was very kind and blamed the computer; 'I told you not to trust those new-fangled fancy gadgets,' he said. I was not worried about landing as the whole country was one glorious landing area, but I was concerned over obtaining more fuel, and a gnawing inside me started up as I began to realise we were going east all the time and there was nothing to show when we had arrived in Russia. Dad didn't worry me with his thoughts, but his mind must have been working on the same lines. I never knew a river could flow for so long through a civilised country without a bridge or village or town on its banks. And then when we had almost given up hope there in front of us was a grass aerodrome, some canvas and metal hangars and a number of military-type aircraft parked on the perimeter. The big question was, were they Polish or Russian, and what sort of a reception were we going to get? We had no choice and I did not hesitate to land, but I was more than apprehensive when scores of scruffy-looking soldiers rushed up as

F

we switched off, nearly all of them stripped to the waist, unshaven and mostly unwashed. Dad and I looked silently at one another. Before we had time to get out of the aircraft an officer forced his way through the men and introduced himself in broken English as Captain Debrowski of the Polish Air Force,* and informed us that we were at Brest-Litovsk, the last town before the Russian frontier. Captain Debrowski was more than kind. He introduced us to his wife, filled our tanks with petrol from open buckets, and when he saw my maps he made me feel better by saying, 'Of course you get lost, there are no roads where your map says. In the winter we travel these routes by sleigh, and in the summer they are only tracks.' He then insisted on loaning me his own flying maps, which were certainly more readable. We left after a drink of hot milk; I had no more difficulty when I used Debrowski's maps, and although we arrived in Warsaw very late in the evening, it was as light as day.

At about that time all sorts of rumours were floating around concerning Germany's revival, expansion and ultimate intentions. To me, the Germans as a whole made a very favourable impression. They were clean, industrious and honest, and there were marked contrasts between their country and most of the others, which was most evident to the naked eye as one flew overhead at low altitudes. This did not mean that I was deluded completely into thinking that the Germans would never again have ulterior motives or take up arms against us, if the opportunity looked favourable. I therefore had an open mind, and, more so, open eyes. I remembered all too clearly how we had once landed on a large aerodome in central Germany. The following morning I had mistaken the hangar in which my machine had been housed, and as it was early with few people about, I had wandered across the airfield and peered into one hangar which had no windows and all the doors firmly locked. Through a gap in the metal structure I was able to see several of

* I was not to hear from Debrowski again until the dark days of 1940, when he wrote to me at Supermarines from Kenley, where he was in charge of a Polish Hurricane squadron. The next time I was to visit Brest-Litovsk was with my wife, and it was then occupied by the Russians, and the aerodrome still bore the marks of bombing and the treacherous invasion.

the Junkers which were then in use as airliners. All the machines I was able to see were fitted with external bomb-racks.

Later during this trip we were going up to the Baltic via Danzig, when near Stettin, over beautiful flat wooded country, we suddenly found ourselves in the midst of many training aircraft. It was difficult to see where they were landing or taking off, and certainly there were no aerodromes marked on my maps for that area. We watched carefully and saw that they were landing on various grass runways sited in between belts of pine-trees which camouflaged them. The hangars seemed to be in the forest themselves, as when the machines taxied off the grass strips into the trees they disappeared completely from sight. We carefully stuck a pinhole in the map at each point where the planes were landing, and on returning to London gave all the information we could to our Intelligence people.

We had to return to England by 30 May as I had entered the Leopard for the London to Isle of Man Race and this was to start from Hanworth. The weather at the start was good, but before we reached Liverpool it began to rain heavily and the cloud was getting too low for comfort. Pandemonium reigned, as well as water, when we landed at Speke, the only control point before the Isle of Man. Many of the competitors thought the race should be abandoned or postponed because of the weather and the sea crossing to the island. Some had lost their way to Speke, and some were falling out with the race officials about a misleading finishing line and an arrogant control marshal. I was more concerned with filling up with petrol, and keeping the rain out of my tanks as I did so. I also had forgotten to bring a raincoat, and but for Scottish Airways Captain McIver insisting that I took his macintosh I should have been saturated. I frankly thought we were going to have a sticky trip as the rain pelted from grey depressing skies. Some of the other pilots were huddled beneath the wings of their aircraft saying very little but no doubt feeling much the way I did at that moment. I passed Charles Hughesdon trying to keep the water pouring off the top wing from flooding the open cockpit of his Tomtit, and close by was Bill Humble sheltering under the low wing of his scratch machine, the Hawk Speed Six. As I passed between them I noticed Bill had taken off his tie. When I asked why, he said, 'I never could swim with my collar on.'

As I swung the Leopard engine into life in the pouring rain there were many dispirited pilots doing the same thing in readiness for the start. Many wanted to cancel the race, but naturally those of us who thought our chances fairly good wished to continue, although I'm sure no one was looking forward to the sea-crossing in such conditions. In a whirl of spray and steamed-up windows we were away. Dad was keyed up and watching every point that might help. We clipped along the sands at zero feet as we made for St Bees Head, and found that the visibility was better than we had expected. It was still raining but over the water I could see a faint horizon, and although it was still pouring hard our side windows had cleared and we could see fairly well. No one was in sight as the dim outline of the island appeared and minutes later Dad slapped me on the shoulder as we crossed the line at Ronaldsway, and shouted excitedly, 'Well done son, we've won!' We had indeed, by a comfortable margin, as I had already climbed and turned before I saw the Tomtit cross the aerodrome chased by Bill Humble in the Speed Six Hawk.

The 6th of June was the official opening of Gatwick, to a fanfare of spectacular publicity. Dad and I decided to go because I wanted to see the aerobatics of an American in a specially prepared machine, who had promised manoeuvres never before seen in the UK. Our landing was not welcomed, as the aerodrome had been closed to all traffic pending the fantastic exhibition they proposed putting on, but luckily the Commanding Officer in charge was Captain Lamplugh, whom we knew very well, and nothing further was made of it. I was disappointed with the show: the best the American could do with his special machine was what he called knife-edge flying, which was simply holding the machine over in a steep bank on ailerons, and stopping the nose from falling away by applying hard top rudder. Not a very convincing performance.

I entered the Leopard in the 1936 King's Cup, with the knowledge that I had nothing up my sleeve and a very poor chance of a place. Dad came along as passenger, and although we were going to do our best, it had to be treated as a fun race more than anything else. The weather was hot and clear and the only enjoyment for us was a private race between Clouston in a Hawk and ourselves. Near Bristol, we were almost cooked in the closed cabin as the sun blazed down from a cloudless sky, and when I saw a flicker on the oil-pressure gauge I suggested to Dad that we put down and investigate. We landed at Brocklehurst, where Maurice Summers, the Gloster test pilot, gave us a most welcome drink and got the ground engineer to look at the oil-pressure relief valve. After a minor adjustment and some additional oil being put in the tank we took off again, but with so much time lost decided to return leisurely back to Hatfield.

In July of that year we were invited to visit Frankfurt and go over the Zeppelin *Hindenburg*. We asked Lewis Tindall, now an instructor at Desford on Tiger Moths, to go along with us as our guest. We arranged to pick him up early on the morning of the 17th, but visibility was down to 500 yards with mist and rain and I had to land at Desford off a turn; if I had overshot in that bad visibility I might not have found the aerodrome again without some trouble. There was a group of instructors waiting with Tindall and as we taxied up to them I saw the Commanding Officer, Wing-Commander George Lowdell.*

After greetings and some banter we prepared to leave for Lympne. The weather cleared before we reached the south coast to give the promise of a beautiful summer day. The *Hindenburg* glistened in the sunshine as we circled over the pine forest, out of which Frankfurt's airport had been carved by the unemployed of a rapidly resurging Germany. The fragrance of the pines, the fluttering of the many colourful flags plus the incomparable sound of a German band made our landing a memorable occasion. It was quite impossible not to be impressed by the façade presented by Germany in those happy days. At that time the ultimate aim of the Third Reich was hidden, and the people

---

* Wing-Commander Lowdell was posted to me at Castle Bromwich later during the war and did valuable work on testing production Spitfires.

were genuinely friendly. Everywhere one could see the happy, healthy bands of youths marching, playing and singing in that glorious summer, stripped to the waist as they vigorously awakened the new Reich that in such a short space of time we were to fear and hate.

The entertainment was lavish and well organised and there is no doubt, as I look back on those days, that we were carried away by our emotions. Before the *Hindenburg* crossed the Atlantic, the British Government had forbidden the commander to use the direct route across England. Amongst others, in the presence of the commander and the designer of the *Hindenburg*, at the official banquet, I loudly condemned our government for such a petty and unchivalrous action. I blush now when I think of all the subterfuges used by the Germans at that time to photograph and obtain information of the highest value on the outbreak of war. However, they were splendid hosts and as the banquet warmed to the spirit of the moment, the champagne flowed unceasingly and the entertainment matched the mood of the party. The girls dancing on the small stage between the tables were beautifully proportioned, and their almost naked bodies, tanned to a golden brown, presented an almost unreal fantasy with the enormous swastika flag forming the background.

We left Germany with the impression of a country reborn. I was filled with admiration as I watched the vigour and vitality of the regimented groups of boys and girls that seemed to dominate the countryside wherever we went: Dad, more perceptive than I, had other views.

I was building up quite a lot of experience by this time and was a lot happier with my navigation and blind flying, which I practised at every opportunity. Even in those early days, however, one had to be a little cautious. It was unusual to see anyone above the clouds at any time, but that year I took Maurice Crouch* and another friend to Brussels for a week-end. As we crossed the Channel I decided to climb above the cloud as the sky was overcast, estimating it would be about 1500 ft thick.

---

* Maurice was a friend of long standing and a fine sportsman. At one time he was Captain of both Cambridge and Northamptonshire County Cricket Teams.

As we entered the cloud it was quite dense, and no one spoke as I concentrated on the compass and the turn-and-bank indicator. Suddenly Maurice gasped and before he could say anything I had a fleeting glance of a biplane flashing by us in a downward and opposite direction. It must have been less than a wingspan from us, and we were all somewhat shaken as we realised what might have happened. We thought afterwards that it was a training machine from the flying club at Lympne practising blind-flying.

The next big race of that year was the Contact Race at Birmingham, and I ached to redeem my mistake of the previous year. This time Dad was going as passenger and would check us in at the various controls. When we arrived at Castle Bromwich for the start, I was somewhat disturbed to see Mr Pobjoy with Seth Smith in a Monospar SP4 fitted with two newly designed engines. I knew Pobjoy would not be there unless he expected great things from his new engines; he had chosen the right type of aeroplane for such a race, and Seth Smith* was a sound pilot for the job. Up until then I had been confident of doing fairly well, but I now suspected that the Monospar would have a good deal more speed than the handicappers had calculated.

The race proved to be the most exciting I had ever competed in. At the first checkpoint at Sywell I swung the Leopard into a vicious steep turn that nearly blacked Dad out, and landed with the machine coming to rest with the starboard wing nearly over the marshal's control table. Dad was equal to the occasion and was out of the cabin like a shot, nearly falling flat on his face in the excitement, and then after a hectic taxi with the tail well in the air we were off again to Leicester. Here I could see we were rapidly overhauling about five or six machines, but whereas I was holding Seth Smith and Napier on the ground they were faster than me in the air. I reckoned that Seth Smith at least would overtake me between Stoke and Castle Bromwich. I pulled out all the stops at the next two landings at Tollerton and Stoke, and when I reflect I easily understand why they made this the last Contact Race. I think the spectators must have had the

---

* Later to be killed as a test pilot with Hawker's.

time of their lives, and the ground marshals nightmares for weeks to come. As I flung the Leopard from right to left in high 'g' turns to lose speed on the last landing at Stoke, I saw the Monospar on my tail. Dad was marvellous at the control point, and we were up again in seconds to see the Monospar still on the ground with Napier's Gull.

We hugged the ground across Cannock Chase, and Dad said he could see Seth Smith behind on the port side a long way back. I was worried because Castle Bromwich is in a steep hollow, and from the Sutton Coldfield direction at such a low altitude it was very easy to miss it by a few yards. I dared not lose a split second in flying higher, and concentrated for all I was worth on picking out every village, church or crossroad that would give me a spot-on fix. As we shot across Sutton Coldfield High Street, Dad shouted, 'There it is, right on your nose, and we've done it.' As I dived into the hollow of Castle Bromwich aerodrome I pulled up into a shallow left-hand climbing turn to see Seth Smith right on my tail and Napier just crossing the line. It was the last important race I was to win with the Leopard.

7 ✳ Finding the Mew

THAT WINTER, DAD AND I planned our flying
for the next summer. It was becoming increasingly obvious that I should never win the King's Cup with the Leopard
Moth, and that we were outgrowing it for long-distance travel.
The real king of all racing machines at that time was without
question the little single-seater Percival Mew Gull, but, to put it
mildly, it was not everyone's cup of tea, and I was not sure that
my own flying capabilities would match the machine. The best
English private touring machine was probably the four-seater
Vega Gull also made by Percival.

In September 1936 the Schlesinger Race from Portsmouth to
Johannesburg had attracted a small but interesting and competitive entry, and it was this race that really made Dad and me
aware of the limitations of the Leopard Moth. I realise now that
I should have entered this race with a Mew Gull, but it is easy
to be wise after the event. A Vega Gull flown by C. W. A. Scott,
with Giles Guthrie as co-pilot, won the race, but it turned out to
be a very hollow victory. Three Mew Gulls were entered and
were by far the fastest machines competing. G-AEKL failed to
start, as Tom Campbell Black, the pilot, when taxying on Speke
aerodrome, was killed by a Hawker Hart, which was also taxying; the propeller of the Hart cut the fuselage of the Mew almost
in half. It was a tragic accident. Campbell Black was engaged to
the actress Florence Desmond, and had flown up to have the
machine christened Miss Liverpool. The second Mew Gull, ZS-
AHM, which was to become the most famous of them all, was
flown by Major A. M. Miller, but he landed at Belgrade and did
not continue. The third Mew Gull, ZS-AHO, flown by Captain

Stan Halse, went down Africa like a streak of lightning. Halse
was one of the best South African pilots, small in stature but very
tough; I think he was the first to fly the tiny Mew through the
night. The cramped cockpit and the continuous flying exhausted
him and he was in considerable pain at Kisumu before leaving
on the leg to Salisbury. When I saw him at a later date he said
he was desperately tired; he observed a large lake or reservoir
approaching Salisbury, and this confused him as he knew the
route extremely well. Convinced that he was lost, he made a
precautionary landing in the failing light; with the machine
touching down at such high speed he was lucky not to be killed,
as it disintegrated on hitting the rough ground. The heartbreak-
ing climax to his heroic flight was the fact that when he woke up
in hospital it was to be told that he was only a few miles north of
Salisbury when he crashed, and would have seen the lights of the
city minutes later had he continued on his course. The whole of
South Africa had watched his stupendous performance with admiration and thousands had flooded on to the airport at Johannesburg, where it had been arranged for Halse to land
briefly and then proceed to Cape Town, where he would have
beaten all existing Cape records.

When Scott and Guthrie arrived to win, it was so long afterwards that the crowd had all gone home and the airport was
almost deserted; those that were left were disappointed and in-
hospitable. The race had taken toll of nearly every competitor.
Max Findlay, Ken Waller and Morgan in the Airspeed Envoy
had crashed at Abercorn. They had the choice of taking off
downhill downwind or uphill upwind on the long narrow strip.
They chose the upwind direction, but in hot air at that altitude
acceleration is notoriously poor and as they lifted off the ground
they had insufficient height to clear the trees and the consequences were fatal, killing Findlay and Morgan. Clouston in
the Hawk Speed Six G-ADOD force-landed in the dark on the
top of bush trees in Uganda when the Gipsy Six 'R' engine
finally expired. It had been giving trouble with pistons and over-
heating from Cairo onwards. He was lucky to survive unhurt.
Llewellyn and Hughesden could not find Abercorn in the dark,

owing to the native bush fires; although they could see the southern tip of Lake Tanganyika as a very good fix. After an intensive and systematic search in the end they had to land on a sandbank, which clearly showed up in the moonlight near the middle of the lake. They stayed in the machine until rescued, as in the dim light they could see the tracks of crocodiles imprinted in the sand.

The race stirred my imagination as nothing had done before. Halse had set a pace that made a mockery of previous Cape record attempts and I dreamed wistfully that I might one day emulate him.

On 20 March 1937 I went down with Dad to Luton to discuss aircraft with Captain Edgar Percival. Percival showed me the Mew ZS-AHM glistening in white and gold, which had been returned from Belgrade, and fitted with a Gipsy Six Series I engine and fixed-pitch airscrew and sold to Bill Humble. On the way home, although the visibility was extremely good, there were line squalls about. I used these to practise my blind flying, so we did nothing to avoid them, and in one of these snowstorms it was so bad that I could not maintain altitude with the Leopard. We slowly lost height on full throttle, and I could not see the ground, only the lights of the cars below as they struggled along the roads with headlights on in the blinding snowstorm. Fortunately, line squalls are of short duration, and we ran into clear conditions before our position became critical. The next day, the Duchess of Bedford was reported missing in her Gipsy Moth, presumed lost over the North Sea. I had met this grand old lady, and have always been convinced that she deliberately flew to her death over the sea, as a woman of her experience would never have entered a line squall or got lost on such an otherwise perfect day. Nevertheless, it still remains an unsolved mystery.

On the 25th of April we flew up to York, where we had many good friends. As we entered the club house we heard voices ragging and pulling Bill Humble's leg. Apparently Bill had bought the Mew on the spur of the moment and was now about to get married; he was having second thoughts and many regrets as the Mew was not the easiest of machines to fly or sell. Bill was a good sport; in fact I always thought of him as the typical sporting blue-blooded Englishman that one unfortunately so rarely sees today. His family were in coal mining, but Bill's heart was in flying, at which he was extremely good. When Bill gave a show of aerobatics in the Avro Cadet, in which he instructed pupils, it was as good a performance as one could see anywhere in the world. He used up very little sky, his programme was varied, smooth, compact and impeccable and seemed to take place almost at your feet. I had raced against him many times and it was always good, keen competitive fun. 'I don't think the missus is going to like it, Bill, you going off in the Mew all on your own,' joked Alex Montief. 'I shouldn't worry, Bill; get rid of the wife, it's cheaper,' teased someone else.

'What I really need is a machine like yours, Alex,' Bill said as we settled down in the club easy chairs. 'Why don't you do a swop with Alex, then?' asked my father.

I frankly was amazed at Dad's suggestion, as until that very moment I had not given it a thought. What took place then must surely stand as a record for the most casual of all transactions in the history of British aviation: no written agreement, no witnesses or legal representatives, just a quiet, 'OK, Bill, I'll hand over my Leopard to you when the Mew is ready for me to collect from Luton.' 'That's marvellous, Alex. I'll write to Percivals telling them to register the Mew in your name.'

The next week we handed over the Leopard to Bill at York with real regret, and on the 8th of May Dad drove me by car to Luton to take delivery of the Mew Gull. It sparkled and looked every inch a thoroughbred as it stood alone on the tarmac in front of the factory doors, only a few hours old and re-registered G-AEXF in place of ZS-AHM. The gold letters and wingtips had been changed at my request to racing green. I stood beside it, speechless with pride and gratitude beyond words to my father, who had made this dream of mine possible; and I fervently prayed that I should be capable enough to prove worthy of the opportunities so generously given.

Captain Percival had moved from a small metal hangar at Gravesend to a new factory at Luton. The airfield on which the

factory now stood was not yet completed, and all the flying had
to be carried out from one narrow grass strip. I was not too
happy doing my first flight from this strip, as not only was it
small but it ran down quite a steep hollow. Dad saw me to the
extreme end of the narrow runway as I taxied out carefully in
readiness for the take-off. With a Gipsy Series I engine and a
fixed-pitch airscrew, the static revs were too low, and the engine
felt very rough as I opened up. The take-off was easier than I
had expected, but the climb was poor as I waited for engine
revs to build up as the machine gained speed. Once under way
at full cruising speed it felt more comfortable, but I was quick
to realise that this was not a machine I could put down anywhere, and if the engine failed then it was God help me. If I had
any misgivings they were soon dispelled from my mind by
fascination at the manner in which I was able to overtake other
military and private aircraft, and the way the countryside slid
by rapidly beneath me.

I did my first landing at Hatfield. It was not a bad landing but
I disliked the lack of vision after I had touched down and it
took me a long while to get rid of the awful feeling that someone
would run across my bows before I could get the machine pulled
up. After all, it could taxi faster than some aircraft flew. It had
been arranged that I should keep the Mew for a time at Waltham
near Grimsby, which had recently had an extension added to the
airfield. They were all somewhat astonished when I first went
there, because as some watchers said my landing speed looked as
if I was shooting up the aerodrome. In any case I used up most
of the airfield before coming to a standstill.

As my first big race was the London to Isle of Man in a few
weeks' time, I was anxious to get as much practice in the Mew as
I could. At first I rather felt it was flying me, rather than me
flying it, and I needed clear skies and large aerodromes to sort
myself out. I remembered that just recently Cardiff had constructed a large new airport. This, I thought, would give me a
decent distance to fly, and, being in Wales, it would not be
crowded with aircraft. The flight down was fast and enjoyable in
good weather. When I was letting down to approach the airport,

I suddenly found myself taking rapid evasive action as I darted amidst dozens of aircraft, and it suddenly dawned on me that Cardiff was having an official opening day. It seemed that every aircraft in the country was going to land at precisely the same time as myself. My first reaction was to climb above the machines buzzing around the aerodrome like wasps over a jampot, and go to Heston or Hatfield. Then I thought: This is ridiculous; if I can't land this thing when and how I like, I'd better pack it in.

My glide-in overtook at least half a dozen other aircraft doing the same thing and I touched down at high speed praying there was no one in the way that I could not see. By the time I had parked the Mew and got away from its admiring onlookers, most of the other aircraft had landed and I thought I would have a quick wash and go home. Then suddenly over the microphone I heard my name called, asking if I could come to the control-tower and collect my prize of £50 for winning the arrival competition. In those days it was a considerable sum, so no wonder it had attracted a large response. The irony of the situation was that I knew nothing about the competition. Christopher Clarkson told me later he had given a great deal of thought to the time chosen and was landing in a Gull IV at precisely the same moment as I was, but out of respect for my rapid approach in the Mew he gave me first choice, opened his engine and went round again.

I took this first-ever prize win by my Mew Gull as a very good omen, and so it turned out to be. The Isle of Man race was on the 29th of May; it was hot and sultry and I had a long wait as scratch man before I was due to take off. Although Hanworth was a most attractive spot, it was by no means a safe aerodrome, being quite small and surrounded by houses. I had not liked landing the Mew Gull there very much as it was extremely gusty; the large clubhouse and trees in the centre of the aerodrome seemed to disturb the hot air, and with the extremely sensitive elevators on the Mew I was working overtime to put it down for a good landing. There was an international entry. Tragedy almost struck before the first half-dozen machines got away. Flying-Officer Clouston had started his engine on the

Hawk a little early, and as he thought it would overheat he had switched off both ignition and the petrol tank control. When he was due to take off he started again at the last moment, forgot the petrol cock, opened up as the flag went down and when about ten feet up his motor cut completely. Fortunately, he had just enough room to land without overshooting the boundary; but it caused a lot of palpitations, including I suspected, those inside the cockpit of the Hawk as the pilot realised what he had done. I then watched Dad as one of several passengers flown by Captain Higgins in the four-engined Rapide go off smoothly with a wave of the hand.

I was now champing at the bit. I was not used to being scratch man and the others seemed to have such a long start on me that I thought it must be impossible to catch them up in time. We were now down to the last three aircraft, including the Germans, when Sid Sparks went off in the Gull III. There was a 180-degree turn after take-off and the only ruling was that all aircraft should clear the boundary of the aerodrome before turning. Sparks lifted off well, went on a little way and then did a sharp vertical turn over the first house: the nose of the Gull dropped and we were horrified to see it plunge into the roof with a dull crunch and in the next second explode into an enormous pillar of smoke and flames. There was deathly silence on the starting line, broken only by the fierce crackle of the fire, and then by the clanging bells of the fire tenders as they rushed to the scene.

There was nothing to say, it was now my turn to start up. Fred Rowarth who was acting as starter as well as handicapper, looked drawn and came up as I strapped myself into the cockpit of G-AEXF and said, 'Two minutes to go, Alex. For God's sake be careful and don't turn too soon.' I put my thumb up to him as I opened the throttle with a reassuring look I did not feel and XF moved rapidly forward over the sun-baked ground. I clipped the boundary trees as the Mew lifted into the air; I was determined to keep the nose well down, and used the smoking pyre of Sparks and his passenger as a turning-point. Once I had completed the turn on to course and reached maximum revs and speed I gently used the bumpy thermals rising from the hot ground to gain as much height as possible on the downwind leg to Liverpool.

My average speed to Speke, the compulsory control point, was 225·9 mph which was a little disappointing, but I had gained so much on most of the other competitors that my chances seemed good. Again I had to wait for the other aircraft to go off, but this time nothing like so long. I had already passed several aircraft before we reached St Bees Head and was beginning to mark off the remaining machines as we sped over the water to the Isle of Man. I passed Dad in the Rapide and waved briefly as I flashed by. I was jubilant: minutes to go and no other aircraft as far as I knew was in front. What I had taken to be land in the distance was partially obscured in cloud and as I raced up to this dark mass my spirits sank as I saw it was obliterating the lighthouse turning-point, whilst only a few hundred yards away the route to Ronaldsway aerodrome was clear. First of all I flew into the edge of the low cloud and then as I realised it was down to sea-level I pulled up and climbing over the cloud, circled in the hope of being able to see the lighthouse below. Being so near the finishing-line with the race won and not being able to complete the last turning-point was frustrating beyond measure. I went back to the edge of the cloud over the sea, pulled the throttle well back, put down the flaps and endeavoured to probe into the mist, if only for the lighthouse people to see me and report me as rounding the turn. All I could see were the waves below; then I ran into such turbulent conditions that I had to open the throttle, close the flaps and shoot up through the cloud into the clear air above. I tried this three times, until once I actually saw close below me the rocks of the shoreline and realised that the cliffs on which the lighthouse stood were in dense fog that I could not hope to penetrate. I flew the last few minutes to Ronaldsway and landed disconsolately. I was relieved, however, to see that the Rapide with Dad on board was now overhead and would soon be landing.

I was quickly followed by the other competitors, who told a similar story. All the pilots expected the race to be re-run or cancelled, except one man, Bernstein in a Monospar, who stated emphatically that he had rounded St Mogul Head lighthouse and claimed first prize. With several others I laughed at this until it became apparent that the Manx Council and officials, in their anxiety to name a winner at all costs, were prepared to accept the claim. Then I became hopping wild. I had nearly broken my neck in my attempts to reach the lighthouse, and I was pretty sure no one could have done better. Captain John Higgins in the Rapide felt exactly as I did; he flew the Isle of Man–Liverpool run daily and knew what bad weather was all about—he told me that on several occasions he had approached the mainland with his aerial trailing as he flew blind, and as he felt it tug on the water he would know just how much height he had to spare. Dad also told me how they had done the same thing as I had, but that the visibility was just zero. The controversy grew into a prize row, with Brian Field, Charles Hughesdon and Bill Humble pushing me in as their spokesman.

We arranged a meeting with the Manx officials and the competitors for that evening at the Castle Mona Hotel. The Manx Council was determined to announce a winner of some sort and I felt that if they had nominated Bernstein there would have been a free fight. The argument waxed hot, strong and bitter; the Chairman of the Council pleaded that in the interests of the publicity for which his Council had subscribed substantial sums to enable them to organise this race, they owed a solemn duty to the taxpayers on the island to resolve this impasse as favourably as possible. Having been satisfied with Mr Bernstein's claim that he had in fact seen the lighthouse he was going to recommend that he be nominated the winner. When the uproar that followed had subsided a little, my father stood up and said, 'Mr Chairman, we have all heard what Mr Bernstein has had to say, but I understand the lighthouse-keeper who was to take down the aircraft numbers as they rounded the lighthouse is in fact present at this meeting; I would like, with your permission, to ask him a few questions.' There was a cheer for this logical request from the pilots, but silence from most of the Council members. Then the lighthouse-keeper was asked to stand up. My father

G

said, 'What was the number of the machine which turned round the lighthouse?' He replied, 'I couldn't get any numbers, 'cos I never saw any aeroplanes.' 'Then what did you see?' 'I didn't see anything until after the race because it was thick fog; the first I knew that the machines had reached us was when I thought I heard rockets going off, but this was the first machine which shot by three times overhead, so fast that it sounded like a rocket. I heard others that followed more slowly, but I did not see a machine turn over the lighthouse until an hour later, when a foreign aircraft went overhead, with letters D-10SA.' There was a hushed silence as the implication of what the lighthouse-keeper had said sank in. Bernstein was forgotten; in one voice we said: 'That's Major Seidemann, number 10—the ME108 Taifun. The race has never been cancelled; he's complied with all the rules; he is the obvious winner.' Peace reigned as a simple and correct solution had been found. Major Seidemann had thought he had no chance from Speke onwards, and had taken it very leisurely for the remainder of the race; when he had arrived over the island, as so often happens in that area, the fog and cloud had moved away and he had had a clear run to Ronaldsway, oblivious of the controversy raging between the pilots below.

8 ✳ *Disappointments*

ON THE WEEK-END of the 4th of June the Sherburn and York aero clubs, with the support of pilots like ourselves who had received hospitality abroad, organised an international rally to reciprocate. It was a huge success. I was asked to demonstrate XF and as this was the first time I had been asked to give a serious performance in front of a large crowd, I considered carefully what manoeuvres would best suit the Mew and the audience. The Mew Gull was not an aerobatic aircraft, but as a very high-performance machine it was adequately stressed if not abused. It was at this stage in my flying life that I made up my mind never to try and perform aerobatics or manoeuvres unless I had previously practised them on my own in safe circumstances.

The Mew had very sensitive elevators, firm to stiff ailerons which stiffened up still further at speed, and good rudder control. With the York demonstration in my mind I took XF up to 3000 ft and decided to stall it; this proved a unique experience for me as it was the first time I had ever heard an aircraft stall. In the Mew, as everything became silent just before losing enough speed for the stall, there suddenly arose a very distinct noise rather like the flapping of a sailing boat 'in irons' in a strong wind.

I next tried a loop. At first I thought the machine was going over smoothly with very little 'G' but when I had just got beyond the vertical and as I gently pulled the control column back the machine stalled abruptly, flicked into one turn of an inverted spin, then into a normal spin and I came out of it at high speed. I was thankful I had plenty of height to spare. Later I found that the Mew must be put into a loop at a much higher speed than I had first thought, if the loop was to be executed properly.

I then tried rolling to the left and to the right, which could be done very smoothly and extremely accurately. I told no one about my practising and for the demonstration I settled on a five-minute show, finishing off with two low rolls across the aerodrome. It seemed to go down fairly well, as Bill Humble said when I landed, 'Christ, Alex, I need a drink. It's bad enough flying the Mew but to roll the bloody thing!'

There was a race the same day, but as one of the hosts I had not entered and helped in the organisation as best I could. Little Connie Leathart startled us all, competing with a Pobjoy Swift, when her engine misfired badly on the last turn and she had to put down on the aerodrome in a hurry, fortunately without damage.

The next big event for me was the former London–Newcastle race, which this year had been changed to an earlier date and was routed from the new aerodrome at Newcastle to York, Thirsk, Sherburn, Carlisle and back to Newcastle. I was looking forward to this race as I had heard that Charles Gardner had entered the only other Mew Gull in the country and it promised some interesting and challenging racing. Gardner had been flying about the same length of time as myself, and I had competed against him on many occasions. He was a man small in stature, reserved, modest and inclined to be absentminded. He was in my opinion the best racing pilot of my day; he had brains and used them. I liked Charles immensely and I found it somewhat refreshing when we were discussing racing methods and procedure, and tuning in particular, that what might have been considered a very subtle and cunning move had been thought of by both of us at about the same time. Charles's Mew was now fitted with the engine from Stan Halse's crashed machine, a Gipsy Six Series II with a variable-pitch airscrew. It was considered to be a little better in performance than my own XF, but as the power was only about 5–10 hp more, I thought that apart from a better take-off and climb with the V/P airscrew there would not be much in it.

The weather for the start of the race was fine and clear; my handicap permitted me to take off before Gardner, and I set off with high hopes and determined concentration. I was streaking along at about 200 ft with Sutton Bank showing clearly ahead as a good guide, when I was suddenly conscious of another machine very close to me; glancing back over the starboard side I was shocked to see Gardner's blue Mew Gull on my tail and about to pass me. I felt utterly dejected. If Charles could catch me up in such a short time from the start, he must be miles an hour faster than I was. I felt miserable because I knew there was nothing I could do about it: the de Havilland Gipsy Six Series II engine in those days was £1200 and a V/P airscrew at least another £300 to £400, even if I could afford, find and fit one in time for the next race. As we left Sherburn the fine weather suddenly disappeared and it started to rain with low scudding clouds and mist. I swung out my special venturi tube from the cockpit in anticipation of running into weather that would force me up into the murk on instruments. It did not get as bad as I first expected but the final run-in over the hills to Newcastle tested most of the competitors and on landing I found that Charles had won, with Geoffrey de Havilland in the TK2 second, and myself third.

I was very despondent over the race and my spirits were not improved when Wilf Dancy the handicapper came up to me and said, 'What happened to you, Alex? Did you get lost? Fred and I expected you to be closer to Gardner's Mew than you were.' I replied indignantly, 'No I didn't go off course at any point, but Gardner passed me like a dose of salts before we even reached Sutton Bank. You ask him.'

Nearly every race had a fastest-speed prize, the result of which was of course a foregone conclusion if you had the fastest machine, and I was somewhat surprised on taxying out to the starting line for the London-to-Cardiff race at Heston, that Charles's Mew was not to be seen. In plotting my course I found I was short of a map from Bristol to Cardiff, and thinking I would easily pick one up at Heston I left the matter until the last moment. The clubhouse at Heston was closed that day and try as I might I could not find anyone who could loan me this particular map. As the distance on this leg was short I made a careful note of the compass course and the general features between Bristol and Cardiff and decided to fly without one. I was scratch man with Bill Humble in the Speed Six Hawk and Geoffrey de Havilland in the TK2 going off before me. I did not see a single machine up to the turn at the Clifton Suspension Bridge, and as I turned on to the new course I cursed myself that I was without a map; I was so near to the finishing line, but with the tide up the river was so enormous that I felt uneasy about the accuracy of my position. So far I had not seen any other competitors; then all of a sudden I saw several, all about 100 to 200 yards to my right, but still no sign of the airport. I decided to ease gently over towards the aircraft I could see as I reckoned they must be pilots who knew exactly where they were; as I did so I saw the aerodrome ahead, with Geoffrey in the TK2 streaking along at almost ground-level. I pushed my nose down to the maximum in an effort to catch him and did so just after we had crossed the finishing line. I estimated I lost by less than 50 yards and to this day I wonder whether it would have made any difference if I had carried a map of the last sector.

The King's Cup was to be the last race of the 1937 season and was to be run on the 10th of September. At the time I had mixed feelings about my chances and I was puzzled because Charles Gardner was not entering his machine in all the small races, so that all the fastest-time prizes were going to me. Edgar Percival was also missing from the scene and it was rumoured that he was building a super Mew Gull, faster than any of the previous models. I was not unduly disturbed as I was enjoying a very good racing season and getting to know my little XF well. We had to land at Roborough for the Plymouth race, which offered an enormous trophy for the fastest time, but the airfield was so small that bets were being made that the Mew would not be able to get in. I landed safely though apprehensively with minimum fuel on board, but I was more worried about my take-off at the start of the race. To get every inch of run I placed the tail of XF almost in the hedge on the boundary and ran the engine up to full throttle on the brakes, before releasing for the take-off. The Mew got off the ground, but if there had been another hedge on the opposite boundary I'm sure she would not have made it. I collected a handsome prize and Dad staggered off with the magnificent trophy, which he picked up for me as I did not want to tempt providence twice by another landing or take-off.

My best race of that year was the Folkestone Trophy at Lympne against eighteen other entrants. I knew the short, interesting course well and although I was sure of the fastest time, the handicap seemed to favour the slow aircraft. On the last lap I had passed most of the other machines before entering the shallow valley which sloped down from the aerodrome and I caught a glimpse of the Hendy Hobo G-AAIG flown by A. J. S. Morris just crossing the airfield boundary. Dad said afterwards that it was the most exciting and astonishing finish to a race ever seen: one moment the Hobo was racing at about 120 mph towards the finishing line, with not another aircraft on the aerodrome or in sight, and the crowd applauding the obvious winner; and then, so Dad told me, appearing to shoot up out of the ground on the airfield boundary there streaked XF, to overtake the Hobo less than ten yards before we both crossed the line. I was of course jubilant: not only did I get the winning trophy, but Anne Davis, who with her husband Eric ran the aero club, knowing that I should put up the fastest time, had chosen specially two beautifully inscribed pewter mugs and now presented them to me.

About this time I began to get bored with the air racing scene. I had come to realise that you were not really racing the other aircraft, but trying to beat or fox the handicappers: they did their best with the information available, but if someone could secretly find a little more speed without them knowing it or having to declare some minor alteration, he was on to a winner, and all the good flying by his opponents would be of no avail. My thoughts continually dwelled on Stan Halse's fantastic flight before he crashed near Salisbury.

The opportunity came when Dad and I were staying at

Shoreham with Tommy and Billy Rose during the early part of August. As I questioned Tommy on flying conditions in Africa, without any prompting he said seriously to Dad, 'You know, Pop, you ought to let Alex have a go at the Cape records in the Mew.' Dad said, 'I should think so, and bump himself off, like poor old Halse nearly did.' Tommy leaned across the table and said seriously, 'Pop, I really mean this; let Alex have a go; he could do it.' I didn't say a word, but my mind was made up.

On the 21st of August I had my most unexpected success of the year in the Isle of Thanet race. To my surprise Charles Gardner had entered his Mew, and he collected the fastest time but did not get a place in the race. I was further surprised when checking the time later to note that he had only just beaten me for the speed prize. Then I realised what the astute Charles was up to: he had only been in one race that year, the Newcastle, in which he averaged 10 mph more than me, and he knew that the handicappers had doubts on the performance of each aircraft because of the weather; now Charles had foxed them by competing in the Thanet race at reduced power, with a speed difference between his machine and mine of only 2 mph. Whilst I had been racing throughout that season, Charles had quietly worked on his Mew with such things as moving the centre of gravity forward, strapping up the undercarriage oleo legs with steel cables and tuning the engine, and he had improved the performance without the handicappers being aware. I was confident even then that Charles was going to win the 1937 King's Cup.

My next best race was the following week, again at Lympne, in the Wakefield International Trophy. This was an event which had been won twice before by a Belgian named Guy Hansey and this year he was making a particularly determined effort by entering a special supercharged Coupe-Deutsche Caudron, to be flown by a well-known French pilot called Arnoux. As I was the fastest British competitor all my friends were looking to me to pull something out of the bag. I said to Fred Rowarth, 'I'm not concerned about winning the race, but I would like to beat the Caudron; what do you think my chances are?' Fred replied,

'Well, it has much more power than your Mew, and if Arnoux flies it well, we think he will be considerably faster.'

Most onlookers at air-racing in those days were of the opinion that all one had to do was to fly your machine flat out and navigate accurately. There was a little more to it than that. Most pilots had a particular method of their own; for myself, having accepted that the first and most important hurdle to jump was the handicappers, then I knew it was up to the pilot. Over the years I had given a great deal of thought and carried out many experiments to perfect what I thought was the best technique. In all cases a thorough knowledge of the course was if not essential of great assistance, and on a short course I would study every dip in the landscape, every hill and almost every tree.

An engine, in most cases, warms itself up before the oil in the tank, so, if possible, I liked to be able to take off once before the start to make sure the engine oil was thoroughly hot. On take-off most pilots let their machines run off the ground; I liked to pick my machine up from the ground without inducing too much drag and then fly along as close to the ground as I could without actually touching it; I had found in many machines that the wheels being in contact with the ground created more drag than the method I had adopted. It was essential to gain maximum revs as quickly as possible, particularly with a fixed-pitch propeller; irrespective of wind direction I would fly as low as I dared until maximum speed had been reached, and then if necessary use every little bump or uplifting thermal to gain the height I needed.

If there was no rule for turning on to course after take-off, then more often than not if the wind lay across the track, it was possible to do the turn on the ground and make the take-off crosswind; mostly however the rules were that all aircraft had to turn at a certain point on or beyond the aerodrome boundary. In my opinion on a short course the turns are the most important part of the race. Theoretically, a turn should be taken so that if it is 180 degrees the turning-point shall be on a radius of a perfect semicircle without any loss of speed to the aircraft. In practice this was rarely so; in the first instance much depends on

direction and strength of the wind, so that the approach to the turn is always different for varying conditions. For instance, a very strong beam wind on the starboard side would mean the approach to a left-hand turn would appear to be wide, but as the pilot attempted a perfect turn his circuit would place him over the turning-point without overrunning the track he was aiming for. Many pilots put on a vertical bank to get round a turn, but this reduces the speed of a machine drastically and the power falls away with the loss of revs with fixed-pitch airscrews.*
Having decided my precise line of flight I would always try to approach the turn with a hundred feet or so in hand; I would put the minimum amount of bank on to get me round and as I did so gently let the nose fall away so that I finished the turn in a shallow dive without any loss of speed. Those pilots who did spectacular vertical turns at low altitude may have looked very good, but they were certainly not getting round the quickest way.

There were a few courses where it sometimes paid off to keep slightly to one side of the true track and take advantage of a wind blowing up a ridge of hills; at Lympne for instance, on one occasion by moving a hundred yards or so to the south of track in the Wakefield Trophy on the crosswind leg, I was getting 10 to 15 mph extra and some free lift from the thermals on a ridge of hills. I am sure this did more to win me the race than a good handicap. As in all sports, experience teaches many 'wrinkles', and in flying one could fill a book with dodges of every sort.

When I looked at the Caudron and spoke to Arnoux, I felt I would have to use every trick in the book to do any good. As we moved up to the starting-line several friends were already consoling me and saying, 'Of course, if yours were supercharged, Alex, you would have at least a sporting chance.' As the flag went down I did not see the Caudron, but concentrated on streaking down the narrow valley between the trees as I built up my speed, I was alone at the first turn and as I straightened out for the second leg I was astonished to see Arnoux still climbing from the aerodrome and about to settle down to make a very

---

* One has to remember that an aileron is also an airbrake, positive 'g' load is an anchor and the greater the 'g' the heavier and more effective the anchor becomes.

wide, casual turn after me. I did not see him again until the race was over. Dad and friends were jubilant; with Dad already being hugged in congratulation by an excited Anne Davis and applauded by many others. They had all been as surprised as I was to watch Arnoux race. The Caudron may have been faster than the Mew, but the way the Frenchman flew it, the further he got behind, and I was happy indeed to finish the race 7 mph faster.

Just before the King's Cup I was on my way to the Eastbourne rally when the weather clamped down and I found myself over Biggleswade. Knowing that R. O. Shuttleworth had a landing field at Old Warden, I decided to call in and wait for the weather to improve. As I climbed out of the Mew, Dick Shuttleworth drove up on a tractor covered in mud and without any preamble shouted, 'I'm glad you've dropped in, Alex; you can give me a hand to clear the road I'm making.' Dick was a remarkable character, and not I think as obtuse as many people thought; wealthy and eccentric, a racing driver who had crashed badly in the South African Grand Prix. It left him with an appalling scar severing the muscles of his thigh and he liked to horrify unsuspecting friends with a macabre display of it. When not racing he spent his time flying, rebuilding vintage aircraft or designing specialist bodies for sports cars. He was killed during World War II in a flying accident, and his mother established the Old Warden aircraft museum in his memory. As we mopped our brows that day after cutting down a large tree, he said to me, waving a damp handkerchief in front of my face, 'Not bad, eh? Three shillings a dozen, Marks and Spencer.'

When we had tired of working on the road Dick said, 'Come and fly my Blériot,' so off we went to carry out a series of hops across the airfield, first in the Blériot and then in the Deperdussin. I would have liked to have flown his Sopwith Pup, but it was not then ready to fly. The weather started to clear but Dick said, 'Stay the night; it will give me a chance to show you my new design on the Essex Terraplane.' I had not brought an overnight suitcase with me, but when shown to my room I saw that a new pair of pyjamas had been laid out for me, and on the dresser was a sealed packet containing toothbrush, paste and hairbrush. After an excellent dinner the butler discreetly asked me when I would like my tea in the morning and how I preferred it. Before I left I promised Dick to fly to Andover the following May for a special exhibition where we would have both the Bleriot and the Deperdussin in the air at the same time. As a parting bit of free advice he shouted, 'If you want any good oil cheap, you can get it from Gamages at five bob a drum.'

On the 6th of September Dad and I borrowed a Leopard Moth from Dick Malone of Airwork, and flew over the King's Cup course to Scotland, Ireland and Wales, and then back to Hatfield. It was a wretched trip, rain and low cloud all the way, and on the first day we were glad to be able to creep into Blackpool, with the tower well out of sight in the depressing murk. As a route-checking flight for the race it was a washout, in more ways than one.

The first day of the 1937 King's Cup was an eliminating race, based on sheer speed; as I was amongst the few fastest machines, I had nothing to worry about and decided to fly the course to Baldonnel at little above cruising speed. I was glad I did so, for although the day was clear the wind was blowing from the northeast at gale force and it was very bumpy indeed. Turning over the control point at Scarborough on the leg to Newcastle, I anticipated particularly rough turbulence as the wind came up over the cliff lip from the sea, so I took it fairly high and at reduced throttle; even so I was glad my harness was tight. Flight-Lieutenant Piper in the Short Scion Senior had two 56-lb weights strapped in the fuselage to keep his tail down in lieu of passengers and these were flung right through the strengthened floor of the aircraft; as far as I know they are still at the bottom of the sea. Wing-Commander Hilton in a Falcon Major G-AENG rounded the turn, and whether he had his harness on or whether it broke away I do not know, but he was flung right through the cabin roof. One of the spectators on the ground took the most remarkable photograph I have ever seen of Hilton crashing through the cabin and forward over the engine cowling to be decapitated by the propeller; the photograph showed

Hilton's head about two feet from his body with Sherren, his passenger, remaining in the aircraft to crash to his death on the rocks below.

I did not rate my chances in the King's Cup very high, because I felt that Gardner would have both speed and a good handicap, but my spirits dropped completely when I saw the entry list. Rumours had been floating around all summer about Percival's new Mew Gull, also about the special racing machine being built by the students at the De Havilland technical school. When I saw the new Mew Gull of Percival my whole feeling on racing changed: I welcomed the competitive struggle with such pilots as Lowe, Humble, Atcherley, Gardner and Broadbent, but I now felt a surge of resentfulness that Percival's should be able to sell two Mews to private owners and then proceed to build one with a thinner and smaller wing section, which would of course be faster. After the initial shock and disappointment I realised my attitude was unreasonable, but I had learnt for the first time the enormous gap technically, financially and in the scale of operations between the amateur and the professional in the fascinating pursuit of speed in the air.

From that moment on I had only one dream, one aim: not to win the King's Cup, but to put up the fastest time; to be able to compete—and win—against all the resources of the manufacturers with their factory backing.

The TK4 was an unknown quantity; certainly it was the most exciting machine of that year and extremely fast for its low horsepower. I never flew it, but Bob Waite, the De Havilland test pilot said he had no aileron control on landing and that on a steep climb the machine would start to turn on engine torque without him being able to control it unless he increased his speed.*

There was great excitement as the machines landed at Baldonnel for the night, and a banquet had been laid on for the competitors and members by the local authority. The Irish

* He came ninth in the King's Cup and then a week or so later, when about to attack the 100-km closed circuit record, was killed as the machine suddenly flicked into the ground in front of all the reporters and photographers watching his demonstration.

would persist in calling it the Big Race, the Blue Riband of the air, the famous air race, but never the King's Cup, and when one of our more outspoken royalist competitors suddenly stood up and proposed a toast to His Majesty the King, only the most diplomatic intervention by one of our Royal Aero Club representatives saved the situation from exploding into a brawl. I was very friendly with Jim Broadbent, the Australian record-breaking aviator, who was flying the B.A. Double Eagle; instead of staying with the others at a hotel, I stayed with Mavis and Jim McNaughton, also friends of Jim.

In the morning everyone was out at the airfield and it was all hustle and bustle for the final preparations. Dad was polishing the Mew with great enthusiasm, but deep down I had the feeling that I was not going to do any good. The leg to Newtownards was upwind and I sped very low over the water, using the mountains of Mourne as an excellent guide. My hunch over Gardner was correct; I calculated as we landed at the first control point and checked our times that he would overtake me before reaching Blackpool. In fact, it transpired that he was lucky to finish the race at all, never mind win it. I had just taxied out to the starting-line at Newtownards and had stepped out of my machine for a few moments, when I saw Charles also taxying out but heading for a large boundary marker, which he obviously could not see; he was about fifty yards from me, and I don't think I have ever run so fast in my life, to grab his port wing just in time and swing him clear before his airscrew and machine ran into the heavy timber marker. As he thanked me he said he often became very absentminded when concentrating.

As I headed out to sea direct for Blackpool I thought I was going to repeat my ducking of 1935, as suddenly the engine began to misfire; I guessed it must be sparking plugs and hoped it might clear itself. As I had worked out, Gardner slipped past me quickly and I followed him, limping into Squires Gate. I shouted for a toolkit on landing and to my surprise, Bill Humble ran over and said he would get one,* but because everyone was on

---

* Bill was not racing that year as he had sold his Speed Six to the Spaniards. I had met him one morning at Heston and he told me that little men in black suits were on

holiday watching the race, there was no toolkit to be found; as time was running out I started the engine, and to the sympathetic looks of Percival, Waite, Gardner and a few others I misfired my way to the starting-line. The engine did not clear itself and I knew I should have to land; as I did so on Stoke aerodrome, it was to see the TK4 and the streaking Mew Gulls flash by on their way to Cardiff and Hatfield. My plugs took half an hour or so to take out and clean so I took off for Hatfield, where I arrived in time to congratulate Charles on a splendid win, and Percival for putting up the fastest time.

---

the tarmac with bags of gold buying any aircraft they could for the civil war then erupting in Spain. Several of my friends had cashed in on this and some had done even better when they flew the machines out in secrecy. I thought this was a good idea, but before I could persuade my father to the same frame of mind our own government clamped down very severely on such escapades.

9 ✳ Comet rescue

THE RACING SEASON over, I had time to take stock. That year I had made the acquaintance of Jack Cross, who ran a small engineering works in one of the metal hangars at Gravesend. He had carried out a top overhaul on the Gipsy Series I engine of the Mew and during that time I had come to appreciate his unique ability. Brilliant in aero-technology, and superb in his practical approach to aerodynamic problems, he could achieve results that would leave others bewildered at his audacity and courage. At that particular time he had just rebuilt the Comet G-ACSS and had made a superb job of it with a fraction of the resources available at the De Havilland factory.

We discussed racing and record-breaking for hours on end and I reached the conclusion that Jack would take calculated risks and chances if the pilot would do likewise. At the same time I knew that if I agreed to the plans we had discussed concerning the Mew it would not only involve many risks but very heavy expenditure as well. I was then nearly 25 years old with capital of my own, so that in a sense I was my own master; I felt that as long as I did not impose upon Dad for financial backing it was my neck that would be sticking out, so eventually I agreed to start upon an intensive development programme. Over the many months that followed, during all the trials and tribulations, the high spots and the disappointments, the frustrations and the triumphs, there evolved as far as I was concerned a tremendous respect for the talents and ability of Jack Cross. I suspect that in some small way this view may have been reciprocated.

The first move was for me to purchase one of the Comet

Gipsy Six 'R' engines from Tommy Lipton and fit it with a Ratier pump-type airscrew.* On the 14th of November, 1937, I was to make the first flying trials in the Mew fitted with the 'R' engine, and at the same time see Clouston and Mrs Kirby-Green take off on their attempt at the Cape record. Clouston was one of the first pilots, in my opinion, who really set about record-breaking in the proper manner. A very fit man, a New Zealander, a first-class pilot, he had a clear-thinking brain not to be side-tracked by a lot of cheap publicity. He spoke very highly of Mrs Kirby-Green, who was responsible for arranging the financial backing for the flight by Burberrys, and although she did not land nor take-off the Comet, Clouston said it was possible to get several hours rest when she was able to take over in the air for long spells. Clouston was successful in smashing all existing Cape and back records with 3 days 16 hours 2 minutes, a margin that was a shattering blow to the aspirations of people like Jim Broadbent, Amy Mollison, Charles Scott and Jean Batten.

Clouston's magnificent flight compelled me to revise all my plans; I knew that I had to beat him if I was to keep faith with myself, but any way of doing it seemed a long way off. The Mew had altered beyond recognition when I saw her for the first time since the engine-change: new cowlings in red and grey priming paint; now fitted with the Ratier V/P prop, newly designed pistons, and special platinum sparking-plugs to cope with the increased power of the highly tuned engine. Because of the high compression, and phosphor-bronze cylinder-heads I had to use an unleaded fuel. This posed quite a small problem as the fuel had to be specially distilled and I found to my dismay that it was going to cost me 13 shillings per gallon as opposed to the normal price I was paying of half-a-crown for high grade leaded high-octane petrol. I was very conscious of the increased power as I ran the engine up and when I used full throttle on the take-off,

---

* This primitive method of operation was merely a football bladder inside the spinner, which when inflated with a bicycle pump on the ground forced the airscrew blades into fine pitch. In the air, as speed was increased after take-off, a Schrader valve pressure disc in the tip of the spinner was forced open, permitting the blades to return into the coarse position, where they would remain until landing and pumping up again.

H

the effect was fantastic: my head was forced back against the bulkhead and the acceleration was that of a very high-powered racing car.

I didn't like the bladder-operated V/P airscrew, which I found unsatisfactory to operate, but the increase in the performance of the Mew in fine pitch was, to put it mildly, startling. I shot along the shore of the Thames estuary and knew full well that the position error of the pitot head was not allowing the ASI to give me anywhere near a true reading, and was elated when I got my first stop-watch check; in fact I thought I had made an error and did another full-throttle speed run to re-check. As I did so I felt the engine beginning to roughen up and I immediately thought of the piston-failure experienced with the 'R' engines in the Comets during the Australia race and in the Hawk Speed Six in Africa. I returned to Gravesend quickly and Cross opened up the cowling to inspect the engine: the pistons appeared OK but the top of the crankcase showed signs of over-heating, so we knew in any case that the engine would have to come out and be stripped down.

It was then December the 1st and for the whole of the next two months I was to be working and testing that engine; the over-heating was in a thrust-bearing due to the increased power, and while we were dealing with this I was able to fit an electrically-operated control to the Ratier V/P airscrew; this again improved the performance still further. While Jack in his enthusiasm was keen to talk about the work and the performance of XF, I was most anxious to play it down; I saw no point in letting Percival think we were producing a faster aircraft than his and for him to put the whole factory resources to work in improving his own machine. So I thought of a simple ruse. Guy de Chateaubrun used to visit both Gravesend and Luton with regularity. Guy was a friend of mine, a product of two of the most noble families in France and Belgium, a man of great charm and intelligence, and moreover so pro-British that one took to him immediately. He was a fine amateur pilot and flew his own aircraft—in fact he was the first pilot ever to win an important event in the Mew Gull when he brought G-ACND in first during the Coupe Armand Esders at 188 mph from Deauville to Cannes and back on the 20th of July, 1935. He had also baled out of a Mew in 1936 over France in bad weather—and he was in contact with Percival fairly frequently. It was always a pleasure to talk to Guy; one day when he said, 'Cross is very pleased with your Mew's performance,' I replied, 'Naturally; he is doing the work. But between you and me, I'm not really getting anywhere and if I do the engine is bound to pack up. Do you remember how every Comet had engine-failure with the 'R' engines?' I knew the message would get through.

I was also helped by the fact that we had decided to buy a Vega Gull fitted with long-range tanks and a comprehensive instrument installation and other modern equipment. Our reasons for doing so were fairly clear cut. First both Dad and I felt that to make a successful attempt on the Cape records I must survey both the East and the West routes over Africa: as well as carefully inspecting the landing-strips on the desert or in the jungle we should determine what facilities they could offer with petrol, oil and landing-lights, to say nothing of such mundane matters as soap and water, and hot drinks, if not food.

The Vega had been in use with such pilots as Jean Batten, Amy Mollison, Charles Gardner and others, so it was well proven. It was in a reasonable price range, about £1600, with another £400 to £500 for extra equipment. Radio or any similar navigational aids were out of the question as they were strictly limited in their benefit to a private aircraft over Africa. I did intend, however, to use every modern blind-flying aid that had so far been developed—by today's standard sparse indeed. The two most useful items I fitted at the time were a large Smiths chronometer which gave GMT, local time, stop-watch time and trip time; and the large P4 compass which could be read to an accuracy of half a degree. Also ordered were the comparatively recent artificial horizon and gyro compass to supplement the standard turn-and-bank indicator. A rate-of-climb indicator was not fitted but the sensitive altimeter was almost as good. We did not have fuel-flow meters so I planned to fit an exhaust analyser, but in the event this turned out to be a waste

of time and money as it was so inaccurate. We also ordered good
landing-lights to be installed in the wings in addition to the
navigation lights, and a wind-driven generator to keep the
battery charged.

Whilst the Vega was being constructed, a matter of some
three or four months, I had ample opportunity to talk with
Edgar Percival; on one such occasion he said he had heard I
was spending a great deal of time and money on my Mew, and
asked how much speed I had gained. I said, 'Very, very disappointing; we are having a parcel of trouble with the 'R'
engine and although I had expected good results with the large
increase in power, I simply am not getting it.' He commiserated
and said, 'No, those extra miles per hour take some getting;
many people seem to think that by putting in a large engine
they are going to get a corresponding increase in performance,
but being subject to the cube law it doesn't work out that way.'

During the early part of February Clouston with Victor
Ricketts as co-pilot was to make an attempt on the Australia and
New Zealand records with the Comet G-ACSS. Cross prepared
the machine at Gravesend although they were to take off at
Croydon. I gave Clouston my parachute for the flight, but because he was unable to borrow one for Ricketts he didn't take it.
Whilst I was working on XF one day, Cross came rushing up to
me and said, 'Clouston's down in Cyprus with a damaged undercarriage and the insurance company want me to go out right
away to repair it. Will you take me?' I had an awful amount of
work on just then, but the idea appealed and also I didn't like
to think of Clouston out in the middle of the Mediterranean and
no friends moving to help him. The snag was a suitable machine
being immediately available for the flight, which involved some
fairly long hops over the water. Our own Vega was almost
finished but had to have starter, generator and some special
instruments fitted, and then to be repainted in our own colour
scheme of white and green, so there was at least two weeks work
before it would be ready. Cross had a Short Scion twin in the
hangar, but the range was too small for us to make the hop from
Athens to Cyprus. I then had the idea of ringing Charles Gardner

and told him the insurance company would pay generously for the hire of his Vega; he immediately agreed and I arranged to pick the machine up from his airstrip at Ramsey Green the same day. Accompanying me on the trip was to be Cross; his best metal-worker, London, with 300 lb of tools and equipment; and an Irishman called McAlpine, then the British chief of the Australian Consolidated Press, the sponsors of Clouston's flight. Mac was a wonderful personality and we got on extremely well together from the start. Salty and down to earth, with a dry sense of humour, he was good company under any circumstances; he had in fact been a Sinn Feiner during the Irish troubles of 1916 and had been condemned to be shot by a firing squad, but fortunately for him the order was countermanded by a dispatch rider just as the rifles were being raised. When I asked him what on earth a man like him was up to fighting with the Sinn Feiners he said, 'Everyone was fighting someone; I was young and Irish and as I couldn't fight against my own people I had to fight for them.'

Our trip started early on the 10th of February and with a strong tail-wind we averaged 180 mph to Lyon, but then our troubles began; gales were blowing in the Mediterranean and at our next point of call the wind was registering 110 kph and gusting higher. I decided it was too risky so we stayed overnight in Lyon. In the morning the gale was still blowing, but not quite so hard, and we took off for Naples with me remembering only too clearly my previous experience in high wind over the Alps when flying the Swift.

It was all as I had expected and we were hanging on to everything as the overloaded machine bucked around the sky with me opening and closing the throttle; Cross and London puked their hearts out and Mac huddled in his seat with his coat-collar turned up looking very miserable. As the wind abated so the rain and cloud came down. We flew from Naples over the sea in a pouring deluge, with the angry white surf of the huge waves a few feet below and the knowledge that we would have to creep all the way round the toe and heel of Italy to reach Brindisi. Jack annoyed me by suggesting that I fly up into the cloud,

over the Appennine range and let down in the Adriatic. I said
sarcastically I didn't think Charles Gardner would be very
pleased when told he could collect his machine from an Italian
mountain peak if he would kindly remove the bodies and clear
the snow away.

We crept into Brindisi in the pouring rain, with visibility at
times down to 100 yards, to find several machines including Imperial Airways grounded because of the conditions. When I spoke
to Captain Anderson, pilot of the Empire flying boat that evening, he told me not to cross the water to Cyprus without proper
sea charts, as in poor visibility I would find the numerous small
islands dangerous and confusing; Jack had lost my scale-rule
over the side when being sick, so Captain Anderson very kindly
loaned me his own charts and slide-rule.

We were all up next day before first light hoping for an early
start; the outlook was grim and all the airline flights had been
cancelled until further notice. We were now working against
time as Clouston had to be back with the Comet within a week
if he was to make another attempt on the New Zealand records.
Looking doubtfully at the pouring rain I said we would try to
reach Athens, but as I opened the throttle and the water
cascaded over the wings and cabin I felt far from optimistic
about our chances.

Fortunately the sea was rough and could be seen clearly
below, whereas had it been calm with the rain and low cloud
and mist the visibility could have been much worse. As it was I
steered to a rigid compass course until ahead and a little to the
left was a belt of blinding rain sweeping out of a black cloud that
was moving in an enormous mass slowly over the water. I edged
over to the right to avoid this and in doing so must have missed
the entrance to the Corinth Canal. A little while later land
emerged with a long, sandy, scrub beach and for a spell I
thought we were lost; as we groped southwards I heard Mac
say, 'At least we're bound to hit Africa if we keep going long
enough in this direction.'

I peered at the map to work out some time and speed figures
and then quickly spun the machine back as I suddenly realised

we were flying along the shore of the Peloponnese. When we approached the Gulf of Corinth the weather started to clear a little and we landed at Athens and quickly refuelled. As we were about to take off for Cyprus an official rushed up to us and said the weather was still very bad over Rhodes, Turkey, Syria and Cyprus. As we had been forbidden by the Italians to land at Rhodes this meant a fairly long sea-crossing and if the weather was really bad with darkness coming on we would find ourselves in a tricky situation. We decided to spend the night in Athens, and to spend the last hour of daylight looking at some of the superb art treasures that the city provided in abundance.

Our crossing the next morning, over a sea so blue and violet that it looked unreal, was sheer delight after our experience of the previous day. As we circled the area of land that had been picked out as an airfield, we could see Clouston and Ricketts waving, and the Comet tilted over at an awkward angle as it had come to a standstill after landing with one undercarriage leg crumpled up. Clouston had been unable to take-off from Adana in Turkey because of heavy rain and deep mud. He had managed to have the Comet towed on to an adjoining road by some camels but in taking-off struck the buttress of a stone bridge with his undercarriage; aware of this and not wishing to return to Adana he made for the nearest British territory, which was Cyprus. He put down with the knowledge that he might have to crash-land, but fortunately the chassis leg stood up to the strain until the last moment, when it collapsed without further damage to the wings or fuselage.

We wasted no time after landing. Jack took a quick look at the Comet and asked Clouston what facilities were available on the island. There was a public works department which was prepared to assist in every way, so we all made our way in a Model T Ford first to the small hotel where we were to stay and then to the public works department to collect Jack's oxygen bottles, steel stakes, sledge hammers, ropes, etc. I was in my element; I loved physical work and a challenge and was soon hammering the steel stakes into the rocky ground with great gusto.

The island was all so lovely after the English winter; with

oranges for the picking the size of small pineapples, with the glorious sunshine and exhilarating mountain air, I felt on top of the world—to such an extent that I think Clouston and Cross must have become a little tired with my excessive exuberance. We all worked from morning until dark; we were loaned two Model T Fords and terrified the life out of the slow-moving locals as we tore up and down the narrow tortuous road which ran from the coast at Nicosia along the side of the mountain to the airfield high above. Even though the scene generally was peaceful, one could sense the animosity between the Greeks and the Turks and the peaceful restraining hand of the British.

When we had the Comet up on high trestles and were assured that the repairs could be carried out on the site, I flew to Alexandria to collect a new replacement V/P propeller, which had been despatched from England by Imperial Airways. Victor Ricketts came with me as passenger and our first landing after the sea-crossing was at Haifa. We had some difficulty in picking out the aerodrome as the desolate sandy waste crept right up to the runway and as we touched down a Jeep with a high-ranking British officer and a soldier with a machine-gun accelerated up to us, warning us of the danger both from Arabs and Jews.

We had a shock on landing at Alexandria; first of all we could not locate the airscrew, and then I was told I had broken a serious regulation by not applying for permission to fly into Egypt. I was told I must see our own Air Attaché and he must apply to the Egyptians for the necessary permission. Victor Ricketts being air correspondent to the *Daily Express* was able to help but all this meant we were forced to spend a night in Alexandria and we only hoped we could get away early the next day. We found the airscrew, which had been put into one of the storerooms on the aerodrome. We were only just able to get it into the cabin of the Vega after it had been uncrated.

We were out early the next morning, but the officials shook their heads when we asked for permission to take off. As far as I could see we might have hung around for days: no one was the slightest bit concerned over our anxiety to get the airscrew to Cyprus in the quickest possible time and we were merely passed

from one official to another. I said to Victor Ricketts, 'Get
ready; I'm going to take off whether they like it or not.' The
Vega was in the open, guarded by a soldier with a rifle. I casually
asked the control officials for my log-book so that I could complete entries in anticipation of our leaving; at the same time I
told them I did not like the machine standing out in the blazing
sun and proposed taxying it into the shade of a hangar. Ricketts
and I then very casually walked over to the machine, started up
the engine and with the guard walking alongside we taxied
slowly along the tarmac. Gradually, without making my intentions obvious, I increased the taxying speed of the Vega and the
soldier trotted along beside us; this was warm work for a man
with a rifle and equipment, and as my speed slowly went from a
trot to a run he began to fall behind. I kept the nose pointing
towards the hangars and then when I thought the moment right
spun the aircraft round and with the throttle wide open took off
towards the middle of the aerodrome; I turned as soon as I
dared and then dived out to sea, thanking our lucky stars that
the battleships below were British. Of course when we landed
again at Cyprus Mac and Clouston wanted to know why we had
been delayed; when I told them of our troubles they were
worried that Ricketts might be held in Cairo on some charge
when they stopped there on the next record attempt.

With the airscrew fitted, Clouston decided not to carry out a
test flight, but to take off at dawn the next day for England. It
was dark when we started and the exhausts of the Comet and the
Vega glowed in the dull light. I went off first with all our lights
twinkling and then anxiously peered down below for the Comet
to follow me, but I could see nothing. Just when I was beginning
to think how unwise I was to take-off first, as the Comet might
have had more undercarriage trouble, way over on the port
side I saw a red wingtip light coming towards me. The Comet
went by at a cracking pace, with Cross, who had insisted on
being the passenger, flashing a reassuring signal to us with his
lamp. In contrast to our flight out the conditions were wonderful,
with little dots of islands showing everywhere in the clear blue
sea and brilliant sunlight. We wasted no time in Athens and

were soon clipping past Mount Parnassus on our way to Naples; we made Nice that afternoon and as we landed on the sandy beach the lights of the town were just coming on. The Negresco Hotel seemed like a palace after the boarding-house hotel in Cyprus and we had our best meal for many days. The remainder of the flight to England the next day was uneventful. As we landed at Gravesend it was to be asked by Cross, with a grin, 'What kept you so long?'

10 ✳ *Algiers non-stop*

THE NEXT FORTNIGHT was a frantic chase to get everything finished on time. I picked the Vega up on the 9th of March, after the completion of the instrument installation; A transmitting radio set in the rear locker which could never be used in flight but satisfied the authorities for the Sahara crossing; and finally the painting in our colour scheme of white and green. This colour scheme had been chosen by us for functional reasons as well as looks: we worried about extreme heat on a wooden aircraft, particularly if exposed for long periods, and the difference in heat absorption between a light colour and a dark one is remarkable. One could play practical jokes in Africa by nonchalantly putting the tender part of an elbow on the white wing as it stood in the blazing sun and then suggesting that someone do likewise; moving on to the green wingtip and pretending to place one's elbow there in the same manner, there was always a yelp as that part of the wing was blisteringly hot.

Most of the formalities for the flight were complete, except that I had not yet received permission to cross from Colomb Béchar to Gao and was not authorised to fly into Turkey on the way back. As I was assured that these documents would be despatched to me at Colomb Béchar and Cairo, we planned to leave Heston at dawn on the 12th of March.

Heston looked almost deserted as we circled overhead in the dimming light of that February afternoon; I playfully demonstrated to Dad, before landing, how the various landing, navigation and interior lights operated on the Vega as it was the first opportunity I had had to try them out. After the tarmac mechanic had got over his surprise at the order for an odd 130 gallons of 87-octane fuel and we were assured everything was finally checked over, we left word that we should be leaving at dawn the following morning. We asked Burke the Customs officer if he would be good enough to clear us right away and save him the trouble of stamping our papers at such an inconvenient hour in the morning. After a light supper in the club restaurant we decided to have an early night. I do not think either of us slept very well: like a couple of schoolboys we both felt the exciting anticipation of England–Africa non-stop; it sounded grand and was our first real long-distance flight.

It was pitch dark as we walked from the club to have breakfast. For the first time I felt a slight twinge of apprehension for the take-off, as apart from the extra load of petrol and oil we had on board several hundred pounds of luggage in the form of clothes, camping equipment for the tropics, guns and ammunition, cameras, and iron rations sufficient to last us a fortnight. After breakfast we carried over the last few items of personal effects to the machine and I remarked to Dad how beautiful she looked as her white and green paint shone and her chromium plated parts glittered under the powerful overhead lamps of the tarmac. We quickly climbed on board to escape the biting winter wind and I pressed the electric starter button; a few compressions burst the engine into life, its blue and orange exhaust flames belching out as if to set the machine on fire. I taxied carefully over the grass airfield to the extreme northern boundary lights, allowing plenty of time for the engine to warm up, and with 'Are we all set?' to Dad, slowly opened the throttle to take off. The initial acceleration was slow but after a run of about two-thirds of the field the machine was ready to ease into the air, climbing slowly with plenty of height to spare over the red warning lights on the top of some low buildings. The wind was blowing the smoke from London in our direction making flying unpleasant, especially as I found the machine was somewhat longitudinally unstable with full load, but as we gained height the slight morning fog and smoke was left in shallow floating layers below and ahead stretching towards the east was a light grey streak signifying that daybreak was not far away.

We set a course for Corsica and Dad took over the controls as soon as we had settled down whilst I worked out a few ETAs on obvious fixes, a flight plan for operating the petrol cocks and also for pumping oil from the cabin auxiliary tank into the main oil tank at various stages of the flight. We saw little of the Channel or Northern France owing to the thin covering of fog and when at last we were able to see the land clearly an argument ensued as to where we were. Dad was right, which put him in high spirits, and I concentrated on working out an alteration of course, partly to hide my chagrin at having boobed so early on the trip.

The rest of the flight over France was pleasant and uneventful, the Alps their usual awe-inspiring magnificence; but when we reached the Mediterranean a nasty dark-looking layer of low cloud enshrouded the land and hid the sea with no sign of any break in it anywhere. Knowing that the rugged mountains of Corsica would show up above this layer we kept on course and very shortly were able to see the white peaks of Mount Cinto towering up from the level plateau of cloud. Now assured of our exact position, and with Corsica being the extent of the strip map I had been using, I asked Dad for the section of North Africa so that I could alter course for Algiers. After some flustered searching in every conceivable spot in the cabin, Dad said, 'I can't find the damned maps; you must have them over on your side.' I knew without looking that I did not have them and at the same time the very disturbing fact dawned upon me that last night I had carefully packed all the maps away in a small leather attaché case, with the exception of the one I had just been using, so that it could always be carried in perfect safety on top of the large cabin petrol tank and would be accessible during flight. But my precautions had gone one stage further: I had taken the case out of the cabin and locked it up in the rear locker so that there was no chance of it being stolen during the night; and there it was at the present moment as safe from us as from anyone else until we landed. My spirits lit up immediately when I remembered that Dad always took it upon himself to look after the *Phillips Atlas of the World* which we always carried when travelling abroad; I could easily plot a bearing from that with the

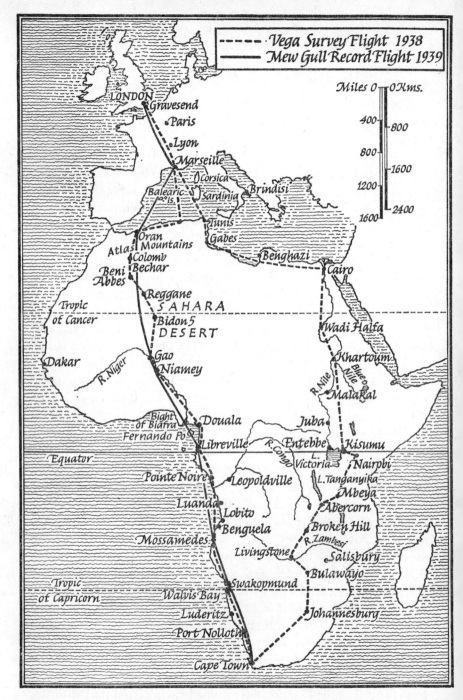

African survey and Cape record flights

protractor without any difficulty. I said to him, 'Pass me over the Atlas; we'll manage with that until we land.' There was another few minutes of frantic foraging in the numerous nooks and corners at the rear of the cabin, and then very red in the face he said, 'I think I put the blasted thing in the rear locker.' 'Well I'm damned if I'm going to fly all the way back to France just to land for a map,' I said defiantly, spinning the compass verge-ring on to due south as if it was all entirely Dad's fault.

We flew on in silence and with little enjoyment from the marvellous sunshine. I knew we were both thinking the same thing: when and where should we strike the coast of Africa, and how low was this endless layer of cloud? I had decided to fly on for fifty minutes from the time we ran off the map and then if there was still no break in the cloud, having checked the accuracy of the altimeter against Mount Cinto, I would throttle back and descend slowly down to within a few feet of sea-level; if we were not out of cloud by then I would open up again and return on a reciprocal course to France whilst we still had sufficient petrol left. As we were flying smoothly along we both nearly jumped off the seats with fright when the engine suddenly spluttered and stopped. I made a hasty dive for the petrol tank cocks: for a few moments there was a silence so still I thought I could hear my heart beating, and then the reassuring roar as the engine burst into life again. The main tank had run dry. I looked at the scribbling-pad again and saw according to our calculated consumption figures that the tank was not due to be changed over for another twenty minutes; this meant that the petrol consumption was higher than expected. We exchanged a few words and decided to try and get below the cloud without delay; if the conditions were bad we would return to France forthwith.

The sun disappeared as we sank into the grey gloom but much to our surprise on descending about 1200 ft we both shouted at the same time that there was the sea several hundred feet below. Very much relieved I opened the throttle and continued to fly due south. We flew on and on, both of us thinking we should have reached the coast ages before; I began to have grave doubts about the course I had so casually guessed and even to wonder if after all there was not another way out of the Mediterranean than through the Straits of Gibraltar. Dad was scratching his head and consoling me by saying, 'We're bound to make a landfall if we keep going long enough,' when almost below I spotted white surf breaking over rocks, to be followed almost at once by the red, green and brown colouring of the North African coast. It was very hazy but as we turned west to follow the coast, we saw we were passing over a fairly large town which had a fine harbour with a good deal of shipping in it; Dad thought this must be Bone. As we followed the picturesque coastline the visibility improved, and shortly we were able to distinguish in the distance a very large port, graced with a magnificent harbour which was literally packed with ships of all shapes and sizes; a good many of them we guessed were bound with supplies for the Spanish Civil War. There was not much doubt that this was Algiers. There was tremendous excitement amongst the few Frenchmen who ran to greet us as we taxied up after landing at Maison Blanche; they thought that because we had flown from England direct we were obviously out to break some records. They all rushed around in a terrific hurry to get us supplies of petrol and oil and notify the Customs official, all laughing, talking, and asking questions at the same time; nothing would convince them that we were really on a holiday and had plenty of time to spare until we took our luggage out of the machine and ordered a car to take us into Algiers; then their disappointment and loss of interest was manifest.

The way the machine and its equipment had behaved on the first long run—which was really a test flight—had given us the greatest confidence for the arduous journey that lay ahead, so as we drove up to our hotel we were in high spirits. The excellent dinner would have been thoroughly enjoyed but for the continuous drumming in our ears, and the table and its contents appearing to be constantly in motion. Neither of us could dispel the illusion which was obviously the after-effects of so many hours in the air: we had been flying 10 hours 45 minutes on our first hop—1500 miles non-stop to Algiers.

As the permits had to be picked up at Colomb Béchar we agreed not to waste any time, for as the French control officer had said, 'You go into l'intérieur.' As we neared Colomb Béchar the country changed again and was made ruggedly beautiful by abrupt towering cliffs, buttresses of red, brown and black rock which by their very bareness and colouring gave us some idea of the aridity in the hundreds of miles of the real Sahara that lay ahead. We were both thrilled and excited when we spied Colomb Béchar for the first time: it was Beau Geste come to life; the little oasis of palm trees, the mud walls and dwellings, the furnace of rock and sand and standing out from all else the white and red walls of the Foreign Legion fort. It was necessary to exercise care when landing on the level but rough aerodrome as the heat-waves shimmered up from the ground making judgement of height difficult; also there was a high ridge of sand-dunes running along the west side which in the heat of day was not easy to see and could be struck with serious consequences whilst one's attention was focussed on a landing-point further ahead.

On stepping out of the machine we first made the acquaintance of Lieutenant Gallois of L'Armée de L'Air; he spoke fairly good English and in his charming manner was exceedingly helpful. We told him our intentions were to cross the desert and that all the various papers and permits should now be awaiting us at the office of the Compagnie Transaharienne. He shouted an order to one of the numerous airmen who had forgathered, and in a few minutes a small car arrived and we dashed off with plenty of noise and dust towards the village. The next few hours were turmoil. Whatever sleepy intentions the few good French people had in Colomb Béchar that day were most rudely disturbed: our plans had gone awry; the Compagnie Transaharienne manager had not received our permits and moreover had not been notified of our proposed crossing. After an animated discussion, despatching of numerous cables and lengthy telephone calls, we went for advice from one commanding officer to another; Captain Pillon of L'Armée de L'Air and Captain Garros of the Foreign Legion put everything they had at our disposal, and a major of the Spahi Regiment assisted us greatly

I

by personally contacting Oran and Paris on his priority line. Satisfied that all the various departments had been notified in Africa, France and England of our plight, we had plenty of time to spare and made the best use of it.

As we went to bed that night we discussed our future plans and decided that if the transit papers had not arrived in the morning, we would go back to Oran where we could live in real comfort and utilise our time until the permits arrived by sight-seeing Morocco and Algeria. I was disturbed during the night by griping pains in the stomach and made a very hurried retreat to the somewhat unwholesome toilet; in fact I spent the rest of the night racing from my bed across the open flat roof to the point where this particular department lay. I woke Dad up during one of these many hasty exits saying in a worried voice that I had dysentery. Dad was throwing on some clothes to go and fetch a medical officer when the black manservant entered with the morning coffee; he sensed that something was wrong and said in broken English, 'You not well.' When Dad told him of my troublesome night and asked where he should find the nearest Doctor, instead of answering the question he asked, 'What you eat las' night?' I told him everything I could remember and to my annoyance his face split into a broad grin: he laughed, 'Ah, *cous-cous*; you will be all right tomorrow.'

11 ✳ *Sahara*

THERE WAS NO news for us on our arrival at Oran nor for some time to come, and in fact we were able to explore most of North Africa. Entering our hotel one evening the manager came up to us with a telegram from the Governor-General at Dakar stating that our flight across the French–Sudan had been authorised and that we might proceed immediately. We telephoned Boumati the Shell agent that we should be leaving at dawn in the morning and spent the rest of the evening pouring over a rather blank map of our route, checking vital equipment and generally analysing the flight ahead. We had coffee and rolls served in our rooms and by 0330 hrs were down in the lounge waiting for the car to pick us up. We spent an entertaining few minutes as somewhat hilarious guests were returning from the various night-clubs and in an exuberant state.

With the aid of the hangar and car lights we attended to the last few essential details. Dad had had the brainwave of bringing along a large inner-tube to act as an emergency water carrier and proceeded to fill it from the tap inside the hangar toilet. He had to stop when about half-filled as it took two of us to lift it into the machine, but it proved far better than metal containers and was most satisfactory as it could be pushed and twisted to fit almost anywhere in the cabin. The radio official having taken down the exact times we should send out a distress call in event of an emergency landing asked if I would like to send out a test signal, but I refrained in view of the haste and my lack of practice in morse and code-signs. All formalities completed and the machine filled to capacity we waved cheerio to Boumati and

the French officials and were soon circling for height over the
fading lights of the town.

It had not been possible to tell exactly what the weather was
like from the ground, but as soon as we started to climb we
realised the cloud was low enough to cover not only the mountains some miles away but the sloping ground adjacent to the
aerodrome. With this in mind we climbed slowly on a due
northerly course up to 3000 ft which would bring us over the
sea, and then in a fairly wide spiral continued the climb until we
broke out of the darkness; from then on we flew in perfect
serenity over a level layer of cloud with the brightening light of
the still-hidden sun gradually forcing out of sight the few remaining stars. For about an hour we flew on over the unbroken
cloud and then suddenly as if peering over a cliff we saw that the
cloud belt had ended and below was the familiar rock, scrub and
sand of the country north of Colomb Béchar.

We were both a little sorry that we were not putting down at
Colomb Béchar just to say goodbye to our good friends, but I
had scribbled out a note explaining that we had too much
petrol on board to risk a landing and thanked them once again
for all they had done to help us. When the colourful little oasis
came into sight we lost height rapidly and circling low over the
aerodrome I saw Gallois waving to us. Choosing the right moment I flipped the sheet of notepaper out of the window; we
saw the paper floating slowly down to earth, but did not see
anyone run out from the little crowd to pick it up.

The regulations controlling the crossing of the Sahara state
that an unaccompanied aircraft must follow the track across the
desert and on no account leave it or strike off on a direct compass course; the search contract is issued only on that basis and
our friends with considerable flying experience over this region
had confirmed that this was absolutely essential for safety, not
only for the airmen concerned, but for those who might otherwise have to be sent into an uncharted part to make a search.

Captain Pillon and Lieutenant Gallois had been so serious and
had shown so much interest and concern for our flight to Gao
that Dad and I wondered if after all we had not underrated the

nature of the journey ahead. The track as it left the aerodrome and winds its way through the barren hills towards Beni Abbès was quite distinct and could be seen without difficulty from 7000 ft; thus the flight to this little outpost was easy, although our interest was retained by the remarkable change in colour and conditions of the country below. To the west of our course the vast boulder-strewn level plateau was ornamented here and there by odd mountains of black jagged rock but to the east the desert was entirely different and appeared to be made up of continuous lines of huge, undulating dunes of bright soft sand, in fact just what I thought the whole of the desert would be like from all the books I had read and the films I had seen. It certainly was enchanting but, with all due respect to lovers of the desert, apart from this small region almost adjoining Beni Abbès and a narrow coastal belt of similar sand which we came across later on near Swakopmund, I found this type of terrain the most forbidding and depressing place to fly over at any time. The track faded a little as we left Ben Abbès so we came down to 3000 ft to make sure we should not lose sight of it.

About this time we noticed well over to the east a long narrow string of oases whose tall green palms stood out conspicuously from the bare rock and sand. I glanced at the map and noticed that the southern end of the oases intersected the main track we were to follow some distance further on, so I suggested to Dad that we went over and had a look. We skimmed over the trees, under which were scores of Arab tents and camels, and laughed at the excitement of the occupants as they rushed in all directions to see where the noise was coming from. We were amazed that so much life should exist on such a concentrated strip so far out in this wilderness; we could plainly see the fertile irrigated plots of cultivation, the hundreds of goats and camels and the Arab families clustered around their tents or mud houses, all this on a narrow sector in the burning sand several miles long but only a matter of yards in width.

We had a glimpse of Adrar in the heat-haze and with the shimmering mirages rising up from the ground were glad we were not compelled to land there. Following the track had been so easy up to now that we had the greatest peace of mind and sniggered to ourselves at the way the French had assessed the dangers, although we fully agreed with them that the best way to navigate the crossing was by the track and not by direct compass-course. We soon had very good reason to change our minds. Until now the weather had been good with the customary heat-haze reducing visibility to six or seven miles; it was hot but not uncomfortably so. As we flew on from Adrar, however, the track became more difficult to pick out and we had to descend from a cool height to one of only a few hundred feet to keep it in sight at all; the heat was becoming so oppressive that we shed one garment after another until we were clad only in slacks, topee and sunglasses. I think we exclaimed at the same moment, 'What's that ahead?' I refused to believe it was fog but it certainly looked uncommonly like it: from the clear hot air with good visibility we entered thick heat-haze.

There were three alternatives we could take and we hurriedly discussed the best one to try. We might climb to a greater height above the fog and fly direct to Gao: it would be difficult to plot an accurate course as our map was a strip and twisted and turned with the track and there was still a very long way to go—the atlas was not much use as it did not show our exact position; also we were not to know whether the poor visibility might extend to Gao or beyond. It would be simple to turn back and land at Adrar or any of the landing-grounds further back, but neither of us thought much of that idea. We decided then to put our wheels almost on the track, feel our way through the haze and see how we fared. Whatever hazards we might have imagined in the crossing, I think this was the very last one we should have thought of. No raw, damp, smoky fog that we get at home in November, but a thick haze that when we were well throttled back and had a wingtip banked over a few feet off the ground just enabled us to keep sight of the precious track. So we groped our way along: if we went too fast we lost the track, as we did time and time again; I kept re-setting the directional gyro to zero and when we ceased to see wheelmarks below gently executed wide S-turns, on the assumption that the track would not turn, until we picked them up again abruptly. Once or twice the procedure proved rather a strain.

Every few kilometres along the track are what the French call ballises, small tin structures put there by the Legion as a guide; one is supposed to count each ballise as it is passed and in event of a forced-landing by simple calculation of the numbers the exact position can be transmitted to the relief party. Dad checked them off but in the more tense moments forgot about it, or realised when we had been flying some length of time without coming across any that one or more had been missed: they were extremely difficult to see even in good conditions and many of them were either destroyed by storms or completely covered by sand. The heat had become terrific; there were black streaks down the windows where the Bostik that sealed in the glass had melted; the icy cold water put in the tube at Oran was now lukewarm. When the visibility had become reduced to almost nothing I made the mistake of lifting up my dark welding glasses which I used as protection against the sun; the effect was almost blinding. Although I put on a grin for Dad occasionally I was feeling terribly worried; I had no idea how long these conditions would last, whether they would get better or worse, and I blamed myself over and over again for getting Dad into such a fix and for not turning back when we had the chance. As it was I dared not climb and lose sight of the ground and I simply could not face the ordeal of retracing our tracks from where we had already come; to make matters worse, the oil-temperature gauge which normally registered 65 to 70 degrees Centigrade had crept up until it was now hovering round 103 degrees. We were crossing the dreaded Tanezrouft whose water-holes were many hundreds of miles apart, and we thought of the mad torturing deaths of many a man and beast in their efforts to conquer that burning waste.

The further we flew the more forbidding became that ocean of burning sand. I will not call it desert as it had lost its appearance as such; the brilliant colours had gone and a mildew-looking grey-brown had taken their place. The visibility was becoming a little better but the faint wheelmarks—there was no recognisable track now—were harder to see and the ballises almost non-existent. We cursed the fools who had instructed that all aircraft must follow this myth of a track for so many hundreds of miles; a direct flight at night would be child's-play by comparison and that was the way I intended to cross it in future. Dad swore about the ballises as it was his job to try and locate them whilst I was intent on sticking to the wheelmarks; he was feeling far from happy and must have been tired by the long hours of tension, although he was too much of a sportsman to show it outwardly. 'Looking for a needle in a haystack isn't in it. Bloody silly idea,' he said. 'Why the devil don't they stick pieces of broken mirror into a ball of wet concrete and put them on top of these tin huts; you'd see the sun reflect in them from almost any angle then.' The needles on the oil and induction temperature gauges gave me cause for alarm every time I glanced at them and I fervently thanked heaven for the Gipsy engine: nearly six hours now with the oil-gauge registering over a hundred degrees Centigrade; I anxiously pumped the remaining oil from the auxiliary tank, to see the needle merely drop an odd degree to record its doubtful coolness.

Neither of us knew when we should reach Gao. We had a very rough idea where we were on the map, but the going was so slow and tedious and ground speed impossible to calculate; there were times when we were forced to circle round a thin mark on the ground at zero feet to determine whether it was a trail left by the Transaharienne car or not and the compass seemed to read anywhere but in the right direction. How we longed for the encouraging sight of a little vegetation or a sign of life of any kind, even if it was only an odd straying camel or goat! We had experienced enough of the Sahara for one day; we were stiff and cramped from head to foot by the constant state of tenseness, wet and sticky with perspiration and our eyeballs red and inflamed by the strain of ceaseless concentration.

We had reached a region which was worse than any we had seen yet; frankly, with things as they were I found it rather terrifying, although I did not say so to Dad. I think he had similar reactions, though, as he said, 'If this isn't Hell with the

gates wide open I'd like to know what is.' Then what we had
dreaded happened. We had not picked out a ballise for ages;
with the greatest difficulty we were slowly tracing out almost in-
visible irregular tyre marks, which ran in any direction but in a
straight line, and suddenly we lost sight of them altogether. That
was not unusual in itself, but this time although we criss-crossed
and circled searching intently we were unable to pick them up
again. We tried going back a little and attempting to search for
the lost track in that manner but it was no use; there was not the
slightest sign of it or a ballise to be seen anywhere. I said to Dad,
'There's only one thing to do now, we'd better "guesstimate"
where we are and draw off a compass track to Gao.' Dad looked
at me, tilted his helmet further back on his head and said,
'We've been flying nearly all day so we shouldn't be far from
this River'—meaning the Niger—'unless the damned thing has
dried up.' He was holding the machine in a fairly steep climb
whilst I made out a course when suddenly he pitched the
machine forward so that we nearly left the seats and shouted
excitedly, 'Look, Alex! What's that over there?' I looked in the
direction he was pointing and saw a small cloud of dust moving
slowly towards us. That could mean only one thing; someone or
something was disturbing the desert sand and it wasn't wind;
there was life of some sort hidden in that dust and this was all we
wanted to see at that moment. In less time than it takes to tell we
had dived to where we saw the dust rising and to our delight
found that it was caused by the large white lorry-van of the
Compagnie Transaharienne which was forging slowly through
the soft sand on its long return journey to Colomb Béchar. We
shot the van up once or twice and as it came to a standstill could
see the occupants leap out and wave to us excitedly; this eased
our minds considerably, knowing that most probably the person
in charge of the van would transmit a wireless message to Gao
that we had been sighted. It was comforting to know that should
we now force-land they would have a good idea in which locality
to make a search.

We were able to see the tracks left by the van and followed
them hoping they would not fade out eventually like the others

we had lost. We flew on with ease except for the awful discomfort from the intense heat; the haze had dispersed and one
could see for three or four miles. The nature of the desert was
gradually changing and had now lost its deathly appearance, the
single tyre-tracks we were following soon converged with a
multitude of others and we were now flying alongside a trail as
distinct as that from Colomb Béchar to Beni Abbès. We were
still not sure of our exact position and our argument on this
problem was interrupted by the sudden sight of some wireless
masts and a white tumbledown shack immediately alongside the
track we were following. A few boundary markers on the ground
indicated a landing ground so we knew without hesitation that
we had reached Bidon 5; the Sahara was as good as crossed. In
our lighter moments we had considered landing at such outposts
just for fun and experience, but when we saw the heat mirages
shimmering up from the sand, making the hut rise and fall and
the masts tremble and twist, we were very thankful we had
sufficient petrol and oil to take us to safer spots.

With the relief of easier flying conditions and the exact knowledge of where we were our minds turned to less serious topics;
we realised for the first time that day that we had been flying for
over ten hours and that neither of us had had a mouthful of food
or water, and now with the day's journey nearly over we had lost
all appetite for any. Dad rummaged amongst the various parcels
and soon found a bag of tempting-looking apples; as we munched
them he wisecracked to me, 'How I crossed the Sahara on one
apple.' It was not long before the road below began to show
signs of life and we were soon regularly passing over little groups
of Arabs, some walking and others riding on the backs of
camels; most of them were driving small herds of goats that
kicked up clouds of dust and they scattered in all directions as the
noise of our approach frightened them.

We were upon Gao almost before we were aware of the fact. I
had expected something different from the typical Arab mud
houses that lay below: both of us had connected the Niger with
darkest Africa and had visualised dark green jungle and a clear,
fast-running mighty river splitting it apart. The desert was still

below us and had it not been for a little more scrub growth to all intents and appearances we might still have been over Beni Abbès. The flat banks of muddy sand revealed a winding stretch of stagnant-looking water upon which as far as we could see were some black boys dressed in Arab clothing fishing from some small boats or canoes. We had arranged to stay at Gao but as we circled the fairly large landing-ground we found the place so unattractive to our disillusioned eyes that with a quick glance at the time and petrol we voted for trying our luck at Niamey some 300 miles further down the river, as I had in mind using Niamey aerodrome on the record attempt. Keeping Gao in mind only as a safety valve, I weighed the place up carefully as we circled round it and deeming its surface to be like most other desert landing grounds I made a few notes and swung the machine on to course for Niamey. The country changed rapidly as we flew south and the monotony of sand was broken by bush-land with occasional trees here and there; also we saw fewer Arabs trekking along the narrow track that ran more or less parallel to the river and more and more black Africans on the muddy banks. At times we came across little homesteads of reed huts built upon rickety-looking wood piles right out into the water some distance from the land. We also noticed naked black figures punting their puny craft to and fro so we guessed that the water in which they had built their homes was fairly shallow.

I don't think either of us had any fixed idea of what Niamey would be like but I think we both expected to see a rather large inland port teeming with activity. In any case neither of us worried much about it just then. We were giving each other occasional looks of self-congratulation at having been in the air for nearly fourteen hours and for travelling from civilisation to a country which was entirely new to us, and which as we looked below intrigued us with exciting possibilities of exploration. There had been no need for navigation of any sort from Gao as we merely followed the snaking ribbon of water until we should come upon the town of Niamey; we had of course worked out an accurate ETA and found we should land there a few minutes before sunset. The watch indicated that we should be almost there so I gently eased the stick forward to lose height in a shallow dive; just as I did so I received an alarming shock by the sight of the oil-pressure needle flickering backwards and forwards with the appearance that the pressure was failing completely, and I snatched the throttle back and pulled the airscrew into fully coarse pitch looking at Dad as I did so with a wry grin and an awful sickly feeling in my tummy. It was my idea in the first instance that we should continue on from Gao and I cursed myself bitterly for having been such a senseless idiot, and prayed earnestly under my breath that I could get my father down safely.

We had to make up our minds instantly what we were going to do. As we strained our eyes looking for a suitable landing-place we saw a few red-and-white stone and tin buildings on the left bank of the river. We realised that this must be Niamey, but had considerable doubts owing to the very small size of the settlement and wondered if it was a small trading post on the outskirts of the town; from that distance we could see no signs of any aerodrome. If the engine was opened up again in an effort to reach Niamey aerodrome I was convinced that by the time we had found it the engine would have seized up: even if we were lucky enough to land without personal damage there would be no chance of repairing the machine, and it would take us months to get back home again by ordinary means of travel. I felt the engine was all right at the moment as the revs had been reduced almost the same second the oil-pressure needle had flickered and I had hopes of it remaining so, providing the engine was kept switched off until the cause of the failure was investigated. This meant an immediate landing, and I anxiously searched the rough bush below whilst at the same time I shouted to Dad that I thought it would be the only chance of saving ourselves. He said only, 'I'll leave it with you, son,' and went on for the few seconds we had left helping me to pick out a spot where we might get down without too much damage. As I glanced at his set face intent on the search I felt desperate with remorse for the awful plight in which I had placed him.

As we silently glided lower and lower we picked out a narrow track winding through the bush as the one and only place where it might be possible to land at all. We could not see what the surface was like; to make matters worse the sun had already set and the twilight was disappearing with its accustomed tropical rapidity. The track was bordered by low scrub bushes and odd trees here and there: I attempted to judge the approach so that we should just miss some of the trees and endeavour to stop, if the surface of the track was firm, before we swept into other trees further ahead. I gritted my teeth to do the best I could; my first hope was that we should escape without injury; secondly, that although the machine might be damaged we should be able to carry out temporary repairs. Thoughts morbid and otherwise flashed vividly through my mind during those last few seconds. Had the decision been too hasty? Should I be taking a lesser risk to open up again and attempt to make the aerodrome? Had I forgotten any vital point?

'Sorry Dad, I'm afraid we're for it. Tighten your straps down hard and pull your legs from underneath that centre-section.' He quickly refastened the safety harness, pulled his legs partially up and then put them back again, giving me a look as much as to say 'If you've got to have your legs crushed amongst the controls, so have I.'

It was too late to argue: the port wing narrowly missed the branch of a tree as the machine was swung out of a steep side-slip and the moment the wheels touched what felt to be solid ground I applied the brakes hard. Luckily the track was made of rock or gravel and we heard the tyres protest as the wheels nearly locked, with the machine lurching badly; my efforts were desperate to keep it from swinging from the narrow track. I noticed that the edge of the track was defined from the bush by a continuous line of small boulders, big enough should a wheel come up against one to send us crashing into the undergrowth.

We were by this time lightly loaded as the petrol-tanks were now nearly empty, and this probably accounted for us getting down as we did. The machine rapidly decelerated as it touched the track and with one last frightening lurch came to rest with the airscrew almost pushing back the leaves of a tree that was certainly far too firmly rooted for any game of tag. I looked at Dad but was too breathless to speak; we both sat there in silence as if mere words would break the magic spell and we would find ourselves writhing amongst the crumpled and shattered wreckage that had once been the Vega.

Dad took off his helmet, wiped his brow and said, 'No more pranks like that for a while; I came out for a holiday, not for a nervous breakdown.' We laughed and climbed out of the machine to take stock of our surroundings. It was almost dark, and although there was not a soul to be seen the night was alive with sound.*

---

* Oran to Niamey direct is 1660 statute miles. We calculated that the route flown that day was over 2000 miles.

THE FIRST THING to do was to try and get some assistance, and although we would have liked to have kept together the idea of leaving the machine unguarded in a place where we had not the slightest notion of what to expect was out of the question. Finally I said to Dad, 'I'll run into Niamey and see if I can find some white people while you stay with the machine; here is the automatic and an extra twenty rounds.' Dad selected a comfortable-looking hummock of grass near the machine, sat down and said, 'OK, son, mind how you go. I think I should take the rifle with you and either of us can fire a shot if we want urgent help.' I couldn't be bothered to turn out the back locker to get at the rifle, so saying that I should not be gone many minutes I started off down the road at a sharp run.

I have no knowledge of how one's mental state of mind affects one's physical capabilities but I do not remember ever feeling so energetic as I did that night. I could have sung with joy the way fortune had favoured us, and to find myself sprinting with un-accustomed, effortless ease after such a gruelling day was ab-solutely beyond my comprehension; I felt that I could run ten miles without any difficulty and as hard as I sprinted there still felt to be plenty of energy left in reserve. It was a most extra-ordinary and exhilarating feeling.

At first I intended following the road until I came to someone, but seeing a light glowing dimly in the distance over to my left I decided to go straight to it by going through the bush. I ran, twisted and jumped over the dry grass and low bushes, but was suddenly brought to an abrupt stop by the sight of an almost naked black man standing motionless a few yards away. For a few seconds we stood still looking at each other and then, thinking of nothing else better to say, I asked in English if he could direct me to the nearest white man. He obviously did not understand me, but jabbered out something that sounded like broken French and waved his arms indicating that I should follow him. I did not feel too happy about it and had the horrible, spooky feeling as I kept a respectful distance from him that I was about to get a spear in my back. To my surprise, when almost stumbling over a large boulder and feeling gritty stone under my feet, I realised we were back again on the road I had just left, and far ahead in the direction I took Niamey to be in were two bright lights moving towards us. I soon heard the sound of a car approaching and stood in the middle of the road waving my arms and hoping I should be able to stop it. With a squealing of brakes a tiny car pulled up, or should I say a chassis, as it was devoid of any mudguards and two seats precariously attached seemed to form the body. I was so pleased to see it, however, that it might have been the best racing model at Brooklands. The two occupants, a Frenchman and his wife, jumped out to view me in the lights of the car and bombarded me with a host of questions; they had apparently seen the Vega in the sky but had no idea where it had landed and were just coming out to look for us. I pointed to the black man, told them how I had met him in the bush and asked them to interpret what he had tried to tell me. I soon found out that the bush was infested with snakes and scorpions and that he had been telling me to follow him on to the open track. I felt very guilty at having been so suspicious and promised to reward him well when we got into Niamey.

By this time two other Frenchmen had turned up and we all set off to pick up my father and make the Vega safe for the night. Dad had an amusing tale to tell when we arrived. He had been kept constantly alert by the noise of crickets and mysterious sounds from the bush, and soon after I had left him had been alarmed by the sight of a black head and whites of eyes peering out between the two tall tufts of grass. He was taking no chances and drawing a careful bead with the automatic on the black

10 Comet rescue, Cyprus: (*l.* to *r.*) McAlpine, Ricketts, Cross, London
11 The Henshaws' Vega Gull at Hagnaby, 1938

12   Amy Johnson in trouble at Colomb Béchar on Cape attempt, 1938
13   Down in the bush near Niamey, March 1938

head told him to come out into the open; the result was an immediate disappearance of the head and although Dad had a
good look round there was not a soul to be seen. He then went
back to his seat near the machine and feigned sleep, and a short
while later out of the corner of his eye he saw the head rise slowly
above the grass again; this time he was more startled by the fact
that near this head was another one and opening his eyes fully
he realised there were scores of heads. In the dim light he saw he
was completely surrounded by them, and he remained absolutely quiet to think out a plan of action. It was obviously a trap
and they would set upon him at any moment: he could not shoot
them all, so his best move was to try and make friends with them
until I returned with help. He then hid the automatic in his coat
pocket, his hand clutching it for instantaneous use should the
need arise, and called out that they should come into the open
and meet him. In a flash the heads were gone and Dad was left
to himself again. At this moment we arrived and listened to his
story in fits of laughter, especially the Frenchmen, who said the
natives would have been more scared than Dad was.

It was suggested that we should clear a way for the machine to
be pushed off the track, as the natives often drove their cattle
along there, and we could arrange for a guard who would remain
with it until we returned next morning. This seemed the best
thing to do, so we started to clear away the scrub; as we were
doing so one of the Frenchmen let out a nerve-wracking yell and
stumbled over to the car. We rushed over to him and, finding he
had been bitten by a scorpion, his comrades rendered first aid and
swept him off in the car to Niamey for further medical attention.
After that the grass was well beaten with sticks to ensure that no
more of the pests were lurking around. I felt sick with the thought
that it might have been my father who was being carried off instead of the poor Frenchman, as the scorpion had bitten him
within a yard of where my father had sat waiting for me to return.

When the little car came back we clambered on to it with the
luggage we required and clung on as best we could whilst we
were driven into Niamey. We were rather surprised when we
were accommodated in a comfortable stone building and served

K

with little delay with a meal that was hot though of doubtful quality. I suddenly remembered whilst struggling through the food that we had not reported to the police or customs official with our credentials, etc., and turned in haste to our companion, the owner of the car. 'Oh,' he said, 'you need not worry about that. We do not bother about laws and formalities out here; we are only too delighted to see any fresh faces and I hope you will be able to stay a few days with us.' We retired early and were shown into two small stone rooms, bare except for hard-looking beds draped with mosquito netting. I spent some time pondering over the events of that long day, and whilst I was truly thankful at the way things had turned out I fell asleep with a worried mind as to what we should find wrong with the engine in the morning.

Strong sunlight filled the little chamber as I leapt out of bed to call Dad the next morning, and after a quick wash and a cup of hot, strong coffee we were on our way to inspect the Vega. We had seen very little of the district in the darkness the night before, but now the daylight revealed many objects of intense interest to us, and in no time Dad was taking camera shots of animal life in the bush and of the natives around their quaint reed-built kraals. In due time we came upon the Vega surrounded by natives; outwardly she showed no signs of her ill-treatment except that instead of shining with her normal immaculate gloss, she was covered in streaks of dirty oil with dark red dust stuck to it. Most of the oil had come from the vacuum pump, and as we had not been able to fit a Pesco separator unit before leaving England this was to be expected. The long broad streak down the starboard side of the fuselage, however, I could not account for and I took off the cowlings to look for a leak in the engine. Having cleaned, inspected and tightened things up in general, the oil filters were taken out and we were very much relieved to find no trace of any white metal in them. The screw-cap of the large oil tank was then undone and I gave a low whistle as I peered into its lower depths: there was barely any oil left. I was dumbfounded, as although I had found a leak in the engine it was only slight and certainly would not account for such a loss. A carefully worked out flight-plan had shown that with the extra loose tins we carried in the cabin to replenish the auxiliary tank, with a normal consumption the main tank should have been almost full after fourteen hours flying. I had thought this would allow amply for any increase due to higher temperatures, but evidently I had not allowed sufficient for those gruelling hours over the desert when the oil was boiling all the time. When we told our French friends that we must have some oil before starting the engine, without delay they chased off in the car to get us some Castrol Aero, but they were some time in returning as it transpired the only Castrol Aero oil available was a ten-gallon drum sent out for Amy Mollison during her attempt on the Cape record in April 1936. It would be sufficient to carry us to our next port of call and we poured some of it into the main wing tank quickly.

A press of the starter-button set up a healthy roar which sent the inquisitive natives running in all directions, and the oil-pressure needle after a momentary lull and a few fluctuations settled down to a fairly high and constant pressure. The next problem was to get off the road and on to the aerodrome, where we should be able to complete the inspection without fear of losing vital tools or parts of the machine. It was fortunate that the road we were now on ran right on to the aerodrome, which we were told was but a few miles ahead: we could either clear the boulders, bushes and trees on either side of it and fly off, or take the longer but safer method of taxying all the way there. We decided to taxi and discussed with the helpful Frenchmen how we were going to do it. They immediately called in all the locals to help us and we were soon slowly but surely feeling our way along the firm but dusty road. Most of the obstacles we were able to manoeuvre round by shutting off the motor and man-handling the machine, an absurdly easy job with so much man-power available; if anything looked as if it might be troublesome, such as a tree or large bush overhanging the track, an over-whelming force of natives would completely erase it in less than no time. After many stops and starts to allow the engine to cool down and to manoeuvre the machine past difficult points we eventually came upon the aerodrome, whose boundaries abutted the road without an obstruction of any sort, and we were able to taxi up to the open tin hut that served as a hangar and laugh to ourselves at what our friends in England would say when they heard of how we 'flew' to Niamey.

The blacks seemed as pleased as we were at having reached the aerodrome and clustered round, no doubt hoping to see this strange bird leave the ground. Acting as treasurer as usual, I thought this would be a good time to reward them for all they had done; turning out my wallet I said to Dad that I had nowhere near enough Nigerian francs, even if we only gave them five francs apiece, whereon he suggested that one of the Frenchmen would change us some English money. I approached the one who had been with us most of the time, but he was aghast when I told what we had thought of giving. 'On no account must you do that,' he said; 'it would cause endless mischief for weeks. Give the chief over there a small sum, but nothing more than that.' Further examination of the engine and airframe confirmed our hopes, and having carefully inspected the fairly large, level sand clearing that was the aerodrome we made notes for future reference. We were now looking forward to penetrating darker Africa as far as we might, and we made up our minds to move on to Duala in the Cameroons that day.

We were keen to see the country over which we flew, but for the first part of the journey our pleasure was spoilt by a thick heat haze, not helped by the numerous bush fires which reduced visibility considerably. In fact at 7000 ft, the height we chose to fly for lower temperatures, the ground could only just be distinguished, and it was easier to relax and keep an eye on the Sperry panel and large compass than it was to peer over the side in vain attempts to pick out any useful landmarks. Later on conditions improved; we were able to see for miles and realise for the first time that we were passing over vast expanses of dark green jungle foliage, with native tracks and villages when we did see them at all very few and far between. The heat although still intense was losing its dryness, and the air that came in through the ventilators and open windows felt thick and clammy; also, when we left Niamey the sky was a cloudless blue, but now it was largely filled with towering banks of cloud which were almost jet black at their base and, when we could see them, with tops that were like billowing drifts of virgin snow. We passed through a few rainstorms of no consequence, which we rather welcomed as a soothing contrast to the dry heat we had experienced so much recently.

A little later we saw a storm some distance away; breathtaking in size and blackness and terrifying in its menacing appearance, neither of us had seen anything like it in our lives before. It swept over the ground at an alarming rate and we could see the trees swaying and bending to the ground as they bowed to its awful fury. We made a wide detour to avoid any encounter with it, but although miles from it the machine trembled and shook as it passed through the violently disturbed air. We were now in a region where typhoons were frequent, although I understood they were only at their worst at sunrise and sunset. I made a note on my pad and was determined however awkward it might be that my schedule for the record attempt would be made out to cover that part of the flight in daylight. (So much for such resolutions! I little realised that less than twelve months later I should be forced to fly through these very storms in a night of nightmare that would live in my memory for ever.) It was fairly easy in the daylight to avoid that storm and the many others that followed, until shortly before sighting the Cameroons we had left the last one behind and were able to fly with comparative ease in calm air. Duala made an attractive sight with brightly coloured buildings intermingled amongst the palm trees and other tropical plants along the waterfront, but on circling the small aerodrome we realised it would be too risky landing a Mew Gull on it. As there was not much point in putting down we decided to go further on to Libreville. I made a hasty check of the mileage and the amount of petrol we had left: I was almost sure we had enough to reach Libreville easily, but as I was not certain of the accuracy of one of the gauges we played for safety and turned back to land at Duala.

There was terrific excitement as we taxied up to the well-built hangar which I noticed already housed a small trainer and a French military machine. Blacks and white men alike crowded around the aircraft, no doubt in their eagerness to find out who these strangers were. We did not keep them in suspense long and the President of the Duala Flying Club introduced himself to us, saying that we had caused an awful scare in the town as they had been certain when we had circled overhead and had not landed that we were Germans making a reconnaissance with a view to an invasion landing. They all laughed heartily when they found out their mistake, mostly I think from relief. I was soon in conversation with two L'Armée de L'Air officers who had flown from Lake Chad in the military machine we had seen on the aerodrome; they were quite animated about their flight and we spent a long time discussing difficulties of weather and navigation over such country. We passed a very pleasant evening, and then at the club President's invitation went to his house where we were to sleep.

The next morning I was awakened by the sound of at least a hundred kettle-drums being beaten with a fanatical fury. It was some few seconds in my sleepy stupor before I realised what was happening and with the sound of running water reaching my ears became aware that it was raining. What rain! I shouted across to Dad but the noise of the deluge on the tin roof was such that I hardly heard my own voice. I took a look out across the veranda and saw that everywhere was flooded; water poured out of the sky in such torrents that it was impossible to see more than a couple of yards and there was every danger of getting drowned just standing out in it. Gasping for breath we agreed that flying was off for the day and glumly wondered how long it would be before the aerodrome dried up. As we stood fascinated by the downpour the president came along and suggested some hot coffee; we followed him along the wide veranda and I ventured to ask how long these weather conditions were likely to last. He shrugged his shoulders and said, 'It is possible that everything will be dried up within an hour or so,' but looking at the swirling flood at the bottom of the veranda step I could not imagine how the ground could possibly dry out for several days even if the deluge stopped, and there did not seem the remotest chance of that happening for some time. We sipped coffee and between our gasps for more air chatted about things in general, then as we were doing so we were suddenly left shouting at each other: the crescendo on the tin roof ceased and there was complete silence broken only by the faint gurgle of the flowing waters outside and the drip, drip from the steep sloping roof. Almost before we had time to finish our coffee the sun was out in all its power and to our complete astonishment within an hour amidst a rising mist of steam blended with the pungent odours of rotting vegetation, everything had dried so completely that it was difficult for us to imagine the torrential downpour and rapidly rising floods of a short while before.

We spent an extremely interesting time at Duala and were rather sorry when the time came for us to move on. We had a slight delay on the aerodrome as although I had given instructions that I wished to be there when the machine was refuelled we arrived at the hangar to find black boys already pouring petrol into the main wing-tanks. I stopped them immediately until I had inspected the filters and the octane value of the spirit, and it was fortunate that I did so as the petrol they were pouring in was an aviation spirit of a lower grade than should have been used in the Vega; however, they had only put in a few gallons so it did not hold us up long. Before taking off I always made a practice on strange aerodromes of walking over the ground to see there were no obstructions: I saw no reason to alter this practice here and told our friends so, but I think they were rather hurt that I should cast any doubts about the state of their aerodrome of which they were very proud. They assured me that the surface was in good condition but as I insisted they drove me out in a car, direct from the Vega over the path that we should use when taking off. I stood on the running-board as it was the coolest spot and would also give me a better chance to examine the ground as we went along, and we had barely gone three hundred yards when I saw something that made me shout a warning to the driver. He swerved and we came to an abrupt standstill a few inches from a large hole several feet deep. I was very silent as I looked first at the hole and then at the faces of my companions; I was thinking of what would have happened if I had taken their advice and taken off as they had suggested. The president and the other Frenchmen were of course dumbfounded and profuse in their apologies: the only explanation they could give was that the boundary fence must be down somewhere permitting some beasts to wander out of the jungle and scratch this deep pit in which to sleep. Instructions were given to fill in the hole at once and after a more searching examination of the ground we were able to say farewell and take-off.

13 ✳ *Two narrow shaves*

A FORCED LANDING of any sort between aerodromes in this region is entirely out of the question and we debated between ourselves as to which is the worst to fly over, desert or jungle. The surf from the Gulf of Biafra broke on a narrow, steep shelf of sand which was strewn with the trunks of washed-up trees; at the top of this shelf the thick, impenetrable jungle began and all we could see landwards was an endless expanse of dark green foliage and an occasional glint amidst its depths as the sunlight temporarily uncovered a murky swamp or slowly creeping river. For hundreds of miles the scene was unchanged but the further south we got the more polluted and stagnant the jungle swamps seemed to be; from them arose a damp, steamy mist carrying with it a rotting stench which we could smell even as we flew high above it. The monotony was broken momentarily by a long narrow clearing carved out of the jungle forest to serve as a landing ground, marked on our maps as Libreville. We circled it slowly, made some notes, took a few photographs and then as we were loth to land without good reason in such a climate, we continued on our way south. I did not attach much importance to this place at the time as I had in mind Pointe Noire as the best stop in that region when I made the attempt on the Cape record. Shortly afterwards we were crossing the Equator but not being in a position to execute the customary ritual we had to celebrate by sorting amongst our tins and parcels for something especially attractive to eat and drink.

As we neared Pointe Noire the low swamps gave way to long rolling hills studded with copses of fine trees, reminding us in a way of beautiful parkland in England. That was our opinion from the air but we had good reason for changing our minds when we got lower down. Port Noire is a small trading port and as its name implies, not very impressive. We circled its forlorn and desolate-looking aerodrome carefully and as the surface looked good came in for a landing. As we flattened out over the thick grass for a touchdown I realised that all was not as it should be: it looked uncommonly like elephant grass. And so it proved. The wheels failed to touch solid ground and the machine dropped with a bump into three or four feet of strong reed-like grass; having half suspected this I was ready to raise the flaps without hesitation and probably saved them from being torn off. The machine pitched once or twice but judicious use of the throttle managed to keep the tail down and with some difficulty we taxied, or rather, cut our way through the tall grass that flew in all directions as the airscrew mowed it down, until we reached the doubtful shelter of a large steel hangar. It was well into the stages of decay and the heavy doors had obviously never been closed for years; from its size and structure we deduced that the owners had at one time great hopes of a thriving airport, but what they thought of it now was easy to see. An unkempt individual sauntered up to us and asked in French what we wanted. When we complained of the dangerous state of the aerodrome, he shrugged his shoulders and said, 'What's the use? Nobody ever comes here, and if we cut the grass one day it is up again the next.'

Having a little time to spare I decided to carry out a fifty-hour schedule on the engine and generally check things over before going into town. It proved an awful job; the heat and humidity were worse than anything encountered before, and life was made a misery by the plagues of mosquitoes and other insects that filled the air. I received a certain amount of immunity from them as I sweated underneath the engine and rapidly became engrimed in petrol and oil; the pests did not like the smell of it, and for the most part they left me alone to seek a more wholesome target. Dad came in for more than his share and I could not help laughing as he mopped his face with one hand and beat frantically at the empty air with his other, cursing and mumbling under his breath, 'If we don't get malaria, sleeping sickness, yellow fever and every other fever under the sun, then it won't be because we haven't tried.'

A narrow track cut in the jungle undergrowth guided us from the aerodrome towards the town which at first sight appeared to consist of nothing but two straggling rows of wooden huts. To one of the largest of these we made our way and I hardly know who was the most surprised as we opened the door and walked in to find it full of black men, who stared at us, showing the large whites of their eyes as we stepped forward. This strange 'hotel' evidently served the neighbourhood as a general store and bar-room. Dad was pleased with the effect as it reminded him of the places he used to shop at when a young man in the Hudson Bay district: he said the only things the place lacked were a pair of snow-shoes and a sleigh. We both had a wash and clean-up and then sat at a table which had been laid for us in a quiet corner of the 'shop' and awaited what they might serve us to eat. Neither of us had had anything substantial that day so when we were served with a steaming dish, we did not worry unduly and tucked into it: I thought the dish must have been made up of small birds such as snipe. Dad said nothing until we had both finished and then suddenly said with a look of realisation on his face, 'They're frogs! That's what they were.' If I had guessed it before I shouldn't have eaten them, but I saw no sense in getting upset; in any case I had to admit it was one of the nicest dishes I had ever tasted. We had a stroll round the little place after our meal but the insects bothered us to such an extent that we voted for bed and beat a hasty retreat under the netting.

We were on the move soon after sunrise the next morning. Our mattresses and sleeping attire were saturated in perspiration, the parts of our body that had been exposed the day before were a red mass of swollen insect bites and we were so gasping for air that we longed to get back into the machine again. When we returned to the aerodrome we found that the grass had not been cut but the blacks were trampling down a narrow runway for us to use; it did not look too satisfactory but as there was nothing much we could do about it we decided to get into the air as soon as we could. We had not a great deal of petrol on board so after a fairly short run over the flying stalks of elephant grass the Vega rose gently from the ground to a height of five or six feet; was it my imagination or did I really feel the elevator control come up against something solid? I lightly eased back on the control column, but to my consternation it would not budge. I at once thought of the cameras and lenses that Dad often carried in his lap, and shouted at him to remove them as the elevator had jammed; he fumbled down amongst the controls but it was quickly obvious that nothing was fouling there—the leather guard was tight and intact. We were now travelling at high speed just above the long grass and heading straight for the tall trees which bounded the aerodrome on all sides. Dad saw the plight we were in and frantically tore at the control covers. I heard him scream out that he could find nothing and then as the trees loomed sickeningly closer, in desperation I hauled back on the stick with all my strength: there was a movement as if something had broken and we shot up into the sky almost vertically. I gingerly felt the controls as we flattened out of the climb; they felt quite normal, but both of us had received a shock and it took us some time to make up our minds whether to land immediately and investigate the cause of the trouble or to go on. Had the aerodrome offered a reasonable surface we should have landed without hesitation, but we decided to go on as carefully as we could to the next aerodrome.

The mouth of the mighty Congo River was passed. Steam rose from its lurid waters to lose itself in the low, ominous-looking cloud through which we could just discern a pale sun throwing out dull beams. We gave little thought to this as we flew by; our minds were centred on the disturbing incident at Pointe Noire and we discussed at some length what might have been the cause of the trouble. Benguela in Portuguese West Africa was to be our next stop and when we saw the prosperous looking sea-port below we were more than satisfied with our choice and gazed ahead for the aerodrome. The sight of it completely changed our minds: after carefully circling round we agreed that to land amongst the thousands of anthills with which the aerodrome was completely covered would be to ask for trouble so we reluctantly flew on in the direction of Mossamedes.

The country had now changed from the low jungle swamps to a dry rocky wilderness and the air sweeping into the cabin felt fresh in spite of its heat after the vile damp stench of a short while before. We assumed the land was rich in minerals as numerous mining camps were to be seen. We flew along a bare, precipitous shore which had suddenly become attractive: surf, now changed to a soothing blue, was dashing itself into a frothy white foam against the red-brown rocks that challenged its progress. Eventually a tiny valley of green vegetation stood out conspicuously from the white heat of the surrounding rock and sand; seawards it ended in a small town which boasted a jetty and a few gaily-coloured buildings—Mossamedes. The level plateau of sand and rock which forms the aerodrome for this small port was a short distance away and we scrutinised its surface carefully before cautiously approaching to land, our minds much occupied with the unpleasant experience we had had when taking off a few hours before. There was not a person to be seen when we landed and as there was no hangar or petrol pump to guide us we ran to a standstill, switched off the engine and jumped out of the machine to inspect the control cables inside the fuselage. As I unscrewed the inspection covers Dad examined the elevator hinges, and we were not working long before Dad shouted out, 'Well I'm damned, here's the cause of the trouble all right, Alex.' I hurried over to see what he had found, and the reason was easy to see: part of a crushed reed was embedded in the metal fairing. The elevator leading edge on the Vega is protected from wear by a light aluminium covering screwed over the wood and small nicks or gaps cut into it where the hinge-pins fit; these are of course left open for movement and greasing. The tailplane shroud extends over the elevator nose with a stiff wood fairing so that when the machine is in level flight there is little or no gap between the elevator and tailplane. A tough stalk of the elephant grass at Pointe Noire had poked its way, probably when we were already on the move over the trampled part of the aerodrome, to one side of a hinge between the aluminium nose and the wood fairing; when the control-column was eased back this not only crushed the reed but the tough stalk acted as a lever on that part of the aluminium over the hinge and bent it, so that when the wood fairing tried to close over it, the metal forced itself into the wood and solidly stopped the elevator from moving. When in desperation excessive force was used on the controls the metal being supported strongly on either side refused to bend or break and cut a piece clean out of the wood fairing as if it was a chisel.

We tapped down the offending metal work and assured ourselves that no more damage had been done; we had, it appeared, plenty of time to arrange future plans before anyone arrived to give us assistance. Mossamedes had looked far more enticing from the air than it did from the ground and we were far from impressed with the place at which we had thought of staying the night. The sun scorched us mercilessly and the sandy rock burnt our feet so painfully that we were continually hopping from one foot to the other. There was not the slightest shade with which to protect ourselves. We tried sitting underneath the wings but soon found the ground so hot that we were forced to give up. Our helmets and glasses undoubtedly gave some respite but as we were not wearing spine-pads we thought it would be safer to climb back into the cabin, draw the overhead blinds and open all the windows. As we slowly cooked inside the machine waiting for someone to turn up we perused the maps for our next landing ground, a short hop of just over 500 miles: it was still early and as we had several hours to spare we decided to push on as soon as we could get some petrol and oil. We were highly pleased with this quick change of plans, we were now only 1400 miles from the Cape and as our map gave more detail than we had seen for a long while we visualised a wide, green, rolling veldt, fruit gardens and cosy farmsteads once we had left this cauldron that was surely roasting us alive. A tiny cloud of dust took our attention and an open car drove up followed by several others; the dark-skinned occupants got out and chattered away in a language we could not understand. It was very difficult to explain what were our requirements as most of the people who had now arrived in considerable numbers were merely sightseers more concerned with asking us hundreds of questions in an unintelligible tongue, than with helping us. But for a tall young Portuguese who understood a little English, we should have been stranded there for the rest of the day; as it was, after a struggle with pencil and paper, words and signs we had the satisfaction of hearing him speak to his companion in the car who at once drove off.

We had a trying time waiting for the supplies to arrive. We could not get back into the machine as out of politeness to our inquisitive onlookers we had to smile and muster up some sort of broken conversation, even if they could not understand it. The Portuguese and the natives seemed quite unaffected by the heat, many of the blacks disdaining to wear even a helmet. Dad gave up in the end and murmured to me that he was going to sit in the machine as his feet were blistering. I was compelled to keep hopping round the machine to save it from damage as the crowd now pressed close in their eagerness to see all that was going on. Fortunately at this moment a lorry arrived loaded with large drums of petrol. Willing hands soon levered down one of the drums and after inserting a small rotary pump with a long pipe into it they began pumping the spirit through a chamois leather into one of the 14-gallon inboard tanks. I guessed something was amiss the moment they started to pump, as the going was far too easy, and also the litre-gauge on the pump was flying round at an incredible rate: according to that, the tank was already full. I tried to explain that they were only pumping air, but they still carried on unheeding, and as one man got tired another took his place. When the pump-gauge indicated they had pumped in nearly 200 litres they shouted some words which I took to mean that the drum was empty. I lifted up the funnel and peered into the small wing-tank, it was barely half-full and as it only held fourteen gallons they had actually only pumped in about six or seven gallons. I went into a lengthy and tedious argument with the well-meaning Portuguese in an effort to explain to them how it was a sheer impossibility for them to have put nearly two hundred litres of fuel into a 14-gallon tank. Try as I might I

could not clarify the position, but the next second I was roaring
with laughter as the problem solved itself: convinced that the big
drum was empty, a hefty individual took hold of the top to
whisk it away. It did not budge an inch. Another fellow assisted
him with an energetic heave, but the result was the same and the
drum remained in precisely the same position. It was a sketch
good enough for a comedy as it was not until four or five of them
tried to push the drum over that it dawned on them that there
must be some petrol left inside. One man had the brainwave of
dipping the drum and was more than surprised when he found
that it was still almost full. The remainder of the refuelling process was unforgettable, a scene that might have been taken from
one of Heath Robinson's cartoons. Fully aware by now that the
rotary pump was not working properly, a noisy and excited
discussion took place amongst the head Portuguese as to the best
thing to do. Repair apparently was out of the question, so a 4-
gallon tin had to have the top cut off so that it might act as a
measure and petrol was pumped from the large drums into this
tin in a series of short squirts before it was eventually poured by
hand into the machine. I thought the job would never end: the
volatile spirit was splashed all over the place, my clothes reeked
of it and as it spilt over the edge of the funnel and the tin measure
to stream down the wing on to the hot ground, shimmering
waves rose up like a mirage in the desert. People smoked quite
unconcernedly and in spite of my entreaties made themselves
quite at home, with the glowing red ash from their mouths
almost dropping into the inflammable spirit at their feet. I held
my breath expecting a terrific explosion any minute. Dad waved
the fire extinguisher and to show his sympathies were with mine
hummed the ditty 'Steamboat Bill'.

Nearly three hours were spent in feeding the Vega with petrol
and oil and even then we only had sufficient on board to get us
comfortably to the next landing-ground; a good deal more time
was spent clearing up the paper-work, but at last I was able to
shake hands, mutter our thanks and crawl into the machine beside Dad. Once in the air we had time and reason to give vent
to our feelings; what I didn't call Mossamedes and the Portu-

14   Hot welcome at Mossamedes
15   Surprise arrival of the Vega Gull at Cape Town, 1938

16   A.H.'s sister Pearl with TK4 at Baldonnel, Eire, 1937
17   Herr Gerbrecht with the Dornier, Isle of Man race, 1937

guese isn't worth mentioning. Dad said they were our oldest allies, and more sarcastically, that there was probably a very good reason for that! (Months later I was to take back every harsh word said against them as they were to prove reliable, staunch friends, and instrumental in saving my machine and probably my life as well.) We set out on a true course for Walvis Bay which would take us inland part of the way for approximately 130 miles from the coast. We had lost so much time refuelling that a few calculations showed we should arrive at Walvis Bay about half-an-hour before sunset, so we were anxious to get on as quickly as we could.

So much for the rolling veldt and fruit trees! As far as the eye could see was nothing but an inferno of rock and sand, not quite so sinister as the Tanezrouft—the visibility was much clearer and consequently left less to the imagination—but nevertheless it was equally forbidding. Every vestige of vegetation had disappeared, there was not the slightest sign of man or animal and the heat was simply terrific. The engine temperatures were rising at an alarming rate and not wishing to repeat the Niamey experience I told Dad that I was altering course for the coast where I hoped we should find it a little cooler. The change in temperature over the coastline was remarkable: we were now able to fly in reasonable comfort, except that the hundreds of miles of complete emptiness, devoid of man, beast or bird was a little disconcerting after our expectations, and it was impossible to feel really at ease. The flight was so monotonous that it felt as if we had been flying over these same desolate wastes for days and days instead of hours. I turned to Dad and said I hoped there was a hot bath and a tasty meal for us when we reached Walvis Bay. The scene remained unchanged as the miles rolled by; Dad once shouted excitedly that he could see an animal on the beach but it turned out to be a log washed up by the surf. There was a low line of fog way out to sea but this was the only variation in the monotony since we left Mossamedes; for a while I took no notice of this fog belt stretching as it did all the way along the coast and a few miles out to sea, except to remark to Dad how abruptly the layer started and how strange it should

L

form as it did in a region of intense heat. We concluded that it was caused by the hot air from the desert meeting the colder air from the sea and that there was no danger of it moving inland. We were very much mistaken however; as the sun sank lower over the water the fog crept in slowly but surely, first over the narrow strip of beach and then further out over the bare desert.

We had now about seventy or eighty miles to go as calculated by the number of hours we had been in the air, so neither of us felt unduly worried at the time. We flew for a while above the thin white layer until it thickened and spread over the desert to such an extent that we were never sure how far we were from the sea and realised we might easily pass a small place like Walvis Bay without knowing it. We crawled back again under the low ceiling until the surf was breaking almost under the Vega's wheels once more, and continued like this for some time skimming over the sand and foam with the airscrew practically cutting swathes in the grey murk above. For a while I thought we should just be able to creep into Swakopmund which was a few miles north of Walvis Bay, but it was evident that the conditions were rapidly deteriorating and we should be in a serious plight unless we could land soon. In a little over half-an-hour it would be dark: to return to Mossamedes even if we had the petrol, which we had not, was out of the question. I dared not risk a landing on the beach which was narrow, sloped steeply towards the sea and had the appearance of being soft sand. I began to have grave misgivings and cursed myself once more for getting Dad into such a fix. Well, it was not much use worrying over that now: we were in a jam and it was up to me to get out of it. I flew until the fog was streaming over the front screen like water and my head was saturated by peering out of the side window. Dad said, 'I can't see a bloody thing,' and as I had also reached that conclusion I anxiously opened up the throttle and put the machine into a steep climb. We shot above the white layer almost at once and could see it covered the water as far as the horizon; the sun had already sunk and had diffused the sky and part of the fog with a red glow as its power slowly ebbed away. To the east we were cheered by the sight of the open desert as it left the groping mist still fighting its way into the arid regions beyond. There was now no chance of getting down on a recognised landing-ground and whilst there was still time we looked carefully for a suitable spot in the desert; after all it could not be much worse than some of the other aerodromes we had seen.

I chose two small wadis running parallel to each other as a guide and keeping them well in sight made a dummy approach over the ground in between them; we stuck our heads out of either side of the machine and searched the area for boulders, gullies or any other obstruction as we slowly trickled along at minimum flying speed. Making another close circuit with our eyes glued to the chosen spot I approached again at a faster speed but this time allowed the wheels to touch the ground lightly in one or two places. Opening up we then turned round and swept low over the spot once more, carefully scrutinising for the deep wheelmarks that we half expected would have been made. To our satisfaction there was not the slightest trace of where the machine had touched down and but for a wisp of dust hanging in the air it was difficult to believe I had actually touched the ground at all. Approaching for the third time the wheels skimmed the slopes of the first wadi and then ran over a surface which but for the noise of the tailwheel as it bounced over the narrow corrugations worn in the scorched rock, might have been a first class tarmac runway. Stepping out of the machine Dad jocularly said, 'I don't know. If we arrive at Cape Town in one piece no one will be more surprised than me.' We had landed on what is known as the Skeleton Coast, on the edge of the Namib Desert.

14 ✳ *Cape Town at last*

WE STROLLED AROUND for a while to stretch our legs, but as the fog was quickly enveloping the machine in the gathering dusk we leaned against a wing and argued over our immediate prospects for the night. We were within walking distance of the sea, that we could tell by the surf pounding on the beach in the otherwise still night; how far we were from civilisation neither of us was quite certain about, but allowing for the time lost groping along in the fog we thought we were about twenty miles from Swakopmond. With this our thoughts turned to food and we were somewhat acutely reminded that the last real meal we had had was at Pointe Noire, over twenty-four hours before and I said to Dad, 'Frogs or not, I'd certainly like a basin full of them now.' We had plenty of food on board but what we wanted more than anything else was a drink; without it the tinned meat and dry biscuits tasted like chalk. Just a mouthful of water would have made all the difference and we criticised ourselves severely for being without such an essential item of our equipment. We had religiously carried an abundant supply of water with us, but when the Union was 'in sight' and we had conjured up visions of a land flowing with milk and honey we had foolishly used up what we thought was now an unnecessary burden by washing our grimy hands and faces.

It was now quite dark and as there was nothing else we could do Dad suggested we should try and get some sleep; at least we shouldn't be bothered by the heat or mosquitoes tonight. I did not relish being cramped up in the Vega all night, so whilst Dad was making himself comfortable inside the cabin I blew up a Li-lo mattress, got out some blankets and prepared to sleep under the wing of the machine. Dad wanted me to sleep with him inside the machine and demurred to some extent when I refused: 'You never know what might crop up out here: we haven't seen any animals, but there might be some snakes about.' I thought better of it when he mentioned snakes and letting some air out of the Li-lo I clambered back into the machine, mumbling something like 'Damned silly to be cramped up like this when you could have a comfortable bed outside.' For hours we sat in silence staring at the luminous glow from the large instrument panel; sleep was not to be found and with every grunt and groan from Dad I knew that he too was waiting for the dawn. I must have dropped off, as I was roused by an elbow digging in my ribs and Dad whispering in my ear, 'Look, Alex! There's something prowling round outside.' It was pitch dark and I could not discern a thing; one's courage is not always at its highest when disturbed from sleep in the dead of night and I said angrily, 'Don't be damned silly! How the hell can there be anything in a hole like this?' I had barely spoken the words when as Dad clutched my arm in a warning gesture, we heard the soft pat, pat of animals' feet or hoofs on bare rock. I slipped my hand into the breast-pocket of my leather jerkin and withdrew the heavy automatic revolver, but it was small comfort to either of us as I snapped a bullet into the breach: facing a hungry lion with that puny weapon was not our idea of big-game hunting. We could not get at the rifle without stepping outside as it was in the back locker, so we sat anxiously whispering to each other in short monosyllables; occasionally we would see a dark form move in the blackness and at times the glint of a pair of smouldering eyes. For a while we were content to leave well alone but soon curiosity got the better of us and breathlessly I switched on the landing lights. There was a scurry as a number of very alarmed animals the size of sheep dogs rushed off into the night. Our courage returned in the manner that it does after a severe fright, and we laughed boldly exclaiming, 'Why, it is only a pack of mangy jackals!' We should not have been quite so brave if we had known that the so-called jackals were the wild dogs that roam these parts, and that because of their dangerous ferocity the Government offered a pound per head for every one killed.

The grey light of dawn was not a cheering sight. As we stepped out to ease our stiffened joints the cold morning air pressed against us in a manner that brought on a shiver, and the fog rolled over the ground in a way that would have done credit to an English November day. How miserable we were; what wouldn't we have given for a steaming cup of real tea. Our mouths were dry and parched and as the fog showed no signs of lifting I seriously thought of trekking out to find the nearest house, but when I worked out how long it would take me to walk an odd twenty miles or so I decided we should get on quicker if I sat and waited for the weather to improve.

About eleven o'clock our hopes were raised by the fleeting glimpse of a small blue patch above the fog and in anticipation we packed away the blankets and Li-los and warmed up the engine so that we might be ready to get away at the first opportunity. With the sun cutting light patches through the rolling fog-banks we took off and were soon above the familiar scene of yesterday: thick impenetrable fog out over the sea, with broken layers over the shore dispersing into nothing as the fierce heat of the sun made itself felt on the bare rock and sand of the desert. Our calculations proved to be right, for in a few minutes without the usual warning of a few outlying buildings we caught sight of a small town, so small in fact that we all but missed it, half hidden as it was below the floating layers of mist. This was undoubtedly Swakopmund. We would have continued on a little further to Walvis Bay but the fog looked to be closing in again so we decided to land without delay. After some searching above the slowly drifting layers we spotted some boundary markers in the sand and seizing our chance were able to nip in and land on an aerodrome that was by no means as good as the improvised one we had just left. I had expected someone to rush out and greet us when we landed; after all it was doubtful whether they ever saw a machine here in a blue moon, and our engine must have been heard plainly as we circled overhead. As we glanced around, the place looked deserted except, I noticed for the first time, over to our left, a man laboriously knocking nails in wooden boxes with his back turned towards us. Not deeming it wise to taxi over the treacherous surface I switched off the engine and said to Dad I was going over to see if the fellow was deaf or daft. As I neared this strange individual who took not the slightest notice I thought it better to warn him of my approach and emitted a squeaky whistle through my parched lips. It was completely non-effective and all I heard in reply was his heavy breathing and bang, bang, as he remained intent on his job with hammer and nails. I guessed he was a German by his close-cropped grey hair and thick glasses so that when I received a 'Gut Morgen' in reply to my own salutation I was more surprised that he should speak at all than at the confirmation of my own guess. I asked him if anyone looked after the aerodrome, where we could get petrol, and if it was possible to get a wash and some food. He replied in a series of grunts in broken German, of which I understood only a few words, but it was plain enough that he was not going to be very helpful. I felt his whole attitude unwarranted and inexplicable and when I thought of Dad suffering the same pangs of hunger and thirst as I was at that moment I lost my temper and swore, but this he accepted calmly until I said something about treatment of travellers who had spent the night in the open desert with no food or water for forty-eight hours. He then paused for the first time at his work and as if relenting his rude treatment said in fairly good English, 'Follow me.'

We both followed the old chap along a winding path up to a wooden house. 'Wait here,' he said, disappearing through a door which he closed in our faces, but he was not gone long and had evidently been conversing with his wife about us, as an elderly woman stared curiously while he beckoned us into the house. We were soon seated on hard wooden seats in a windowed balcony overlooking the sandy wastes and in a few minutes were served with a steaming jug of hot coffee and some deliciously baked bread rolls. It was plain enough fare but we remarked together that never in our whole existence had bread tasted sweeter nor coffee more delicious. To have eaten our fill would have been to have abused such hospitality so having eased our aching stomachs and soothed our swollen throats we thanked these strange Germans and asked where we might get some petrol for our machine. I nearly fell off the chair with astonishment when he said politely that he would ring up for some to be sent out to us. In due course a car arrived driven by a young man, another German, who said that his stores could not supply the grade of spirit we required and that we should have to obtain it from Walvis Bay. The weather had not improved a great deal and still feeling hungry and wishing to get rid of the dirty stubble on our faces we suggested that he might drive us into the town. The young German agreed without enthusiasm but with a formal politeness, and after a short but dusty drive we pulled up outside a barber's shop in the main street of Swakopmund.

Somehow the little place seemed strange and unreal, not like part of the British Empire but as if we had stumbled across an outpost unknown to the world, the inhabitants of which were suspicious and aloof of the two strangers who had dropped in from the skies. The wooden buildings reminded me of the large beach huts I had so often seen near my home. The streets were of soft sand and to stop it drifting into the low buildings and doorways one stepped from the street on to wooden platforms such as one would expect to form deckchair verandahs overlooking the sea. There were none of the customary noises one expects from a village or town; as we shuffled by the shops in the loose sand we remarked on the deathly stillness, and this coupled with the reception we had from the shop attendants—which although it could scarcely be called rude was coldly polite— made us reflect that the sooner we moved on the better. All the people we met were Germans and although normally we might have been angry or depressed by their stand-offishness, obtaining what we required put us in a good humour so we merely smiled at such truculent attitudes. Feeling tremendously refreshed we prevailed upon the driver to take us back to the machine and having paid due respect to our earlier benefactors, who had again withdrawn into their shells, we started off for Walvis Bay. Although the fog had cleared completely at Swakopmund it was still fairly thick at Walvis Bay, but by following the railway line and telegraph poles twisting in and out of the rolling sand-dunes which linked the two towns, we were able to creep into the small aerodrome, also with a surface of sand but much firmer than the one we had just left.

Here we were met by a cheerful and willing Englishman who quickly ordered supplies of petrol and oil for us. When we had finished refuelling he suggested that we had a drink before leaving and ran us over in his car to a small hotel in the town. The manager-cum-bartender, of whose nationality at a glance we had no doubt, came to serve us. When our friend asked us what we would have, Dad mentioned several drinks, but the bartender grunted with his face half turned from us that he did not have them and it was plain that he did not care whether he served us or not. Eventually we settled on some concoction or other, but the manner in which it was served so riled Dad that barely lowering his voice he said to our companion, 'What's the matter with this bugger? He's like a bear with a sore head.' The petrol agent then explained that there were many Germans in South-West Africa, especially at Swakopmund, Walvis Bay and Luderitch. Normally they were quiet, amiable people but just recently news had reached them that their Fatherland had marched in and taken Austria, and Nazi propaganda was leading them to believe that it was only a matter of time before the German fleet sailed in and reclaimed by force all the old pre-war colonies; hence the feeling towards us at Swakopmund.

With enough petrol and oil in the tanks to enable us to reach Cape Town we were not tempted to stay and it was not long before we set a final course south on what we thought would be our last hop. I intended climbing to a good height above the rapidly diminishing banks of fog and setting, after a reasonable fix or two, an accurate course for Cape Town; the time was now fairly late and we should not arrive until well after dark. Whilst climbing from the aerodrome Dad, who had been staring down at the scudding fog layers below, shouted for my attention and pointed to something on the seaward side. I looked in that direction and caught a glimpse of a mass of pink and white colour floating underneath the low banks of mist. Flamingoes! Their wealth of brilliant colouring has never failed to fascinate us and without more ado I dived after them whilst Dad hastily prepared the cine camera in the hopes of getting some good shots. We lost sight of them for a few seconds as we chose a clear space to come down under the fog, but spotted them again weaving low over the sandy beach like some gay streamer from a boy's kite. They twisted and turned in all directions as we quickly caught up with them, and for a short time there was a terrific dog-fight as I strove to place Dad in a good position to work his cine. The banks of fog were still very low, which restricted our movements into a series of turns, and as the efforts of the flamingoes became more and more frantic in their attempts to evade us I have often wondered why they did not elude us by the safe and simple method of darting into one of the many banks of fog. I felt somewhat sceptical as to the results of Dad's photography under such conditions and said as much at the time, but when we were to run the reels through at a later date we were astounded at the detail and colouring: not only had he got some fine shots of the flamingoes but the film showed vividly the weather conditions and type of terrain.

Having used up all the film we continued on our way. The fog was now clearing rapidly and with such excellent visibility we were already making plans as to what we should do in Cape Town the next day. There was still no sign of the green veldt although the desert of bare sand had given way to a more rocky scrub-covered country and occasionally we caught sight of small herds of deer as they bolted away frightened by the noise of our engine. Just before reaching Port Nolloth we were dismayed to see the familiar low-level layer of treacherous fog stretching far out to the horizon on the seaward side, and already covering parts of the land in rolling banks over which we were flying. Cursing to ourselves that we had no wish for any more nights in the desert we agreed without hesitation to land at Port Nolloth. We were by no means enthralled by the idea, for the little mining camp looked poverty stricken and depressing with its wooden shacks as we circled overhead once or twice in the hopes that someone would come out to us when we landed. I approached the aerodrome with extreme caution and felt for its surface gingerly: our map stated that it was a salt-pan, with a hangar and fuel supplies available, but when we looked carefully before landing there were no signs that man had ever put his foot on the place. I have yet to land on a smoother surface; it was like a billiard table, a slight crust acting as a cushion, and we had actually landed before being aware of the fact. The salt-pan was saucer-shaped and allowing the machine to run to the lip nearest the mining camp the engine was switched off; having nothing better to do we sat in the aircraft and waited. We were not kept long; a large saloon car travelling at high speed towards us pulled up with a jerk and out stepped three big husky-looking men dressed in rough, dust-covered working clothes. They were obviously very interested and pleased to see us and whilst we were locking up the machine and making it safe for the night one of them said he would go and fetch us a black man to guard it. The black proved to be self-assured and demanding: he asked how much he was going to receive for staying with the machine all night and when a sum was mentioned comparable with what we had been used to paying he flatly refused to stay and argued in a surprisingly subtle manner, that it was better to have a good man who was well-paid and who would remain awake all night on guard than one who was ill-paid and might even harm the aeroplane out of spite. Dad and I were somewhat taken aback but we agreed to pay him what he asked.

We were driven to the largest of the wooden buildings where we were able to obtain accommodation for the night. Our friends with the car said that they would see us later on in the evening and one of the senior mine officials had asked us if we would care to have dinner with him that night. It was then we learnt just how wealthy and important this destitute-looking little place was. Our host was a genial and good-humoured sort who appeared at first to be hesitant and on guard when we were introduced to him, but he quickly changed his manner as he listened to Dad's tales of our flight over the Sahara and down the west coast. He admitted to us before we left that the object in having us to eat with him was to find out what we were after. Apparently the whole district was under Government control and no one was allowed there without proper authority: the men who had driven out to us were his patrol men and had been given instructions not to lose sight of us. The diamond mines here were shallow and numerous and many attempts had been made by land, sea and air by sometimes desperate persons hoping to make themselves wealthy for life by getting away with some of the fabulous quartz. He told several amusing tales about such incidents.

We were quick to make many friends during that short stay at the camp as the unfortunate people very rarely had visitors and were allowed leave from the minefields only once over a very long period of time; they were hungry for news of the outside world and plied us with so many questions that we were soon tired out in answering. Before going to bed we listened to the late news over a tiny and crackling radio receiver and as we strained our ears to catch what the announcer said we heard with a breathless hush that Clouston and Ricketts had reached New Zealand having broken the existing record. I was proud to think of the small part I had contributed towards the success of this fine achievement and Dad of course just had to tell our friends clustered around the radio of the repair of the Comet in Cyprus; he kept them spellbound for so long that it was very late indeed when we sank on to our cold but comfortable beds. For the first time in many nights I was able to snuggle up against thick warm blankets and enjoy a good sleep undisturbed by insects or oozing perspiration.

It was daylight when I awoke. Cold wet fog streaming in through the open window was an excuse to turn over and go to sleep again. When we did stroll down for a late breakfast I remarked to the landlord what an awful day it was and he replied that it was always like this in the morning but would most likely clear after lunch. We spent the rest of the morning touring the camp and then after a meagre lunch with sun at last piercing the swirling mist we said goodbye. For a while we flew above the now very familiar banks of fog but as the sun grew stronger they disappeared and we were able to see some of the more desolate mining camps as they worked the hard dry rock close to the foreshore. Slowly the country changed its coat and we were now flying very low over hilly scrub, watching herds of deer and numerous ostriches scurrying along thin, winding tracks to get out of our way. It was not until we were within sight of the Cape that the country could be called at all bountiful and it was then as we neared our journey's end on the west side of Africa that we realised we had yet to see the famous veldt. A glorious sight met our eyes in the warm sunshine of that afternoon, the soothing colour of green vegetation bedappled with red and white buildings, a fine luxurious city outlined by a pounding border of white surf on a sea of tranquil blue; the knowledge that we were here on holiday for as long as we liked to stay was bliss in itself.

There was little activity on the well-kept aerodrome of Wingfield as we landed, but the look of amazement on the faces of the few ground engineers and the control officer as we taxied up was laughable. Sergeant Gayney, the control officer, introduced himself and in the same breath asked us where on earth we had flown from, as he had been in touch with Johannesburg a few minutes before and they had not mentioned anything about a private machine passing through. When we told him we had come via the west route he was amazed, and when the aerodrome manager, Colonel George Fisher, arrived some few minutes later he said it was the first time a machine had landed there without them expecting it.

15 ✳ *Confined in Khartoum*

IT GAVE US a strange feeling to be driving along the wide, crowded and traffic-filled streets of such a large and busy city. We had become so accustomed to the primitive methods and habits of jungle and desert that I remarked to Dad that we might have been away from civilisation for years instead of days. We both intended to explore and enjoy every part of this beautiful Cape Town region which had so much to offer after the rough and austere way we had lived since leaving England, but first we had to clean and examine the engine and airframe of the Vega thoroughly. Wingfield was warm, friendly and relaxing. We chatted with Louis Kraft of the *Cape Times* and were chided by Winnie Beardmore, the attractive Intava representative, for not using her fuel. Slowly we were able to complete our work and we finished happy with the condition of our faithful machine.

Days later, refreshed and eager for our return flight home we pushed the Vega out of the well-kept hanger and with the first streaks of light now in the sky we left a few of our newfound friends waving as the reliable Gipsy engine surged its way to Johannesburg. Although the weather was good, there was cloud on the high mountains so we decided to keep well above and although we could only see the ground in patches the navigation ought to have been safe and easy; we had been flying for some time without a fix when the cloud cleared and I saw below in an open space the letters B-e-a-u-f-o-r-t W-e-s-t and was shocked to realise on perusing the map that we were miles off course.

Having made the necessary correction to the compass bearing we decided to make for the main Johannesburg flying club at Baragwaneth. I had often heard recounted how treacherous aerodromes were at over 5000 ft in the heat of a burning sun and the number of unusual accidents that had occurred, both on taking-off and landing, so that I brought the machine in over the airfield boundary with extra caution; even so I was unprepared for the suddenness of the stall after flattening out. There was absolutely no 'cushioning' of the air between the wings and the ground as the Vega settled down and even after levelling out only a few inches from the ground the machine stalled from those few inches and hit the rough grass hard. There was nothing really dangerous about it but in bumpy air conditions it might have caught out the unwary.

Knowledge of our arrival had somehow preceded us and a welcoming party awaited as we taxied up to the clean and attractive clubhouse. In the party was Colonel Rod Douglas, Managing Director of De Havilland South Africa, Stan Halse, my hero in the Mew Gull still recovering from his injuries and their wives and many friends. But our time in Johannesburg was short—we did not like the raw city. Nevertheless, although we spent only a few days we met many nice people including Victor Smith of earlier Cape record attempt fame and Major Miller who had flown my Mew in the UK–South Africa Race and re-tired at Belgrade. Just before we took off for Livingstone I asked for my compass to be checked and it was found to be out 10° on northerly bearings. This made me feel a little better as I had worried about my navigation from Wingfield.

The route north was packed with interest. On our approach to Livingstone we first saw a spiral of cloud in an otherwise perfectly blue sky. For some time we discussed this phenomenon until we realised with a thrill that it was caused by the huge volume of spray and steam given off by the Victoria Falls, still many miles away. The country was such as to test my dead-reckoning into Abercorn. As on many other landing-strips here were the rusting and rotting remains of aircraft that had failed to land or take off in this hot, rarified atmosphere and they were a sober reminder to me that even if I did have a V/P airscrew the engine was nearly fifty per cent down on power in the heat of the day.

I think it was between Abercorn and M'beya that I began to feel unwell. I do not think either of us was in a particularly happy frame of mind at that moment as we both knew Abercorn area for a place with a bad reputation, at least as far as aviators were concerned. The weather had now deteriorated and we could not make any immediate plans but Dad looking at me said we ought to rest at Abercorn awhile until things improved. I was stubbornly determined to get away as soon as we could: I felt weak and at times my head reeled so that I was certain something was wrong, and although I did not say so to Dad my one desire was to get to a large enough town where there would be a decent hospital and a comfortable hotel. It was only a comparatively short distance to M'beya, for which I was thankful, as the broken cloud, isolated rainstorms and mountainous terrain confirmed Dad's view that we should have remained in Abercorn.

To my surprise M'beya, isolated as it was, provided the only tarmac runway we had seen since leaving Oran. I muttered to Dad as we taxied up after landing that we hadn't much time left before dark so that if he would look after the petrol and oil I would try and get a weather report. Switching off I stepped quickly out of the machine, but as my feet touched the ground a horrible spasm of sickness took hold of me and my head swam so that I clutched at the wing of the machine to save myself from falling. It was all over in a few seconds and I hoped that Dad climbing out the other side had not noticed anything. A tall blue-eyed man in a pith-helmet coming towards us looked at me intently and said softly with a Scots accent, 'I think maybe ye have a wee touch o' fever, the noo.' Dad joined in and said we ought to rest up here awhile at least until I felt better and the weather improved. I irritably replied that I was sick of Africa and wanted to get out as soon as I could.

The next morning I thought I felt a little better. It may have been the quinine the kindly Scot had given me or wishful thinking. The weather was now perfect and in spite of my father's enthusiasm I could not rise to his exuberance as we swung low over the vast herds of game that roamed over the enormous plains, almost untouched by the destructive hand of man. For a long time we were silent with our own thoughts, mine to get my father home in safety and he with great patience and understanding to curb my stubbornness and get me well again. Suddenly my father let out a shout and pointed to the north-east. I looked and what we had first thought to be cloud glinted in the morning sunshine with the brilliance that only new formed snow and ice can give: the full majesty of Kilimanjaro rose to nearly 20,000 ft from the shimmering plains below. It was impossible not to be impressed with this wonderful spectacle and the more so as it remained in view for hour after hour.

Nairobi would of course have been a good place to stop and rest. In our anxiety for each other however, I think we both thought that if we could manage two more long hops this would get us to Cairo, where we could take all the time in the world to recuperate and we would at least be in close touch with those nearer home. So with only one thought on our minds we had a brief meal in the little Nairobi flying club, took on enough petrol for Kisumu and started the climb over the highlands for Lake Victoria.

Mount Kenya soon came into view but after Kilimanjaro I am afraid it received only a casual glance and exclamation of appreciation. Having started off so badly with the foul weather at M'beya this morning and leaving the rain belt behind us from now on we already had visions of spring sunshine over the English Channel and were anxious to reach Kisumu without delay.

Sweeping down from the heights in a shallow dive over Kisumu, it was difficult to see such a vast expanse of water with its busy little harbour and realise we were thousands of miles inland and not on the coast. The aerodrome with its flying boat slipways into the lake showed up very well and we were soon rolling to a standstill across a level grass landing ground to pull up beside a large hangar which was spacious enough to house a score of machines like the Vega if necessary. Kisumu impressed neither of us and we both felt a little sorry for the blacks as we noted the number of the very commercially minded asiatics who seemed to have gained possession of the place. However we were in no mood for extensive sight-seeing and with myself thinking

M

what an awful hole it was in which to be really ill, we decided on an early night and a still earlier get away in the morning.

I had no sleep that night and as I tossed and turned, shivered and sweated on the hard clammy mattress I realised only too well just how big Africa was. Here we were in a machine that could fly all round England in a day without refuelling and yet we had been flying day after day covering large distances and we still had a long way to go. I wondered between the bouts of nausea just whether I should be able to make the whole journey home or not and what was going to happen to Dad. As the long hours dragged on I consoled myself that in a short while I should be sitting in the machine again and that I would not leave those controls until we reached Cairo. We should have to land once for petrol and oil but Dad would attend to that; at all costs we must at least get to Cairo.

In complete darkness and silence we were driven down to the aerodrome and with a murmured signal I went to start the machine whilst Dad collected the log-books. I felt so weak and giddy that it was an effort to climb into the Vega, but it was a relief that the engine started with a touch on the button; the familiar sound made me feel a little better so I switched on the lights and taxied out to warm the engine and let Dad know we were ready to go.

We were supposed to land at Juba to clear certain formalities before proceeding through the Sudan but it was evident to us both as darkness turned to dawn and dawn to the merciless heat of day that our next landing was going to be the last one for some time. Perspiration was pouring from me, my breathing was in short gasps and I could focus my eyes on an object only with concentration. It must have been a veritable nightmare for Dad, as I insisted that we must go 1000 miles on to Khartoum, which I knew was an RAF station. As I write I vaguely remember crossing the dreaded swamps where Brigadier-General Lewin and his wife had force-landed and so nearly lost their lives; also the terse argument with Dad as we looked down at Juba: it was almost lost in a shimmering heat-haze, which made me determined that whatever the consequences I was not landing for all the regulations in the world, when it meant we should be stranded in such a desolate spot waiting for me to recover from whatever disease I had caught. So we had set a direct course for Khartoum quickly losing sight of the narrow, twisting Nile as we did so. The sun now high above us in a clear sky did nothing to alleviate what was fast becoming a journey of torture. For the most part we were travelling over a barren, scorched wilderness with no signs of life, and as Dad said later on I began to have hallucinations as I pointed to non-existent hangars and aerodromes with large runways down below. I do remember my eyes burning like red-hot coals and the pith helmet feeling like a ton weight on my head; the compass disappeared in a swimming blur and I gasped to Dad that we would turn off track to pick up the Nile so that if anything happened he could follow it into Khartoum. I do not know how long poor old Dad was left to struggle with me as he juggled with the controls and at the same time tried to mix a concoction of orange juice and brandy, but we were over Khartoum when I came round; my cracked lips smarted and the horrid-smelling sticky liquid oozed down the side of my face, dropping on my sweaty shirt front to form a little pool in my lap which slowly seeped through the khaki shorts to add to the stains and discolourations of many other mixtures that Dad had tried to revive me with during the flight. How we landed I am not quite sure. I only remember Dad switching off the engine and getting out of the machine, a long wait and then some RAF mechanics lifting me out of the aircraft, and one of them saying as they hoisted me up on to a mobile fire-tender, 'Coo lumme, 'Arry, ain't 'e in a bloody mess.'

What happened then is not very clear, but I think Dad said there was a quick examination by the aerodrome medical officer, a transfer to an ambulance and a trip to the nearest hospital. Anyway, I woke up one night in a room dimly lit with surroundings most unfamiliar and vague, white forms moving silently around my bed. Another shock, especially when I blushingly realised it was a nurse, who was holding out my wet pyjamas which had been taken off me, and my birthday suit was covered, inadequately I thought, with warm dry towels. I must have shouted aloud for a cheerful voice said 'Ssh! You'll wake the whole ward. You must be quiet and rest, you can ask all the questions you want later on.'

The first dose of medicine soon informed me that I had malaria, as the bitter taste of the quinine clung to my mouth; I came to dread those only too frequent doses. Dad came round the next morning and was quite cheerful when he was told the fever was leaving me, although he had a sorry tale to tell of what had happened during the short time we had been at Khartoum. He had gone in the ambulance with me to the hospital and when the Doctor had reported upon my condition after a blood test, realising it was to be a long stay he went back to the aerodrome to get extra clothes and toilet equipment out of the machine. As he went to unlock the cockpit door an African soldier with rifle and fixed bayonet barred his way. Now Dad was not a nice man to upset when he was in an ugly mood, and the prospect of weeks in a hot desert town with his son in hospital was not likely to conjure up very pleasant thoughts; as the sentry refused to budge when told that the owner of the aircraft wanted to get some bags out of the machine, there was a lightning move and quick scuffle and before the soldier realised it the rifle was out of his hands and he was being booted out of the way. To add insult to injury, Dad threw the rifle after him and disdainfully turned his back to open the door of the machine. Non-plussed, the poor sentry paused then ran to a field telephone a few yards away: in less than no time a car arrived in a whirl of dust and out stepped an army officer who told Dad that the machine had been impounded and his instructions were that no one was allowed near it. Dad thoroughly riled said, 'I'm taking these things to my son; if you think you can stop me, just try. As to the aircraft, you know where you can stick that, don't you?'

After four days in hospital I recovered completely to find we were in serious trouble. We should not have flown direct from Kisumu to Khartoum as strict regulations demanded that landings be made at Juba and Malakal. However, everyone was very nice to us at the hospital and the Governor-General, whom Dad had to see, was sympathetic with our plight and after much pondering agreed to release the Vega and permit us to get on our way.

The faithful Gipsy started at once but I was shocked when I checked the controls. The aircraft had stood out in the burning sun since our dramatic landing and the wooden machine had dried out to such an extent that the control column felt as if it was attached to loose string. I debated with Dad whether to take up the slack or not and in the end decided to proceed cautiously on to Cairo: I think we made the right decision, as by the time we were half way across Europe the controls had returned to their normal tension.

The few days in Cairo certainly did us both good and we were very confident on leaving that we could reach Tunis non-stop. This was not to be however. The weather was clear and cool across the North African desert but we bucked a gale-force wind in our teeth for hour after hour. I had recently read an article about Mussolini and the number of emigrants he had transported to the Garden of Eden in Libya, so we amused ourselves from time to time by making derisive remarks as we passed some particularly destitute spot with scarcely enough vegetation to keep an ant alive; we wondered as we passed over hundreds of miles of similar territory whether this so called paradise was just a myth and what the thousands of poor Italian colonists in this empire of theirs thought about it all. We had to admit however that the Italians knew how to build roads and must be very fond of them to build one such as this from the Egyptian Frontier to the Tunisian Border. Also they were most considerate towards the poor aviator, for along this road every few kilometres was a landing ground, nothing elaborate it is true, but each had corner boundary-markings and although we never saw any machines on any of them or anyone residing there, we came across odd whitewashed dwellings as if built in anticipation of things to come.

As we reached the border between Libya and Tunisia Dad was pointing out to me the Mareth Line when I calculated that we could reach Tunis with but very little fuel to spare. I was in no mood to take chances so we landed on the rough, stony track near the road and pulled up to some old-fashioned petrol pumps which were situated to serve both cars and aircraft. Doubtful of the octane rating I took only ten gallons of petrol from the pumps at Gabes and we quickly got under way. Tunis looked soft, warm and inviting after the glare and harshness of the desert. It was also friendly, comfortable and the food was without fault. But for our impatience to get home we could have relaxed in the balmy atmosphere for some time and enjoyed the history of the past as we recuperated from the strain we had both suffered over the previous week or so.

Early on a beautiful sunny morning we moved slowly with a heavily-laden machine from the concrete apron of the large hangars at Tunis and set course direct for home. We saw little of the Mediterranean lost below us in the cloud and haze that persisted, but we made such good time that Dad suggested we break our flight-plan and drop in for lunch at Lyon. This we did, leaving enough time to reach Heston, clear Customs and reach our own airfield as the sun settled over the young green corn of the English countryside. As we pushed the Vega into the hangar Dad patted the spinner and said, 'Well, Alex, no one will ever know how much we relied on the old girl, will they? I only hope any other machine we have will be as lucky.'

IN OUR ABSENCE Jack Cross had done tremendous work on the Mew Gull and must have had many sleepless nights as he puzzled and worked on the problems involved. The Mew was ready for more speed trials, now fitted with the electrical variable-pitch Ratier airscrew, and the intake designed not only for forward thrust, but for ram effect from the airscrew. The chassis had been altered and new type wheels fitted so that the frontal area was narrower, and around them Cross had fitted his special racing spats. I was always concerned about this speciality of his, for the spats fitted very snugly over the wheels and riveted to them were strips of spring steel, which were permitted to rub directly on to the tyre. From a performance point of view the idea was excellent, but the smell of burning rubber as I took off made me very conscious of what would happen if I had a burst tyre at the most critical moment. It was fair to say however that although I never ceased to worry about this, at no time did they actually give me any trouble. We had also rebuilt the underbelly of the fuselage. The take-off was now more startling than ever before and I really knew I had a tiger by the tail. I should have been elated by the terrific performance, as I flashed by Southend pier on my way over the Thames estuary, but as I built up speed to the very maximum, noting the exceptionally high boost and the revs exactly regulated, I felt that the engine did not sound right, so I throttled back and returned to land. As we took the engine cowling off, the paint was blistering on the top of the crankcase and as Jack and I looked at each other we both knew we were back with our old bogey.

If we were going to be ready for the Kings Cup there was still an enormous amount of work to be done, even without the worry of problems such as overheating bearings, and although I was prepared to work day and night with Cross and his wonderful team of enthusiastic young engineers to achieve success I must say, on reflection, that I was very despondent over our chances. I had intended not to race in any other event until the Kings Cup, but after days and weeks of testing, modifying, failure and success, retesting and still work to be done, I reached the conclusion that we should enter one race as a trial run. I would not use full power but it would have to be long enough to prove worthwhile. I chose the Hatfield to Isle of Man race on the 4th of June. There was another machine entered from the Essex Aero stable, prepared by Cross, which I had raced five years previously; this was the Comper Swift G-ABWW flown by Stanley Lowe. Also in the race was Charles Gardner's Mew, now owned by Giles Guthrie, and the TK2 flown by Geoffrey de Havilland, now much modified for the 1938 racing season.

The weather for the race was good and the race itself was un-eventful, I came in second behind Lowe's Swift, at the fastest speed of 247·5 mph, with Geoffrey de Havilland third. I was very happy with the result, as I knew I had had speed in hand and could have won had I wished, but I was less happy the next day when I ran the engine up in preparation for the Manx Derby. It misfired so badly that I had to switch off. Fortunately I had arranged for some Essex Aero mechanics to fly over, and they went to work with me to find the cause of the misfiring; it was soon diagnosed to my relief as plugs, the special platinum ones which we had fitted with so much faith.

The Manx Derby over the mountains and round the island was always an exciting race. I found little enjoyment, however, for first I could not afford to win the race and secondly the engine did not feel right. I managed third place in the Derby, and of course fastest time again, without I think making my tactics obvious, but when we looked at the machine the plugs were again faulty, and worse still, the enormous one-piece spinner had started to fracture. I returned to Gravesend with the certain feeling that whilst I might start in the Kings Cup, I would never finish the race. Jack however was more optimistic: we changed the type of sparking plug used and re-spun a new spinner, and our biggest relief was the fact that we appeared to have cured the overheating thrust bearings.

We were now entering on the final and most critical stages of modification. Rules for the Kings Cup race did not permit the use of foreign parts or equipment, so that I had to replace the Ratier airscrew with a De Havilland variable-pitch propeller. The big problem was that the De Havilland propeller was hydraulically controlled by oil from the engine passing through the crankshaft and the snag was that the 'R' engine crankshaft was not drilled for this purpose. Cross got over this problem by fitting an extension to the existing crankshaft with a special billet of high-tensile steel, which he designed, machined and drilled himself. I helped him at the lathe on a very intricate piece of work, and was filled with admiration for the confident, meticulous manner in which he set the job up; I could not help wondering to myself, though, how he would have felt had he the job of flying the aircraft as well. The final modification on the Mew structurally was to rebuild the cockpit and fuselage, so that this fitted me like a suit. When it was finished, by taking out the seat cushion and replacing it with a thin piece of sorbo rubber, the top of the cockpit canopy just cleared my head but left me no room to sit completely upright.

My hopes sank on the first test take-off. After all this work had been completed, the new V/P prop had only two positions, so that I took off in fine pitch and changed into coarse as the revs built up; this detracted from the take-off performance, but worse still the maximum speed had fallen as the Ratier was obviously a more efficient airscrew. Getting the basic pitch-setting right was also difficult as this had to be done on the ground after a series of test flights. The more I tested the machine, the more I worried about my chances, I had the occasion to speak to Major Halford, famed as the designer of the Gipsy engines, and asked his views; he said that it was really a critical design modification and if done by them, would require a very severe test programme. He said basically the idea was sound, but the high stresses would come as I turned round the pylons during the race at maximum speed, when very high gyroscopic loads would be set up and he could not say without more technical information and many calculations, how high the loading was likely to be.

Apart from the personal problems of testing and getting the Mew ready on time as the great day drew nearer, I was having to face up to doubts in other directions. I was sure that I had made a big mistake in entering for the Isle of Man race. Although I had not hoodwinked the handicappers a great deal, the speed of my Mew and how it had left Charles Gardner's old machine way behind, had shaken the air-racing fraternity; rumours were now rife that Percival was pulling out all the stops to improve his own machine and imagining his whole factory working overtime, I saw my chances of the fastest time slipping further and further away.

Normally I would have given a great deal of time and thought to the route we were to take, but this year as it was on such a short circuit, it was going to be the machine rather than the pilot who would win. Day after day we continued various adjustments and tests but on the eve of the race I was still not happy with my basic setting on the coarse side of the variable-pitch airscrew. I had to test at sea level and in bumpy conditions it was difficult to obtain a positive reading; as I landed at Hatfield for the check-in I was only just inside the time limit for the acceptance of the machine and I asked for another fifteen minutes test time before handing over. This was readily agreed upon and I was delighted that as the sun went down the air became still; I was able to satisfy myself that I ought to fine-off the basic setting half a degree and landed so that Jack could re-adjust and I could sleep sound in the knowledge that at least we had done all that was possible to get the best out of the Mew.

As I was deep in thought, with Jack and the boys carefully adjusting the airscrew, a prize row was going on between Geoffrey de Havilland and Harold Perrin, the secretary of the Royal Aero Club, and I was embarrassed to hear Perrin say to Geoffrey de Havilland, 'Alex Henshaw requested fifteen minutes further time for testing; you've now been an hour overdue and if you don't toe the line I shall report you to the stewards.' Geoffrey made a caustic reply and I moved away so as not to get involved. I can't remember where I slept that night, if I slept at all.

Hatfield was swarming with almost everyone in British aviation and the betting had already started on the race, I was unhappy to see my name up as one of the favourites, which I always considered a bad omen. Then I had a real shock; Harold Perrin came over to me in the clubhouse and said, 'The handicappers want to see you, right away.' I went quickly over to the Mew to be greeted by Rowarth and Dancey with very serious looks on their faces and not at all pleased. Fred Rowarth said, 'Has the fuselage been altered, because if it has and we have not got a record on your entry form, I'm afraid we have no alternative than to disqualify you.' I said the fuselage had been altered but I could not vouch for the entrance form as for the first time in racing I had not filled it in, and this had been done by Cross. There was a huddled and whispered conversation and a search through the various forms; apparently the entrance form had been sent off with certain information and the remaining details by letter. In the end Wilf Dancey said, 'We must remeasure.' When they put the tape round I could see they were puzzled, as although the top of the fuselage had been reduced, the lower half had a slightly different shape than originally. I was asked to climb into the cockpit and Dad said the sight of me trying to look smaller than I actually was when the measurements were taken was as funny as a lady with size ten feet getting into a pair of shoes size five. I didn't think it was funny at all, particularly when Fred said, 'I'm sorry, Alex, but we've got to penalise you.' I was so fed up I said, 'You're the handicappers, but I don't think you'll have anything to worry about, as I shall be surprised if I survive half a dozen laps.' Until that moment I did not know what the handicap figures were; I thought the penalty had made me scratch man, but I was surprised to note that Edgar Percival's Mew was just behind me. This gave me hope, because I felt I was faster than Percival if I could only keep going, but this knowledge I kept to myself. Not so Dad. As Percival was putting his Mew into position as scratch man, he said, 'What are you lapping at, Edgar?' Percival replied, 'About thirteen minutes; what is Alex doing?' Dad replied casually that the last run had been under twelve. Percival snorted and said, 'Oh yeah, pull the other leg.'

As always the atmosphere on race day had a quality all its own. I was never quite sure why this was so: it was never called the Kings Cup Air Race but always the Kings Cup. I suppose it meant different things to different people. To the pilot it gave a chance for the amateur to compete with the professional and in some instances the mediocre to defeat the brilliant and for the ordinary to meet the famous. For the manufacturer it was his day as well—the factory had entered a new or revamped machine and win or lose it was on show to the most discriminating and the largest audience in the country. The accessory and gadget firms also displayed their wares with varying degrees of enthusiasm and applauding the fact that so-and-so would be racing with some item supplied by them.

To the fore in all this and certainly contributing more to the glamour, gaiety and colour of this festive air were the banners, flags and bowsers used by the oil and petrol companies. Amongst the military of course the RAF predominated and were represented, if not with military aircraft, by some of the best pilots of the day. It was also impressive to see high-ranking sailors and soldiers in glamorous uniforms looking important and knowledgeable as they showed foreign visitors round the competing machines.

It was also a great social occasion, sometimes with Royalty, certainly with a strong cross-section of the British aristocracy and always with a bevy of actors and actresses usually trying, not very successfully, to behave as if they did not wish to be recognised. Perhaps last but not least it was a wonderful party for the inebriates—what better excuse could you have?—meeting old friends of long standing and the booze free. Whatever your own interest or feeling it was an atmosphere charged with excitement, challenge and expectation mingled with the sound of powerful engines on the ground or in the air and the smell of cellulose, petrol and oil as you walked down the line of England's finest light aircraft as they prepared for the test to come.

There were several fast machines entered for that year; apart from the Mews of Percival and Guthrie, Bill Humble was in a Sparrow Hawk, Louis Fonties in a Speed Six Hawk, Geoffrey de Havilland in the TK2, and but for an unfortunate accident the Comet with Chris Staniland and a passenger named Hopcroft would have been in the race. I saw the accident happen. The Comet had arrived and approached in such a professional and confident manner that I thought Staniland must have got very well used to the machine in a short time, as he made the landing and approach look child's-play. Later I watched him take off and in the same confident manner the tail was pushed up neatly and then to my surprise with a quite short run Chris picked the Comet off the ground, expecting I suppose for the machine to pull into a steady climb on power; the tapered wings of the Comet would not take this kind of flying, however, and to the gasps of everyone watching, the Comet flicked to starboard. Only the wingtip hitting the ground stopped the machine from doing a flick roll and killing both on board; as it was, the machine bounced off the wingtip on to its undercarriage again and as the throttles were snapped back, came to a standstill, when everyone breathed a great sigh of relief.

It was difficult to get any peace from wellwishers, officials, photographers and press, and I was glad when I was able to get away for a few hours. The morning of the race was perfect, for which I was thankful, as the alterations to the Mew restricted visibility so much that I could not see at all forward and had to judge landmarks from the side; the chance of hitting a machine on such a short course was a real and worrying problem, particularly if the weather were to be bad.

I saw that Dad's remarks to Percival had got him worried, as the cowlings were already off his machine and he was discussing basic pitch-settings with his general manager, Summers. Although it was still very early, Hatfield was bursting with activity. In the past I had been thrilled and excited to be privileged to be a part of this big spectacle. This time I felt worried and harassed; my Mew as more and more experts in the aviation world examined it created a sensation, but the driest remark I think must go to Group-Captain Willy Wilson, who was later to break the world speed record. Bill Humble brought him over, full of praise and enthusiasm, and said to Willy, 'What do you think of it?' Willy replied, after a meditative look at the machine, 'I think it would have been cheaper to have bought a revolver.'

I wanted to be near the machine and I needed to be able to think and concentrate in peace. This was impossible, I knew a great many people and they naturally wanted to wish me good luck. The cream of the British aircraft industry were now gathered on the airfield, so that I had engineers, designers and heads of manufacturers wanting to discuss various points with me, and then of course there were the inevitable autograph-hunters, the press, photographers and the BBC. Dad and my brother Leslie could see I was getting so edgy that they tried to provide a shield, but this was not easy when so many friends were milling around. The tension eased in one sense as we were marshalled on to the starting line, as although I did not take off for a long while after the first machine, only a few authorised individuals such as stewards, marshals and judges were allowed there. Dad, Jack and I could now discuss problems with less interruptions. Jack had measured the fuel for Stanley Lowe in the Swift G-ABWW to the last pint for his first heat, but I said to him I did not want to cut things so fine and made him put in a safer margin. None of us were sure I was faster than Percival, so that was really an unknown quantity. I knew more than anyone else of course, but I refused to allow myself to be optimistic. There had been wild speculation when the handicap figures were released but no one really knew who had the best chance. Sammy Morton had been burning up the course impressively in the B.A.Double Eagle as I had arrived the day before, and it was rumoured he was getting a lot of extra speed from it. Clouston was flying the other B.A.Eagle, Broad the Parnel Heck, and Ken Waller a Vega Gull.

I had no fixed favourite in mind, I only wanted two things, to put up the fastest time and finish the course.

The day was warm and sunny and as machine after machine took off my own tension rose and I was glad as I watched for what seemed hours the slower competitors roaring overhead and doing neat vertical turns over the pylon in the middle of the aerodrome. Then I was signalled that I had ten minutes to go, and it was time to start the already warm engine. The course was a pylon at Buntingford, another at Barton and then back to Hatfield to the pylon in the middle of the aerodrome, a total distance of 50·607 miles, of which there were to be twenty laps, making a total of 1012·14 miles in all, with breaks for refuelling every fifth lap. I had my own lap board on the instrument panel

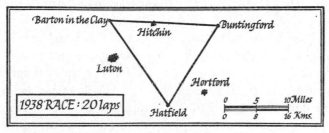

King's Cup 1938: circuit 50·607 miles, total 1012·14 miles

as I think had all the pilots, to avoid silly mistakes. I drew my Sutton harness tight and Dad and Jack lifted the perspex canopy over my head for fixing as Reynolds, the starter, gave us the five-minute signal. The flag went down and as I opened the throttle I cursed inwardly that I had not been allowed to use the Ratier airscrew, nevertheless we shot forward and I clipped over the boundary trees and turned right towards the shredded-wheat factory at Welwyn Garden City, my first fix. Since I could not see forward I had selected points along the course, mostly on the starboard side, such as a church, a haystack, a garage on the Great North Road, and a sharp belt of trees as the ground rose slightly on the homeward sector. All fairly easy and straightforward; the turns were the most difficult to judge, the ailerons on XF at maximum speed were very nearly solid and it was hard and exacting work placing myself in the precise position and then easing the machine into a perfect turn without too much 'g' and intercepting the pylon at the correct point.

Several of the pilots were going into the turns at almost ground level, well below the race ruling; pulling over hard into a really vertical turn and then straightening up immediately, they looked very professional and spectacular and as I waited impatiently on the scratch line for my turn to take off I had heard the crowd shout with delight. I did not propose using this technique: in the first instance, I did not want to risk a disqualification by being too low, and as was my usual practice I liked to approach with height in hand so that as I straightened out I could allow the machine to fall away in a shallow dive and regain speed lost in the turn. It was hot work and I was soon in a bath of perspiration; this made me look at the oil temperature gauge, which had climbed to an alarming degree, but the boost reading was satisfying and the maximum revs just within tolerance. As I came in for the first landing, I felt breathless in anticipation of hearing the results; I guessed they were favourable before the machine came to a standstill, as Dad had a grin from ear to ear and there were scores of people smiling and waving to me with their programmes as I waited for the canopy to be lifted off, and clambered out of the cockpit. 'How have I done?' I shouted. 'Fastest ever,' was the chorus. 'Best lap just under 240.' I felt a wonderful surge of satisfaction go through me and I said to Cross, 'Well done, Jack; do you think we shall finish?'

The cowlings were now off and the Essex Aero team were going over every nut and bolt. I could hear the glug-glug of the boiling oil in the tank and I knew I could not afford to be over-optimistic. I was wet with perspiration and my hands shook as I drank the fresh orange juice Dad had given to me; I think many thought this was nerves, but I think it was tension and the handling of stiff aileron controls so intently for so long. The heat in the cockpit was mainly due to my refusing to spoil the clean lines of XF with ventilator louvres. Jack spoke to me, as he was concerned over the lack of ventilation, and said he would drill some small holes in the canopy. I would not hear another

18 Mew Gull 'The Golden City' before it became G-AEXF
19 Collecting G-AEXF from Luton, 1937

20   Tense moments on the starting line: King's Cup 1938
21   Dad assisting to refuelling point: King's Cup 1938

word about it, however, as I had visions of a split canopy suddenly breaking up in flight. The slide-rule experts had now been
busy and Jumbo Edwards, who was not racing that year, had
plotted each competitor for every round on a chart and told me
that apart from the fastest time which was now obvious, I was a
certain winner. I did not like this line of talk and said, 'That's
all very well, but there is an awful long way to go yet.' Of
course the commercial firms were getting very excited and preparing telegrams and adverts for fuel, plugs, oil, tyres, paints
and so on, but Dad kept most of them away from me as he
knew how I felt.

It was soon time for the next series of laps and as I moved to
the starting line again I noticed Percival with his spinner still on
the ground arguing with his senior staff, Summers and Lavender,
about the pitch-setting. I thought, if he has not got that airscrew
adjusted accurately by now, then he never will. All that day the
racing continued, in hot, perfect conditions and I became more
tense and apprehensive as I got nearer and nearer the finish. Dad
and Jack in contrast appeared to be more relaxed and confident, but then this may have been for my benefit. I finally
flashed over the finishing line for the last time with the knowledge that I had put up the fastest time in the race and won it
at the fastest winning speed ever recorded, and at the same time
beaten the handicappers. I ought to have been jubilant, but
somehow something nagged at me inside, and although the victory was by no means a hollow one, it did not feel quite right
and I started to try and analyse myself. I reasoned as I circled
overhead before landing, that this was really Cross's victory and
yet I was accepting all the glory and ballyhoo. That so much
effort, time and money had been spent to win and yet all this
would have been of no avail other than the fastest time prize, if
the handicappers calculations had been unfavourable. This
point came home to me when after I had landed I was told that
Giles Guthrie in the other Mew Gull was second at some 16 mph
slower, and Cliff, a comparatively unknown pilot with an almost
untouched standard Hawk machine, was third at 91 mph
slower. My elation over the fastest time was dampened as I

N

taxied in front of the huge crowd, who were waving and cheering. As I saw Percival taxi his own Mew to the parking area, somehow I felt a little sad and sorry for a man who had for many years always achieved the fastest time with his own design and own production, in his own factory. To be beaten by one of his own machines flown by an amateur, was I should think hard to take.

The presentation of the Kings Cup, with the cheques for the fastest time, was made by the Secretary of State for Air, Sir Kingsley Wood, a jovial cherubic man. Everyone was in tremendous spirits and although the only thing I really wanted to do was to get to bed and sleep, I had perforce to go over to the Comet Hotel and invite all my immediate friends to a party. I had cause for sober thoughts at the party when Geoffrey de Havilland, said to me, 'Christ, Alex you put the fear of God up me on that last lap.' I said, 'I'm sorry, I'm not with you, what do you mean?' He said, 'You know when you passed me just before Buntingford, when your wing went over me, I reckoned you were less than six feet away.' I felt numb as I replied, 'My God, Geoffrey! You will have to believe me when I say that I never saw you at all on the last lap.' On reflection I can only assume that I was looking out on the starboard side and that Geoffrey's TK2 was slightly lower on the port side and I had not seen him.

What a night that was after such a wonderful day; I never realised I knew so many people in aviation, never mind friends. I was given all the accolades of course by all the numerous well-wishers and I think I did my best to give credit where it was due. There were no television cameras in those days, so that all live broadcasts were through the BBC. Charles Gardner, not to be confused with Charles Gardner of Mew Gull fame, was the air correspondent and compere; when he asked me to broadcast after the race, I paid due tribute to Jack Cross, his splendid team, and the small works of Essex Aero at Gravesend. Gardner was not very pleased about this, as he said he would get it in the neck for advertising. All the de Havilland family were at the party and I realised they were just as joyful as me that the 'R' engine had stood up to such a pounding. I took the opportunity of telling St Barbe and Major Halford, Hugh Buckingham and Captain Sir Geoffrey de Havilland that I was going after the Cape records in October, but would have liked to replace the 'R' with a new Series II engine, which although of less power was more reliable. They all agreed and said they would see what could be done for me.

The next day I could not take the Mew away until the scrutineers had finished examining the engine. In the meantime Jack rang me up and said we were in trouble. I immediately thought he had made a mistake in the cubic-capacity measurements or the compression-ratio on the race application form, but he said it was something to do with the Air Ministry and that Harold Perrin the Royal Aero Club secretary was getting in touch with me.

Later that day Commander Perrin rang through and said that the Royal Aero Club had been informed that certain alterations had been made to my Mew Gull, which had not been approved by the Air Ministry at the time, and that I was to meet the Royal Aero Club race committee with Cross the next evening at 119 Piccadilly. Apparently drawings of some structural alterations had been sent off, and when these had not been approved in the normal manner, Cross had telephoned the department concerned; after some argument it was agreed that an approval would be forthcoming, but in fact this did not arrive in time for the race. Jack had not wished to upset me and said nothing. When Dad asked what I was going to do, I said, 'This is a lot of nonsense and in my opinion has nothing to do with the race, even though the Air Ministry may claim it could have effected the safety of the aircraft. I'm going to take the Cup to the club and tell them what they can do with it.' Dad being much wiser said, 'I shouldn't. Why not wait and hear the committee's views; they might think the same as you.'

Dad, Jack and I went to the Aero Club together. Jack was asked into the committee room first and then Harold Perrin came down for me a little time later. He said, 'Don't worry about this business, Alex; we shall talk a bit, but we have already made up our minds.' When I stepped into the somewhat majestic committee room, with all the members sitting very seriously round an enormous oblong table, I had to check myself from laughing, as nearly all of the committee members were friends and I am quite sure they would have been more embarrassed than me if they had had to declare me disqualified. After some very polite cross-examining the Chairman said, 'We are unanimous in our opinion that the infringement is of a purely technical nature and in no way affecting the results of the race; we recommend that a letter of apology be sent as a result of Mr Cross's misunderstanding with the Air Ministry.' We all then went off and celebrated together in the club bar.

17 ✳ Choosing the route

WITH THE KING'S CUP now satisfactorily behind me I could give all my concentration to the planning and preparation for the Cape records. I lived with this night and day, turning every conceivable possibility of failure over in my mind. I was convinced that my schedule had to be timed to minutes and that this was the most important aspect of the flight on which to work—playing it by ear was just not on: there had to be one meticulous flight-plan and one only.

The Automobile Association had done a very professional job in preparing maps, distances, sun and moon phases, and detailed schedules out to Cape Town and back. One glance showed me however the many weaknesses and high risk points in their planning and I realised there was only one person who could work this out and that if I made a mistake I would also have to suffer the consequences. For days and nights I worked on this difficult problem: I had only a limited number of airstrips that I could use with such a machine as XF; I had no aids to find places in bad weather or darkness; without weather forecasts I had to calculate the limits of my range, bearing in mind the possibility of head winds and bad conditions forcing an extension to my estimated time in the air. Above all I must not be greedy or over ambitious and demand a performance beyond my capabilities. The times, places, distances and facilities kept crowding into my mind so that I would become confused. In the end I traced from an atlas my route over Europe and Africa and then on semi-transparent graph paper I marked off the hours of day and night at a scale equal to that of the cruising speed of the Mew on the tracing. I then coloured in red the period of sunrise to sunset on the graph paper and in blue the phases of the moon. I could now slide this transparency on top of the map tracing and at a glance could obtain a clear mental picture over the whole route using a datum time for my first take-off from England. The key to a successful flight-plan was without question the manner in which I chose to make my landfalls after a long night-flight on to poorly equipped airstrips and also the approaches at night or at sunset. I felt that I could cope with all this, but the one thing that I could not calculate or allow for would be fog, ice or those violent storms that sweep over the Equatorial regions of West Africa. The forced landing with the Vega Gull in Nigeria had already shown me that the margins could be very narrow—at twilight, for instance, one moment it is possible to see and the next you are in complete darkness.

As I worked and studied various possibilities a pretty clear picture was forming in my mind as to the advantages and disadvantages of the Western route to Cape Town with respect to the better known Eastern route.

The important controlling factor was the range that I might squeeze out of the tiny Mew. I was working on the assumption that I had a safe 1500 statute miles range which would give me a reasonable margin for headwinds, loss of time in bad weather or circling a bad aerodrome at night waiting for first light; but it was an assumption, because the difference in fuel-consumption when flying over Europe in cold, damp conditions and those of the summer heat along the Skeleton Coast of Africa was very marked indeed. I was also restricted in my methods of controlling the fuel consumed by the Gipsy Six Series II engine. The performance of XF was so good that it was a little in advance of the Hamilton/DH airscrew I intended to use, in that there was not sufficient pitch range: if the basic setting gave me full power on the take-off then I would be over-revving the engine at my maximum power at rated altitude and would have to throttle back slightly; conversely, if I adjusted the basic setting to give me all the control I needed at 7000 to 8000 ft then I had lower engine revolutions and consequently less power on the take-off. In addition to this technical information on power, revolutions and altitude in relationship to speed, range and endurance was not available as it is today, and even had I been given this knowledge it is doubtful whether I could have made good use of it, for I lacked the necessary instruments: flow-meter, fuel gauge, exhaust-gas analyser, and cylinder-head temperature gauge. I had to settle for my own knowledge of the engine. I would adjust the mixture controls by sound and hope not to overdo it, for my first accurate consumption check would only be when the large bulkhead tank ran dry and the engine momentarily stopped. I would work on the basis of seven to ten per cent loss of power in the tropics but expect a comparable increase in range as a result of this.

As can be seen, all this ruled out any chance of XF reaching Cairo from England in one flight, as had the Comet. Normally, pilots flying to Cairo went down the Rhône Valley and then via Italy or the North African Coast. I could not afford this detour and if I chose the Eastern route I must use Athens or Brindisi as my first stop, traversing Central Europe and crossing the Alps. There was no problem to this but having experienced some of the February weather in those mountainous regions, I would not have been happy letting down through cloud at night purely on a dead-reckoning fix.

Ideally, I would have liked to complete the Cape flight in three long stages but the more I studied each route the more I realised I should in fact be lucky to be able to complete it in four. Cairo to Khartoum was easy, a short leg of approximately 1000 miles, ending in the junction of the White Nile with the Blue and adjoining a large city prominent in desert surroundings; at night I was unlikely to miss it if I flew accurately. Moreover, Imperial Airways used it as a base, so I was assured of good facilities and lights for a night-landing. After Khartoum I had the pick of Kisumu, Entebbe or Nairobi. Entebbe had the best runway and as with Kisumu was easy to find, located as they were on the northern shores of Lake Victoria, and both had night-landing facilities. On leaving the Equator I then had the choice of several quite good airfields. All of them were however on the high East African plateau and subject at times to excessive temperatures. Comforting though the reports on these well maintained aerodromes might have been to examine on paper, I have to confess I was more afraid of this aspect of the flight than I ever cared to admit. In the worst circumstances many of these airfields could have a pressure height of over 9000 ft and the heat so searing as almost to guarantee a vapour lock, usually at the most critical point of take-off. I really needed an aircraft with a low wing-loading and adequate supercharged power; in XF the power output would be less than half and with an overload of 90 gallons of volatile fuel, I had neither. If in my most optimistic dreams I dismissed this particular hazard from my mind, I was brought back to sober reality when I thought of all those red rusting and often charred remains that like an unkempt graveyard gave notice of what had taken place around these solitary, peaceful but deceptive airfields. The rotting debris gave ominous warning.

The most misleading aspect to be found in flying from these high and extremely hot airfields was the difficulty in selecting a point at which to abort a take-off. If the wheels did not leave the ground, then at a critical point with luck it was possible to throttle back and bring the machine to a standstill; so often however, particularly on a good tarmac runway, I found that some aircraft would become airborne in less than half the length of the airfield but would float along just above the stall on the ground-effect cushion of air, deluding one into expecting a build up of climbing speed before leaving the aerodrome. Instead it could happen that the boundary would be crossed, and if nothing happened to be in the way the machine would stagger on a few feet above rough ground whilst with bated breath one avoided with the most gentle of manoeuvres any large boulders, praying at the same time for a slope in the ground or for a hefty thermal to give that little bit of extra speed and lift that was needed so desperately. It was not an experience that I relished or would recommend. My choice of a suitable selection was made still more difficult when considering the night landings. True I should not have the intense heat on leaving any airfield as in the sunlight of day but there was the problem of bushfire haze in the hours of darkness.

Mountainous terrain in this part of Africa was also cause for some concern. Without radio or any other form of communication, even with very careful dead-reckoning and outstanding navigation, although one might be sure of one's position, if it was not possible to see the ground because of darkness or cloud the altimeter became a vital instrument. Also, there was no knowledge of change in barometric pressure and in fact many altimeters did not have a millibar scale, which came into general use only with the sensitive altimeter. Although one was quite aware from the map information as to the height when flying from sea-level to the comparatively level plateau, say, around Johannesburg, it was nevertheless a little disconcerting when flattening out for a landing to notice over 5000 ft registered on the altimeter. It certainly gave warning against casual complacency when calculating a course in cloud or at night in the much higher regions with which this part of Africa abounded.

On the outward flight this sector would be encountered when I would undoubtedly be relying upon the last of my physical and mental reserves and I was frankly fearful of repeating the disaster which befell Stan Halse. Having met him recently, I was impressed by his character and also his unquestionable ability as pilot and navigator. Like myself he was not big in stature so that a cramped cockpit would present similar discomforts to both of us, and as he had been extremely fit at the time of the Schlesinger Race there was no guarantee that I should not suffer the same degree of exhaustion that had enveloped Stan, impairing my airmanship and clear thinking on navigational problems just when they were needed most of all.

The final landing at Cape Town worried me least of all; the chances of fine weather during that period of the year were good and the night landing facilities probably the best since leaving England.

Thinking about using the Western route with XF, I must confess, gave me many sleepless nights. Gravesend to Oran was easy. If I had any doubts about the high Pyrenees with ice and cloud I could deviate slightly to Marseilles and time my descent down to the sea before I struck the North African coast. From then on my difficulties could begin and were of an unknown quantity and complexity. I had many pilot friends who knew the Eastern route intimately and could offer sound advice; not so for the Western route. Those with whom I did discuss a flight plan spoke of poor airfields vast distances apart and the complete lack of facilities or communications. All spoke of three formidable obstacles which were well known: first, the Tanezrouft, where it was possible to find oneself 800 miles between watering holes in extreme temperatures; secondly, the tornadoes that swept over the jungle at frequent periods in the region between Nigeria and the Congo; thirdly, the almost perpetual fog which persists from Mossamedes to Luderitz in conditions that are unpredictable. I knew that Victor Smith had attacked the Cape records using my proposed route several times, and that in spite of the most courageous determination on his part each time he had been compelled to abandon the attempt. A Romanian prince had almost lost his life over the jungles of West Africa when attempting the record in a specially prepared and meticulously equipped twin-engined Caudron. Amy Johnson was the only person I knew who had been at all successful on this route to the Cape; nevertheless, on the first attempt she tore the undercarriage from her Gull Six G-ADZO in the soft sands of Colomb Béchar, and although she broke the existing record down to the Cape on her second attempt she returned via the Eastern route for her attack on the record from Cape Town to England.

Early difficulty came with the first planned landing. I wanted to use Oran because it was at sea-level and I would not have to cross the Atlas Mountains at that stage, but regulations insisted that I call in at Colomb Béchar and clear my authority to cross the Sahara. Having accepted that I must use Colomb Béchar, then, I proposed to do it in one flight from Gravesend and from there to proceed direct to Niamey, both these legs getting near the limit of my range. The real stumbling block to this flight plan was the fact that south of Niamey there was no suitable airstrip that would allow me to land in the night or even at first light: Duala was too short a leg; Leopoldville I considered too dangerous because of the persistent cloud and rain that swept down to the trees; Pointe Noire would have been suitable for range, time and flight-planning but my experience here had proved that not only was it dangerous to land on with a high-performance machine but taking-off would be out of the question. Finally, Libreville was acceptable but made such a short flight from Niamey that I was really throwing away time in the loss of a full night of flying. Colomb Béchar was a French military aerodrome 1312 by 656 yards and 2558 ft in altitude and I did not anticipate any real problems there. Alternative aerodromes were in reality emergency landing strips used by the Foreign Legion and French Air Force, such as Beni Abbès and Bidon 5B and Bidon 5A; here the petrol was kept in tins buried in the ground, and although the strip was given as 656 yards long and only 1148 ft above sea level, in the shimmering heat of day I would not have relished the job of landing safely.

Leaving Oran and having crossed the Atlas Mountains one is faced with what can only be described as an ocean of sand for 1400 miles or so without a solitary fix most of the way—even if flown in the daytime and in good conditions. Information I had received on Gao said that it was a military aerodrome 1202 by 1202 yards at an altitude of 850 ft, firm grass and serviceable throughout the year. The person who prepared that description should have been jailed for misrepresentation! But I decided there was no alternative to landing at Gao. At this juncture I could see no way of pruning my flight-plan and taking off immediately I had refuelled and set out the hurricane lamps from either Gao or Niamey: not only would I have the problem of finding the Duala or Libreville strips in the dark without sufficient reserve of fuel to keep me in the air until first light if I failed, but also if either of these small places on the edge of the jungle were in the path of a tornado during the time that I wanted to land my chances of survival would be slim indeed. Another fear that was constantly on my mind in using these isolated spots was the possibility of a misfortune as silly as a puncture or minor mechanical adjustment; and worst of all there might be a structural failure as a result of the burning heat, rough rocky plateaus or unstable soft areas of sand that constituted most of the airfields from Oran to Cape Town.

I think the best that could be said for the route so far was that, particularly during a night-flight, when I broke cloud I could, certainly over the Bight of Biafra, allow my descent to continue blind almost to sea-level, always providing my navigation had been accurate and I did not strike the Island of Fernando Po which happened to be far too close to my track for comfort. Libreville had a long, firm sand runway carved out of the jungle and as far as I could see at the time presented few problems unless one struck the tall trees surrounding it. It had one distinct advantage—the altitude was recorded as 2 ft! There were alternative landing places, but Benguela was made up of earth and grass, with numerous holes and was liable to become soft and unusable after rain; Loanda had appeared a possibility until I saw it on the survey flight and dared not land because of its rough, stony grass surface covered in anthills; Lobito was also available, but it was recommended only to be used in an emergency.

I now came to the sector where only Mossamedes could be used; this had a hard, rocky sand surface listed as 792 × 792 yds in size and at an altitude of 200 ft. It was one of the hottest places I had ever been on in my life and save for the few whitewashed corner stones I would defy anyone to tell where the aerodrome ended and the desert began, but it was probably better than some of the other places I would eventually choose to use. The real danger here, I felt, was landing at night without lights and the very real risk of fog forming once the sun had gone below the horizon. In between Mossamedes and Cape Town were the airfields of Luderitz, Swakopmund, Port Nolloth and Walvis Bay; none of these were good, but I reckoned that if I were compelled to use any one of them, then my flight would have been a failure. In considering all these possibilities and churning over and over in my mind the numerous obstacles and difficulties to both routes, after days and nights of balancing each against the other I was left with two salient points which to me seemed to rise above all others. The route across the Sahara and the Congo was two hours shorter in time and my worst airfield would be less than a 1000 ft in height.

Whilst I fully appreciated the inherent dangers that lie along the Western route I was of course obsessed with saving any time, no matter how small; and the knowledge that I should take off with a heavy load of highly explosive fuel literally wrapped around my body, with an aircraft C of G aft of all normal limits, gave me the jitters every time my mind dwelt on those scorched airstrips way up on the rocky central African plateau. My father knew how absorbed I was in analysing every aspect of a myriad of items, showed great restraint and although we discussed my plans at some length he never tried to pursuade me one way or the other. He had been able to judge many of the problems for himself as we flew up and down Africa and although I am quite sure he would have preferred that I flew via Cairo, Khartoum and Entebbe, he was wise enough to know that only someone who had flown XF loaded as it was for such a flight and in the circumstances which were likely to prevail, could possibly offer any constructive judgement.

I am not sure when I finally made up my mind. I do know that I had many mixed feelings particularly when good friends like Arthur Clouston and Tommy Rose said, 'Use the Imperial Airways route, it is the only safe way across Africa to the Cape.' I can honestly say this; when I said to my father, 'Dad, I have decided to use the West route,' and he replied, 'You should know what you're doing, if anyone does,' I did not have one single misgiving nor did I at any time feel I must change my mind.

From now on everything I planned was related to overcoming the problems that lay ahead and to reducing the inherent dangers.

18 ✻ *To the very limits*

THE MODIFICATIONS to the Mew took up all my spare time as Jack and I assessed the possibilities of loading more fuel into XF. It was a matter of finding the space and at the same time keeping within an operational C of G factor—to say nothing of designing and fabricating the tanks to carry the fuel. In changing the engine to a Gipsy Six Series II De Havillands, whilst extremely helpful and friendly, would not loan or give me an engine, but offered to discount a new one at £1200. I was a little hurt over this as I had been friends of all the de Havilland family for some years. It did not need any flight that I might undertake to prove the reliability and worth of the Gipsy engine, but the 'R' engine had brought the De Havilland Company into some disrepute owing to its failures in the Comets of the Australia Race, and in the Hawk Speed Six of Clouston; and it was Cross, and myself to a lesser degree, who had redeemed the name of the 'R' engine in no small way. I felt that had it been left to Sir Geoffrey de Havilland or his sons Peter or Geoffrey there would have been no problems, but I realised that now as a large public organisation the decision must be based on hard economic facts. Luckily I knew of a new Series II that had been dismantled from one of Miles's experimental machines, the Peregrine, and I was able to do a much better deal with Shackletons, who were handling the sale.

The long-range tanks both for petrol and oil posed a big problem; although I was already cramped in the cockpit, we had no alternative but to enlarge my main fuselage tank by bringing the instrument panel closer to my face. As I was unable to sit completely upright and in any case was slightly inclined backwards,

I thought I should be able to manage. Another petrol tank was built and designed so that it came up between my legs and over the top and on either side of my ankles. When we fitted the large P4 compass and the mixture controls there was so little room that the airscrew control had to be attached to the face of this tank— between my legs.

The Series II engine was thirstier on oil than the 'R' or the Series I, so that I could not increase the range without provision for more oil. There was now no room whatsoever in the cockpit, nor could the existing oil tank be enlarged, so this posed a real problem. Jack solved it by designing a saddle tank which replaced part of the engine cowling. I was horrified when I first saw this, envisaging a fractured tank, fatigue failure or connections wearing or tearing apart and a slow death in the jungle or desert. Credit was due to Jack that the complex installation never gave any trouble: the saddle tank also acted as a radiator to keep the oil temperature within reasonable limits.

To survive days and nights of flying in such a cramped space, I knew I should have to be really fit, so I spent more time running, riding and playing squash than I had ever done before. The riding part was easy as we had four hunters at home that I would ride and jump barebacked for hours; Dad was a superb rider and was always with me to praise or criticise. The running part was a chore in which I persisted every morning before breakfast. For squash I used to fly to Cambridge at weekends and play Maurice Crouch in the courts at Jesus College. During the week I would play every other night at the Three Counties club at Peterborough.

I absorbed myself in work to such a degree that I found I was often getting up at four in the morning to cope. I could not afford to have a hitch of any sort when the time came, so every minute item concerning the route was set down and sent to all the parties concerned. Permits and visas were obvious requirements and routine but all had to be dealt with, and a compulsory insurance policy had to be taken out against a possible Sahara search. If I was to be successful I had to go further than just planning formalities, even arranging for such small items as a bowl of cold water, soap and a towel immediately after landing, and tea or coffee, etc., to say nothing of lamps or flares for take-off and landing. I asked that owing to the unusual method of filling the oil tank and the petrol tanks, nothing was to be put into the aircraft unless I saw to it personally. As I was going through Portuguese territories and could not speak their language I had the essential sentences typed out in my log book.

That August I was invited to visit the Zlin works in Czechoslovakia and as we were thinking of importing them for the newly formed Civil Air Guard, Dad and I decided to accept the invitation along with another one to the Frankfurt Air Rally and Races which had come through Herr Gerbrecht, President of the Berlin Aero Club. He wanted me to race XF and jokingly said that he had arranged the handicap so that I should win. The Mew's extensive modifications made it unflyable for a while, so we decided to go with the Vega as onlookers and asked Joe Scholes and Fred Rowarth as our guests.

About this time the small war clouds in the sky were becoming a little darker, larger and more menacing and many people began to wonder what was really going to happen. In Germany, as far as we were concerned, not a great deal had altered; the Germans were hospitable and certainly made me very welcome. I was sorry I had not brought XF as so many German pilots asked about it, and when I saw my name and the Mew entered on the list for the race the next day with the handicap figures, I calculated that it would have allowed me to win hands down.

There was if anything more pomp, saluting and clicking of heels than before, and one got a little peeved with the constant 'Heil Hitlers'. When we flew on into Czechoslovakia the atmosphere was solemn and the people sober to the point of being morose. There was little doubt that if the Germans persisted in coming into Sudetenland the Czechs would fight: their army was small but considered by many to be the most efficient fighting unit for its size in the world. I flew several of the Zlin machines and was impressed with their performance on such a low horsepower, but thought the quality of finish left much to be desired.

22 Between laps, Hatfield
23 Dad checking harness before the last lap

24   XF leaves Hatfield on the final lap: King's Cup 1938
25   King's Cup winner 1938: A.H. lands XF at Hatfield

We moved on to Vienna, but the plight of the Jews was heart-rending and more apparent than before, as the Germans now made little or no attempts to hide the true position. We returned home with mixed feelings and I wondered if I ever should make that attempt on the Cape records. The whole business came to an anticlimax with the now historic speech of Chamberlain on his return from Munich: 'Peace in our time'. Most of us snorted at the naivety of such a man, but we did not think Hitler, who had done so much good for Germany, would be fool enough to throw this away in another world war.

In the meantime I carried on with my own problems, which were causing many headaches. One of these was the question of finance; not having a sponsor or allowing an oil or petrol company to back me, I had to evaluate the cost on a practical basis. Some time earlier Jack Cross had asked for help with capital to keep his company going and both Dad and I had taken up shares in Essex Aero Ltd. Now Dad came to me and said that Jack had asked for more finance and he had promised I would help out. I was not very pleased, but realised that we had gone too far to turn back now and I bought another block of Essex Aero shares. I had come to know Jack extremely well and looked upon him as a very close friend. In matters of commerce we did however have differing viewpoints. As a pilot there was nothing I would not do to make his enthusiastic ideas work and no risk I would not take to prove his ability as a designer and engineer. Above all I wanted him to succeed and show the world of aviation his true capabilities.

We were working against time and even if ready for the full moon in October I knew I should not get in as much flight testing as I would like. This time it was not a question of short bursts of speed, and then landing, but rather a test of day and night flying in all weathers for long durations. I was able to do my first real long night flight in the Mew on the 9th of October, three days before I was due to take off for Cape Town.

I left the aerodrome at Gravesend at 2.30 a.m. a little apprehensively as the sky was overcast and I really did not know how the Mew would behave if I ran into icing conditions on full

o

load at night. In any case my night-flying experience was extremely limited. I set off for the north of Scotland and as I broke cloud at the operating height of 7000 ft I settled down to enjoy the stars and the dull grey carpet of cloud below, carefully checking everything from time to time. At this stage I was too nervous to let each tank run bone dry and cut the engine, so I ran so many hours on each tank and then switched over. When I returned to Gravesend in daylight and landed I was sure I had plenty of petrol left, but to my astonishment as I taxied towards the hangar the engine coughed and suddenly stopped. Jack, who was waiting for me, ran forward and opened up the main fuselage tank filler cap and peered in. It was empty. Shaken by this news I told him what I had done and decided without delay that I must carry out more accurate fuel consumption tests. We filled up the machine again and I took off. As there were no fuel gauges fitted, to be positively accurate, I now had to run each tank dry in the air and risk air or vapour lock, and I was alarmed to find I was going to be very tight on range. There would be enough fuel but only just, and the feeling was not comfortable. There was now so little time to spare that I knew I must rest up before I took off for the Cape, so I left the Mew in Jack's hands for the final touches, whilst Dad drove me off to try and get some sleep.

I returned to the aerodrome on the evening of the 12th of October with the intention of leaving that night, which would give me a night landing and take-off at Oran; I wasn't too happy with this, but as it was October I did not anticipate any trouble with weather on the first leg. I had told hardly anyone I was expecting to leave, but to my surprise a large number of my friends had turned up to see me off. It was soon apparent that things were not quite right. As my estimated time of departure approached I carefully sorted out my essential equipment in the cockpit and asked Jack to move the machine outside the hangar for an engine test. He said somewhat shamefacedly, 'We shall have to hang on a bit Alex; Harry is waiting at the Air Ministry to collect the C of A.' I was so flabbergasted that it left me speechless. Unknown to me the approval to validate the Certificate of Airworthiness had been held up until welding samples had been submitted for stress tests; this had been done, but unknown to all of us at that moment, one of the sample pieces had failed the tests and further examples of this welding were requested. To me the situation was unreal.

No one can deny that there is a big nervous and emotional tension building up inside a pilot who has worked and planned on a project so long; there are enough difficulties and dangers without having side issues disturbing the situation still further. I had made it perfectly clear that I would not leave late on schedule and finish up in trouble. My flight plan was cut and dried to minutes and I was not going to alter this for anyone: either I left on time or I did not leave at all. Jack was pretty upset, more so because he could not get hold of Harry on the telephone and expected him to arrive with the approved documents at any time. The tension was building up inside me and either I had to blow my top or make a joke of it; I chose the latter but the joke was very sour in my mouth. As we waited I played table tennis in the club room. Just when I had said to my friends, 'I'm sorry, but it's off for today; I'll be leaving all being well at the same time tomorrow,' Harry arrived, hot and bothered and told us the bad news. The C of A could not be renewed until further weld samples had been submitted for test and this could not be done in time for me to leave in October.

In my planning of the flight I had reached the conclusion that the two most favourable periods to fly to the Cape via the west route were either October or February; and now I knew that October was out I must replan for February. Jack said that we could now be ready for November full moon and both he and his fiancée, Ivy Teesdale, who also acted as the company secretary, tried hard to persuade me to make another attempt then, but I was adamant and said I would spend the next three months in testing and preparing XF to as perfect a standard as we could get it. Inwardly I was not sorry when I'd had time to simmer down: I had not been happy with the fuel consumption and I had not done much night-flying. This would now give me a chance to put in some more long test flights and see how I was going to stand up to the discomfort of the cramped, fixed position for seven and eight hours at a time. I was consoled later on to learn from friends at the Cape that had I arrived on schedule in October it would have been in the worst weather they had experienced for many years.

The first test after we had finally got the C of A proved to be worthwhile. Jack had stripped the carburettors down and had reset the float levels and put in some slightly smaller jets. I was happy to find from this first check that there was a marked improvement in the fuel consumption. The Mew was now running perfectly and I was testing in all conditions. The constant-speed airscrew was a big improvement on the two-pitch type, but still I did not have quite enough pitch range on the basic setting.

The only real trouble I experienced was in icing conditions. Once I was icing up very badly in cloud, and as I saw the build-up on the wings I knew I should have to take great care; I could also feel the ice on the tail affecting the elevators and decided to descend out of the cloud whilst I still had control. I dived slightly and the engine started to over-rev. I closed the throttle and was soon out of cloud, but as I went to open up, the airscrew had stuck in fine pitch. I guessed the oil had frozen in the control head and I kept operating the constant-speed valve until eventually it did clear. Glad to be made aware of this particular danger I came in to land cautiously, and could still see the ice on the wings as I pulled to a standstill; suddenly there was a sharp crack and I saw one of the mechanics stoop down and pick up a solid, clear piece of ice about eight feet long, which had formed perfectly over the leading edge.

On December the 4th there was a strong northerly wind blowing; it was cold but the skies were clear and I decided to do a trial run across Europe and back. I climbed steadily to operating height and set my course. I had a glimpse of one fix as I glanced below the nine-tenths cloud, but could not believe it: then I saw through a small gap the Arc de Triomphe standing out clearly. I looked at my stop-watch and it was exactly 44 minutes from take-off: this was the shortest time any aircraft had ever taken from Gravesend to Paris. Further south the weather cleared and

I circled over the port of Marseilles exactly 2 hours 23 minutes after take-off: again the fastest time ever. I returned and flew up to Scotland and back, making a total of 7 hours and 3 minutes in the air before landing. We had fitted a small funnel and tube on to the floor of the cockpit so that I could 'spend a penny' if pressed, but I had felt no need. I was happy with the way things were shaping up, and in particular with the range and performance we had achieved.

In no time at all it was the end of January. I was putting the final touches to everything for a take-off on the 5th of February, but this time at 3.30 a.m. My last item of equipment was fitted discreetly and no one spoke during the process; I had acquired a small Browning automatic for the flight and now I checked that the magazine was full. Ivy Teesdale sewed the gun into the harness pad of my parachute as I held it, and when finished the job was so neat that no one would have guessed what was inside. Finally, we moved the machine away from the hangar for a compass check. I felt that no more could be done.

19 ❋ *Off—but only just*

THE 4TH OF FEBRUARY 1939, was this to be my last day amongst the things and people I loved? The die was now cast; everything that could be done had been done. It was now up to me. Dad and I were acting a part; he was doing his best to make sure nothing upset me and that the final hours were smooth and untroubled; I was determined to remain relaxed and calm. Dad drove me carefully down to Gravesend from our home; I closed my eyes as he drove and quietly went over in my mind all the thousand and one items which might make or mar the flight ahead.

One final check over the Mew and all the papers, maps and loose items such as slide-rule, flashlamp and rations, then I was ready to spend the few remaining hours before take-off sleeping at Jack Cross's little cottage. The Air Ministry Met Department had promised me a weather report for North Africa and it arrived as I was leaving with Jack and Dad. It was not very helpful, patches of night-fog over the Channel and South England and parts of Northern France; ten-tenths stratus over Southern France and Spain; a front with rain and low cloud over the Mediterranean at deep intensity, position and timing a little uncertain but not expected to clear for 24 hours. I paid little attention to it: I had made up my mind that there would be no turning back. If I waited and depended on weather reports then I might as well forget about the whole idea of breaking records. I stuffed the report in my overcoat pocket and muttered something about it being fine.

How the devil can one sleep? I do not remember having felt more awake: the dull booming chimes from the large clock

below in the lounge tells the house that it is nine o'clock and me
the fact that there is the opportunity for six hours sleep if it can
be taken. Cross's house is only ten minutes in the car from the
aerodrome and Dad will make sure everything is ready and that
I am called on time.

I must nip out of bed and look at the sky through the open
window. Looks clear enough, but no signs of the moon yet! This
is no good, must try and get some sleep.

Aspirin, benzedrine, sunglasses, pocket compass, mirror, quinine, flashlamp. Damn, Dad did not put those Mallock-Armstrong
ear defenders in; something else to be remembered . . . This is
no good, must relax and try to sleep.

Just at that moment there was a slight noise outside the bedroom door and Dad peeped in and whispered; 'Time to get up,
son; I've got your breakfast ready for you.' 'OK, I'll be down in
a jiffy as soon as I've slipped some things on,' I replied more
cheerfully than I felt.

By jove, it's cold in these shorts; it ought to be warmer than
this with the leather jerkin and flannels over the top. Wonder if
I ought to have worn something thicker, can't be all that hot in
Africa, still, no time to think about that now . . . Eggs and
bacon! Looks good and the tea tastes fine, trust Dad for that.
Wish he wouldn't fuss round so much though, and behave naturally. Come to think of it, what is wrong with everyone this
morning, tip-toeing around and whispering as if someone were
dead in the house? Thank God there's only going to be Dad and
the Crosses to see me off anyway.

'3.15. Time we were getting down to the aerodrome, don't you
think, Dad?'

By golly, it's cold; wish my teeth would stop chattering. Don't
know whether it's the raw winter morning air or excitement in the
knowledge—or rather lack of knowledge—of what may lie ahead.

'Well I'm damned!' In spite of all the secrecy and of the un-
earthly hour on a Monday morning, the aerodrome was alive
with activity; I noticed in the poor light scores of friends mingling
with the press and photographers.

All the family here as well. Oh Lord, I purposely said goodbye

at home and tactfully suggested they should remain there, but
they evidently have other ideas on the matter. These farewells
are the very devil.

First of all I must clear the log-books, etc., with the customs
and immigration officer and then check over every detail on the
machine for the last time. What the dickens is Jack up to now?

All the hangar lights had gone out and he was probing into
the Mew with a flashlamp. Dad rushed over assuring me that all
was well and the machine was about to be pushed out, but his
tone of voice that I knew so well made me feel uneasy. 3.25. By
this time the machine should have been on the far side of the
aerodrome near the north landing-light with the engine ticking
over ready to go.

Late again, I might have known it!

Whilst I was fretting and fuming Cross appeared quite un-
ruffled and with a very pleased look on his face tried to soothe me.
I afterwards heard that during the night while everything was
going perfectly he was as miserable as could be: 'It's not right,'
he said. 'It's a bad omen. We've never had a machine ready on
time yet without a snag—look at Clouston last March.' When all
the hangar lights went out as the Mew was having her final
adjustments and inspection, his relief was manifest.

Everyone was huddled up inside the hangar wrapped in heavy
overcoats and scarves. This probably made me feel the cold more
than I normally should have done and my friends evidently
sympathised as I strove not to shiver visibly in the ridiculously
light clothing I had thought fit to wear. Stamping with cold and
livid with exasperation, I counted the minutes rolling by. After
what felt an eternity, with a few quiet words of instruction from
Cross the mechanics were moving the machine quickly on to the
tarmac to start the engine. Shaking hands with everyone hastily,
I asked that only Dad and Jack should accompany the machine
to the edge of the aerodrome. As I moved away Charles Hughesdon kindly pressed a pair of warm gloves into my bare hands,
but as I could not write with gloves on, noticing at the same
time that they happened to be very nice and practically brand
new, I handed them back with thanks and jokingly said that if

he loaned them now it would probably be the last time he would ever see them again. As I started taxying out all the brilliant floodlights sprang on.

What a gorgeous night! Strange that the far boundary lights are not visible; perhaps they've not been put on yet.

Dad looked a bit down in the mouth, I hoped he was going to be all right. 3.35 a.m.GMT. Five minutes late. 'Goodbye, Jack! Goodbye, Dad! Don't you worry about me, I shall be all right. See you on Thursday.'

My God, what putrid luck! No wonder the boundary lights are not visible.

A thick ground fog had rolled across the field and it was now scarcely possible to see the main floodlight barely twenty yards away.

Blast!

Dad was tapping on the cockpit roof. I knew perfectly well what for, but there was going to be no turning back on this trip! I was thankful we had taken the precaution to point the nose of the Mew exactly in the right direction for take-off just before the fog had rolled over, and after cheerfully reassuring Dad as well as I could through the dimness of the coupé head, I uncaged the directional gyro and opened the throttle.

It may have been the pressing closeness of the fog, the long vortex of petrol vapour streaming over my head from the air vent in the main petrol tank, or the cold air improving the power output of a very well-tuned engine, but the machine appeared to accelerate with astonishing rapidity for the extremely heavy load it was carrying. The centre of gravity of XF when loaded was much too far aft for comfort and it was some time before the tail would lift from the ground. At first I thought it would be easy enough to keep sight of the ground until the machine was ready to fly off but the moment the throttle was opened this proved to be impossible; as the directional gyro was now the only means of telling if the machine was heading in the right direction under these conditions, it was not wise to attempt looking in different places at the same time. For a few worrying moments I recollected that when we had positioned the machine near the floodlight before the fog had obliterated everything, the take-off track went by the large hangars, leaving them about a hundred yards to the left. With this very much in mind I cautiously eased the rudder a little to the right at the same time watching the directional gyro carefully. At all costs the tail of the machine had to be kept well up until ample flying speed had been reached: a take-off with the tail down meant the probability of being rocketed into the air in a semi-stalled condition which would just invite disaster.

The aerodrome was large and there was room to spare, so for a few seconds it was almost like travelling in an express train going through a tunnel, the wheels pattering over the hard ground; out of the corner of my eye the reflection of the exhaust flames against the dull fog produced a sensation of phenomenal speed. When the oleo legs were hammering to the ever lengthening bounds the control column was gently eased back so that the artificial horizon indicated a slight climb; at the same moment the wheels must have struck a slight rise in the ground as the Mew simply shot up into the blackness, and where one second before it had been a matter of intense concentration on instruments I was suddenly able to relax and gaze with relief at the marvellous starlit sky with the light of the moon illuminating the fog below.

Turning exactly on to course the machine climbed steadily until the throttle was wide open and the correct manifold depression registering on the boost gauge. The next job was to synchronise the independent mixture controls; this was always tedious and required both care and patience. Also the various petrol tanks must not be forgotten; to eliminate the danger of any syphoning taking place it was thought advisable to operate independently on each individual tank for a matter of five or ten minutes before settling down to the main fuselage tank. All times had to be recorded accurately at the change-overs, otherwise as no fuel gauges were fitted it would be impossible to work out the petrol consumption or tell precisely how much longer the engine would continue to run if I ever got down to the last few gallons.

Hello! What was that light?

A glance at the large chronometer and stopwatch together with a check on the slide-rule and map indicated that the South Coast was about to be crossed. I wasn't sure if this was so: climbing most of the time with nothing below but fog it had been impossible to obtain a definite fix and check the ground speed. Nothing to worry about of course as quite likely the coast of France would show up soon. An occasional light here and there glimmering dully through the white blanket below, but it was impossible to tell whether they were beacons from a lightship or neon signs advertising some cinema or shop.

Wish the beastly stuff would clear; been in the air 50 minutes now. That's strange, I should have thought there would have been some signs of Paris before this, surely all those lights along the grands boulevards and Champs-Elysées will make some sort of a show in the murk? Let me think, 202 miles, say at 230 mph, yes, that should take just over 52½ minutes. Well, should be able to see something now surely . . .? Compass course is OK, and there can't be much wind with this fog about . . . Is that a light glowing over there or just my imagination . . .? No, thank goodness! That's Paris all right . . . 53 minutes 15 seconds. Let me see, that gives a ground speed of 227·6 mph from take-off. Not bad! Better reset the stopwatch again; may get another better fix soon to re-check that ground speed.

Having generally assured myself that everything was in order and content that the machine was on the correct course, there was time for reflection.

Just gone 4.30. I expect Barbara's below there somewhere; wonder if I shall ever see her again. Wonder if I can pull it off . . . Why the devil wouldn't they let me pick up those permits at Oran instead of that lousy dump Colomb Béchar? As if I hadn't got enough to worry about without that—just like the French—anyone would think I liked landing on their damned desert. Still, wouldn't be any worse than Libreville, I suppose! Wish it wasn't amongst all those trees: too narrow for my liking. I hope that report on the surface condition was accurate.

In case the weather happened to be bad over the mountains I

very much wanted to get another check on the true speed and
drift, if any, but apart from a small cluster of lights here and
there, and an occasional glint from the light of the moon
shining on glass or water there was nothing to be seen. A glance
at the clock showed that if the first check was correct, over
600 miles should have been covered.

Nevers should have been a good fix with the Loire and railways; strange I never spotted it . . . might of course have been
in the fog belt I've just left behind.

At that moment a glint of white appeared ahead and a little
to the east, and a few moments later awe-inspiring mountains
covered with glistening ice and snow, with the moon throwing
eerie shadows in the valleys, came into view. I thought at first
that it was the Alps, but then realised that I was miles off course
if this was so; in any case they would be a good deal higher
than these. There is a lower range of mountains, the Massif
Central, just off the Rhône valley and in their winter garb they
looked very much like their larger brothers.

There's no mistaking that myriad of lights away in the
distance: that's Marseilles all right.

Here was the chance I had watched for since passing Paris,
that would enable the drift and ground speed to be worked out
accurately. I wished again that XF were more stable and
would fly hands off; what a help it would have been! A glance
at the watch and a little juggling with flashlamp, map, ruler and
slide-rule satisfied me that the old Mew was now cruising along
at a steady 233 mph, which would mean that if this speed was
maintained I should arrive at Colomb Béchar a few minutes
ahead of schedule. A comforting conjecture!

It was noticeable then that the moon did not seem so bright
and in fact had taken on quite a watery appearance; it was not
long before it had disappeared altogether and I realised very
quickly that I was flying in cloud.

Ice! That's frost on the screen without a doubt. Must be careful now: this is how Clouston nearly came unstuck in the Comet.

With these conditions it was advisable to sacrifice speed for
safety and change the carburettor intake over to hot air: how

different the engine sounded, almost as if the throttle had been eased back. The boost gauge indicated a considerable drop in power with this changeover but of course Cross's beautifully designed forward cold air intake would account for a good proportion of the difference. The danger of ice formation had been given much thought so I was not unduly worried at this stage: XF would fly for quite a considerable time before becoming unduly dangerous to handle.

In XF all the tank vent pipes led to a common junction, and thence by a single pipe which led into the cockpit and then out again into the atmosphere. Where the pipe came into the cockpit it was drilled and an adaptor fitted to take a small wooden plug, so should the outside vent become frozen over, all one had to do was withdraw the plug and all tanks would breathe from the warm air inside the cockpit. In view of this carefully thought out if somewhat primitive installation there was no need for anxiety when running into this ice-belt over the Mediterranean. As I had by now used up a fair quantity of fuel, the machine was reasonably stable; moreover, dawn was not far off and things would probably look a little brighter in the daylight.

Time I checked up on our position again: at a guess should think we are near the Balearic Islands . . . Some hope of Franco's fighters intercepting me in this stuff; that's a consolation anyway! Yes, if we're averaging the same speed, should just have passed Majorca. Give it another hour, then I'd better start climbing and hope we can run out of this cloud. Much lighter now, anyway; shan't need this flashlamp again for some time . . . Ice is clearing, no wonder, it's starting to rain cats and dogs . . . Nearly eight o'clock; better start climbing; don't relish running into a stuffed cloud over those damned Atlas Mountains.

At 9000 ft it was beautiful, with a perfect sky above. The low rising sun was shining brilliantly on a level, snow-white carpet of cloud below. Ahead I could just discern the Atlas Mountains almost completely enshrouded in cloud; of course this would clear once the desert side of them had been reached.

Yippee! That's Africa in record time, anyhow. Think I ought to celebrate by trying some of Dad's egg and orange. Let me see, which pipe do I suck? Try this one—no, that's coffee, better keep that for tonight. This must be the flask then, yes . . . not bad either; egg seems to resent being sucked up Cross's pipe-lines though.

That's strange, I'm sure we're beyond the main mountain ridge and yet there is still ten-tenths cloud ahead . . . No, can't be, I must be out on my dead reckoning.

Colomb Béchar was a place that could easily be missed if I was a little off track; there was a railway line which ran at right-angles to the correct compass course only a short distance from Colomb Béchar and I had aimed to pick this up and carefully check my position before striking off into the desert looking for a needle in a haystack. I had been assured some considerable time before that although there might be cloud on the Medi-terranean side of the mountains, almost invariably it would be found that the desert would be clear; also it was with confidence from experience gained on previous trips in that locality that I expected to find Colomb Béchar in little or no cloud, irrespective of conditions elsewhere.

Must be getting close now; wish this blasted cloud would clear . . . Where the devil are we?

A little more juggling with map, pencil, paper and slide-rule indicated I was only a hundred miles from Colomb Béchar pro-viding of course there had been no change in strength or direc-tion of the wind in or above the cloud.

Must find that railway at all costs . . . or should I strike for Colomb Béchar and hope that the cloud is not down to the ground? Might hit it off all right—daren't: if I don't find it first go, I shan't have enough petrol to get back to Oran. No, must go down now and hope for the best. Ye Gods, this is horrible. I'm sure these hills are in the stuff . . .

My God, that was a near one all right!

After closing the throttle and slowing up the machine to put the landing flaps down, I had just entered cloud at approxi-mately 4000 ft when in the groping mist the brown-black shadow of a mountain-top slid by underneath the starboard wing. I slammed the throttle open and the machine rapidly climbed back to the sanctuary of the glorious sunshine, and how glorious it was after that filth down below. What was to be done? I dared not risk going on into the desert, I should have to go back to Oran for more petrol and have another attempt by flying well over Colomb Béchar and if I managed to get down through the cloud trying to approach it from the Sahara side.

Better work out a course and time to bring me out over the sea beyond Oran: these damned mountains in cloud give me the willies ... Good Heavens! Nearly half an hour late on schedule already. Oh well, half an hour isn't all the world; soon make that up with a bit of luck. Oh Lord, if I land at Oran for petrol and then again at Colomb Béchar for those permits, that will make me at least two hours late. I hadn't thought of that. Let's see: dark at Gao 1815 hrs and I'm due there according to schedule at 1730 hrs; that means landing there in the dark if I'm lucky enough to find the damned place. Oh hell, I've boobed on the first lap. How the devil can I expect to cross that lousy desert and then land on a patch of sand no different from the rest near a village which I shan't be able to see in the dark anyway?

What a miserable failure. Charles said I should never be able to do it. What if I fill the tanks right up at Oran and then just land at Colomb Béchar for the permits? Blast the permits! ... Hmm ... that's taking a chance, landing at over 3000 ft; aerodrome's rough with all those boulders strewn about and it'll be as hot as Hades by the time I land there—and it's not very large either. Besides the French will want to spend an hour or so telling me what not to do and loading me up with water, smoke bombs, iron rations and heaven knows what. Then there's the transmitting set ... No, it's out of the question, there are enough risks to take without asking for trouble. Shall I go home and make another start? No, I just couldn't face all that over again. By gad, there is just one chance left ... too bad if I trip up ... if I were to fill right up at Oran and bluff the officials into the fact that I intended going to Colomb Béchar to collect all the necessary papers and conform with all regulations they would of course let me go and I should either be across the Sahara or have come unstuck before they woke up to the fact. Yes, it's worth a shot, in any case it's the one and only way I can possibly hope to pull the thing off.

My plans now made, the next stumbling block was to find Oran as there was still no welcome sign of a break in the clouds. I thought it wise to allow a further five minutes on top of the dead-reckoning time to make doubly sure of coming out over the sea before dropping into the cloud and attempting to get underneath it.

Here goes . . .

The floating mass of soft cotton-wool soon lost its brilliant hue and appeared very black and forbidding after the dazzling brightness of the reflecting sun above; the lower I descended the darker it became, with an ever increasing deluge of rain.

My God, it's damned thick! 900, 800, 700, 600, 500 ft; surely I must break through now or the stuff is right down on the water. I suppose I am over the sea . . . too bad if I've slipped up on time. Wish I had given it another five minutes. 400 ft . . . Phew! what a relief . . . Golly, the sea looks rough: not much blue about it today, more like the English Channel than the Mediterranean.

There must have been a strong wind blowing at the time as the sea was running fast with huge troughs of bluish-green water topped with white foam that played leap-frog as they rolled along. The rain was falling in a steady downpour which made it impossible to look forward, but out of the little side window I could see, uncomfortably close, huge black rainclouds sweeping down so low that they appeared to mingle with the angry sea. I realised it had been a lucky break coming out in a clear patch at 400 ft. After a few minutes of snaking in and out between the worst storms, a large rock swept with foam flashed by underneath, to be followed closely by the welcome sight of the rough North African coastline. I did not recognise this part of the coast, nor was I likely to do so as visibility was restricted to the red boulders and frothing waves beating up against the cliffs below. As no allowance had been made for drift and as evidently the wind had been blowing from the east for some time, it was obvious that I must be to the west of the true track; so that I turned east and followed the coast along with a certain amount of confidence. The weather was now improving; the storms were less violent and more widespread, with patches of light in between as the sun made a brave effort to pierce the thinner layers of cloud.

At Oran the rain had stopped, but it was easy to guess what the conditions had been like a short while before by the state of the aerodrome, which was flooded in places with large patches of water. There was a tarmac runway on one side of the aerodrome, but I did not think it advisable to land there: I remembered it was nearly always under repair and more often than not was obstructed with little heaps of stones the same colour as the tarmac surface, which could not be seen until it was too late. The Mew touched down on the driest looking piece of mud there was in between two small lakes of water and then gaily plunged on with mud and water flying up in all directions. Finally coming to a standstill on the right side of the aerodrome some distance from the control tower, I saw a short figure whom I guessed to be Boumati, the helpful French Shell agent, waving frantically for me to taxi over to him.

P

I BROUGHT the machine to a standstill near the pumps, leapt out of the cockpit and after a quick handshake with Boumati, grabbed the special tank spanners from their hiding place and prepared to refuel. Having shown the reliable little Frenchman which tank to fill first I began the intricate business of pouring oil into the engine; due to the particular design of the tank and cooling system, the oil had to be replenished through an awkward filler-cap cut in the extreme top of the saddle-tank that bridged the whole engine and formed part of the top cowling. It required a high platform to reach over the nose of the machine, a specially designed spanner to remove the locking-down cap after the covering flap had been lifted and then a good deal of patience and care when actually pouring in the oil to ensure that the small adaptor-funnel was not over-filled, and that none dropped on to the delicate unshielded magnetoes immediately below. Whilst this tedious work was being carried out, a customs official came up and demanded to see my passport, log-books, permits and various papers. I hurriedly handed them over to him and went on with the refuelling. To my surprise the oil-tank took a very small amount considering the flying time: I thought that owing to the small aperture and unusual shape of the tank there might have been an airlock, but in spite of all my careful attempts no more could be forced in. I noticed that the resourceful Boumati had filled one tank and had found another one to start on: good work. But I also saw that he had sealed up the full petrol tank before I had had a chance to glance at it. Mistakes are easily made and it would have been just too bad to realise that one had been made when about a 1000 miles farther on, so with a hearty exchange of verbiage, understood I should imagine only by each speaker himself, and many gesticulations, the irate Boumati was persuaded much against his wishes to take the cap off. I could only see petrol up to within three or four inches of the neck of the tank, so made him pour more spirit in until it almost overflowed.

The customs officer came back again and was babbling something about Colomb Béchar, radio and *permission d'intérieur* amongst many other things. I knew very well what he meant and said, 'Ah, oui, Colomb Béchar. Je comprends très bien.' And then in English so that he would not understand quickly mumbled, 'I shall pass over Colomb Béchar on my way to Gao.' Anyway, they couldn't very well say I had lied. The log-books and papers were handed back to me with further assurances that I should land at Colomb Béchar, but as Boumati at that moment shouted that the last tank was full and awaited my inspection, I paid little heed. Making absolutely sure that everything was tightened down and that all papers and spanners were in their correct places, I asked Boumati to hold the engine switches on contact whilst I swung the airscrew. The engine burst into life on the first swing with a note that was delightful to hear, and with a wave of farewell to the little group of onlookers, the cockpit hood was quickly fastened down and I taxied out for the take-off. There was only a slight breeze but its direction necessitated going over to the extreme opposite side of the aerodrome if I intended making full use of it. As every minute counted in making a successful landfall across that ocean of sand that lay ahead, I was sorely tempted to open up from the petrol-pumps and take-off downwind. I thought better of it, however: more haste, less speed seemed appropriate, and I taxied out as quickly but carefully as possible, picking what I thought would be the best runway in between the immense puddles. Amidst huge splashes of water and mud, after a long run XF laboured into the air; a ninety-degree turn on to the constant-bearing course; a press on the stop-watch button; the machine put into a steady climb and I was free to deal with other incidental items.

Oh hell, I'd forgotten about mountains . . . still no break in the cloud, can't afford to make any detours . . . shall have to go up through it. So much for the resolution of no blind-flying with full tanks. Had better spiral up over this low ground and then swing on to course when we break through the top. Not as bad as I thought, by jove. She's touchy on the stick, though; hope I don't have to do this when I'm tired . . . Getting lighter, be out of it in another jiffy . . . Lovely!

The Mew seemed to leap out of a blanket of white wool into a world of brilliance; how stimulating and peaceful it all was.

Wasted seven minutes making that spiral, still, can't be helped; better to be seven minutes late in this world than 25 years early in the next . . . will set a course for Colomb Béchar and if I can't see it when the ETA is up, will strike for Gao and hope for the best. What shall I do if I do spot it? . . . If I circle, Gallois isn't a mind reader and may get in an awful flap . . . I know, I'll drop a message. Better write it now, just in case . . . What shall I put? Can't explain everything but must put an excuse of some sort. I know . . . 'Dare not land with full tanks. Am proceeding direct to Gao' . . . Hope I find the damned place, otherwise when I don't turn up they're going to send out search parties and wireless messages all over the place . . . Of course, they'd pick that up in England as well . . . Oh Lord, I hope Dad won't worry too much. Nearly an hour, this is about where I just missed that hill I should think . . . not much chance of finding Colomb Béchar in this stuff . . . Well, of all the luck!

As if cut by a knife the cloud finished and there, nestled in a picturesque setting of lofty green palms against a background of red hills enshrouded with faint blue haze, entirely surrounded by the dazzling brightness of the Sahara sand, was Colomb Béchar.

Flashing over the aerodrome it was possible to detect a small crowd near the fuel dumps and in my imagination I saw my good friends Gallois and Pillon in their smart L'Armeé de L'Air uniform, ordering their men about and threatening them with worse than death if they did not get me away in good time. What a disappointment for them: I seriously thought of landing but for the fact that I was so far behind schedule that I might have had to find Gao in the dark, I think I should have done so.

However, I made a low circuit and tearing the note from the knee-pad, flicked it out of the little side window and hoped they would be able to see it falling to the ground. With a pang of remorse I thought of the struggle I had had for twelve months to get permits, all of no avail. Losing no time, with a rapid climb I pointed the nose of the Mew into the endless desert beyond.

Strange, I feel sick; must be the excitement . . . think I'll put on those sunglasses and panama hat, pull the sun-blinds well over and see if I can relax a little. Why, I haven't eaten anything since leaving Gravesend; no wonder I've a headache and feel sick . . . I'll try one of Dad's Coxes . . . Ugh! What an awful taste . . . something on the skin, must have come off the linen bag they're in . . . Good heavens! The bag is saturated . . . petrol tank leaking . . . I knew something would go wrong . . . must open up all the ventilators and get some air in or I shall pass out with these fumes. Funny I didn't smell them before. Well, that's strange; how on earth can petrol leak on to those apples, they're nowhere near a tank. Great Scott! Do I deserve a kick in the pants. Of course, the air-vent plug.

I had forgotten to replace the wooden plug in the main petrol air-vent line after coming out of the icing conditions, and with filling all tanks to the brim at Oran surplus petrol had forced its way along the air-vent lines and leaked into the cockpit via the plug orifice. I may have detected the smell at first attributing it to petrol overflow during the refuelling; and then I suppose when the fumes did not disappear, the senses had gradually become so accustomed to them that they continued unnoticed. Still, it was remarkable that the fumes had not been detected: with petrol dripping into the small cockpit as it had, and considering the amount of lead it contained, I was truly thankful to get off so lightly.

How beautiful the desert looks when there are a few palmtrees and signs of life about; but how terrifying when one realises that for hours one has been travelling in a fast machine, as straight as a compass can steer, unhampered by making detours, and yet not a trace of life, man, beast or bird: nothing, nothing but sand, it may be boulders and sand, wavy dunes of sands, sand level and smooth, sand red, sand white, sand gold, but sand it is and still more sand, and even from 8000 ft it looks as hot as hell.

Splutter, phut, phut, phut: the engine stopped as the main tank ran dry.

Wish I'd turned on the wing tanks before ... puts the wind up you, engine cutting out over this lot ... devil of a long time cutting in again ... Ah that's more like it, marvellous engine the old Gipsy. Why that's incredible ... must be a mistake ... Just goes to show what a little judicious use of the mixture controls and pitch setting combined with the best operational height will do towards fuel economy. I'll work those figures out again; something wrong somewhere. No, 9·24 gallons an hour, what a difference as against the consumption over the sea; expected some but not all that ... enough petrol to get me over, thank goodness, unless I get lost ... Hello, what's that down below? ... looks like cattle ... Why not eskimos? What next! Cattle in the Sahara ... I'll go down and have a look anyhow ... By golly, it is ... life at last, thank God for that ... looks like half a dozen camels, some arabs and a herd of goats ... Am I glad to see them, must have got over the dreaded Tanezrouft by now then ... I should think they're on one of those tracks near Gao ... nearly 1700 hrs, should be quite close now ... wonder what sort of reception I shall get from the officials. Oh Lord, what a fool I am ... Oran would have wirelessed Colomb Béchar when I was to be expected; Colomb Béchar would wireless back that I had passed overhead but had not landed; and Oran, of course, would immediately communicate with the Ministre de l'Air in Paris or the Governor General at Dakar controlling the Sudan for instructions as to what action to take ... There's no doubt they'll take a very serious view, worst luck ... I'm sure the officials themselves will be the same as those we met at Niamey, so pleased to see a fresh face they won't care a damn what regulations are broken ... this is going to be very different, there is no doubt about that ... yes, headquarters would wireless that I am to be detained pending an investigation ... What an idiot I've been; why on earth

didn't I chance a landing at Colomb Béchar? All this way for
nothing, the whole trip ruined because of red tape. Ye Gods,
something has got to be done ... wonder if I could get the
machine filled up on some pretext and then sneak off before
they were aware, force my way if necessary ... no, that wouldn't
be any use, they'll certainly have armed guards there and in any
case I've got to come back this way ...

Hello, what's that ahead? The desert is looking different
surely ... yes, that's water, without a doubt ... the Niger at
last. Thank Heavens for that ... lot of dwellings over there to
the right ... By golly, my luck is in today after all: that's Gao
without any question; never expected to land here in daylight ... 1725 hrs ... good going, very little behind schedule;
marvellous after all that business at Oran ... Now to face the
music ...

Gao below looked very attractive and picturesque after the
desolate barrenness of such a vast wilderness. The sun, rapidly
disappearing, threw a glowing beam of dull red which glinted
on the Niger and reflected its slow majestic presence over the
numerous mud hovels and the already colourful terrain. Black
rocks peeped out of the burning sand, like will-o'-the-wisps in
the strange shimmering mirages that probably caused everything to appear very much hotter than it actually was. In the
distance towards Kano and along the sloping marshes that
served as the banks of the Niger I could just see, in the dimming
light, small bonfires ablaze; whilst over the innumerable tracks
Bedouins in their peculiar picturesque attire, accompanied in
many cases by camels and herds of goats, trudged their way
amidst small clouds of choking dust towards their own particular goal; no doubt, in an effort like mine to defeat the
quickly gathering darkness.

From the air, the aerodrome at Gao looked a flourishing airport in comparison with most of the other places in that part of
the world: it boasted a small corrugated iron hangar or two
in one corner of the more level strip of sand boundaried by a
few boulders, and fairly adjacent were a small number of mud
and stone buildings intermingled with wooden and tin huts, no

doubt to accommodate the personnel of the Foreign Legion and
L'Armée de L'Air. I now regretted deeply that we had not
landed here with the Vega instead of hurrying on to Niamey . . .
how much better a landing would have been than those quick
notes, mental and otherwise, that we had made before proceeding on our way. There was not a breath of wind, so carefully
choosing the longest run of aerodrome, I gently eased XF round
for a landing. In the hot, still air the machine seemed to be
gliding in at a terrific rate, although I was warned by the feel of
controls that there was by no means that margin of speed above
the stall which the pace that we were moving over the ground
led me to believe. The Mew touched down nicely on an almost
bare rock plateau and then clattered along at high speed until
it struck an unexpected soft patch of sand, causing it to swing
violently to the left and almost nosing over as it did so; there
were a few breathless seconds, momentarily relieved when the
machine suddenly ploughed away from the soft sand to scuttle
along again over more solid rock—only to strike another soft patch.
This time it swung viciously to the right with the tail bounding
up dangerously from the ground and finally it came to a standstill with the nose pointing in the wrong direction. Nothing
makes you forget about one worry quicker than another greater
worry taking its place. The fact that an armed escort should now
be waiting for me was completely forgotten: the last few moments had created an obstacle worse than I had faced so far.
The landing, yes, that had been precarious enough, though no
damage had been done, more by good luck than by judgement.
But I realised that the machine was extremely lightly loaded
with all tanks practically empty and moreover the daylight although fading fast was adequate enough for vision: what was
going to happen attempting to take-off in the darkness of night,
with so much petrol on board that even on a good aerodrome it
was very much an overload?

The sand swirled in clouds penetrating everywhere, leaving
behind a soft musky smell, an odour so peculiar and rare that it
is completely beyond my powers to describe it; but I can never
think of Gao without imagining I can detect that elusive aroma.

As the engine had to be opened almost to full throttle to move the machine and again there was a threat of a nose-over, I jumped out of the cockpit and with a little manoeuvring, with the assistance of a few blacks and Europeans who had suddenly turned up, managed to taxi from the treacherous soft patch on to the hard level floor of a fairly large hangar. On switching off the engine it dawned on me that here I was at Gao with a lot of explaining to do. Glancing around apprehensively I quickly took stock of the situation. At least I could see no signs of any menacing troops with fixed bayonets: only a few blacks and dirty-looking Arabs in the background, an odd inquisitive rating of L'Armée de L'Air here and there and a respectable looking man dressed in civilian clothes desert-style was making his way towards me.

'Ah, Monsieur Henshaw, it is you, n'est ce pas? We expect you and yet we do not, vous comprenez? I had word from our London office that you had left England and then no more; so we wait and voilà, here you are! Did you have a pleasant voyage? You will see we have made all the necessary arrangements for you here. You have 1000 litres of Shell 87 octane and 80 litres of Castrol Aero oil. Perhaps when you have refuelled you would care to come with me where I have prepared for you a place that you may wash and eat, non?'

I could have shouted with joy. So they had not wirelessed Gao, did not even know I was on the way. Why, that was marvellous. Having had such wonderful luck so far, surely there was some way of overcoming this greatest hazard of all? Now I was safely on the ground surely I could pick out a smoother part of the airfield for my take-off in the dark?

21 ✳ *A line of lamps*

WHATEVER WAS TO BE DONE had to be done
quickly. Perhaps I might be able to taxi the machine off
the aerodrome on to the Gao-Niamey road and with petrol
flares on one side, take off from that . . . No, that was too risky,
the track surface was not likely to be any better than the aerodrome and furthermore there would be those nasty little boulders
spaced along either side: touch one of those with a slight swing
and it would be just too bad.

Quick! I have it: Niamey, that had a fairly good surface, in
fact a real billiard table compared with this dump. Yes, get
Gao to wireless Niamey to put flares out; I could take off now
with very little petrol on board and be there in less than an
hour and a half . . . navigation's easy, just follow the river . . .
Fuel supplies! There's the snag; whatever I do I must find out
if they have sufficient oil and petrol before I leave. We used the
last drum of Castrol XXL they had for the Vega . . . Still, we
can easily find out what they have; after all, we're only 300
miles away.

I turned to the Shell agent and informed him of my plans; he
looked at his watch, shrugged his shoulders in doubt, but suggested that we saw the Commandant. The Commandant, helpful
and charming, explained in French to the Shell agent that this
was not possible but begged that if Monsieur Henshaw was concerned with the surface of the aerodrome he should borrow his
car to select a good runway where he would then instruct flares
to be put down. This seemed the best idea and in any case there
was no alternative now; without more ado, to make full use of
what little light there was left, we rushed off leaving clouds of

dust in the wake of the tiny Citroen. The Commandant struck off from the hangars in a direction which would give the longest run, drove as straight as he could until the small car was slowed up in the soft sand and then attempted to zig-zag on to firmer ground. We became bogged or *ensablé* as my companions called it, and had to get out and push with the engine screaming. My hopes of taking-off seemed well nigh hopeless.

At last managing to extricate the car, we leapt on to the running boards and this time zig-zagged across the sand at higher speed, memorising as well as we could the firm spots from the soft. On completing this manoeuvre a number of times, we drove in a straight line over what we had considered the best part of the aerodrome; but the more we drove over the precarious ground the less I liked it. Having satisfied ourselves that we had chosen the best track, the Commandant drove back to the hangars, leaving me to attend the refuelling of the machine whilst he showed his men where to put the flares. The blacks and arabs, all smiles, were clustered around the machine babbling away like so many monkeys and when they saw that at last the machine was going to be filled their willingness knew no bounds. They hacked holes in the tops of the four-gallon petrol tins with murderous looking steel spikes as if they were made of cardboard and then light-heartedly splashed the volatile spirit about as if it had been water; a shimmering vapour rose from the hot floor to fill the place with a sickening smell. When the petrol tanks were all filled I am afraid that I rather hurt some feelings by proceeding to clean most thoroughly the drums containing the oil before opening them up. On examining the chamois leather through which the petrol had passed there had been a noticeable deposit of grit and sand, although they had most conscientiously cleaned the tops of the drums before using them; I concluded that this must have fallen from either side of the tins, or the bottom when being tipped up over the large filter funnel; and as the oil was not to be passed through an external filter, it was as well to ensure that drums, measures and my own hands were free of the fine sand which penetrated everywhere. This time XF had been rather more thirsty on oil, no doubt due to the considerable increase in the engine running temperature; but the tedious job of pouring the oil into the small aperture was helped tremendously by the tropical heat which caused the new oil to have a viscosity almost akin to water.

The refuelling completed, my next thought was to get the helpful officials to stamp the passport and log-books so that I could put them away safely together with the maps and navigational aids in their respective places inside the cockpit. Also I had to check the chronometer for accuracy and change my wrist-watch over to local time so that there would be no mistake as to when the flares should be lit. Satisfied that nothing had been left undone and that the machine was ready except for starting, the cockpit hood was fastened; nearby stood a fierce-looking Legionnaire sentry complete with rifle and long bayonet, faithfully on guard with precise instructions from the Commandant on how to deal with anyone daring to approach the machine. We then climbed into the little Citroen again and roared along to a wooden hut which proved to be the officers' mess. It appeared comfortable and stylish inside, furnished in what I suppose would be termed Bohemian style. A glance at my wrist-watch showed that I had just over two hours rest before take-off; the kindly Frenchman, reading my thoughts, beckoned me to a large, luxurious hassock where he explained I could rest whilst eating my supper.

Supper, of course! The last solid food I had was Dad's egg and bacon . . . what about all the serious advice on eating regularly without fail to keep the tummy muscles working . . . Oh well, I feel fine now, anyway . . . I'm not the least bit hungry . . . Ye Gods, I hope they don't bring me any cous-cous like they did at that Foreign Legion dinner last year . . . if they do, the only records I shall break will be running down the corridor . . .

Silently in came a dusky batman bearing a tray with many dishes, steaming and exuding an appetising odour. It looked very nice indeed: some cold meatlike substance, probably canned or bottled pâté and a variety of piping hot vegetables, undoubtedly from cans too. It would have been sheer ingratitude not to have eaten, as these splendid officers had evidently put themselves to a good deal of trouble to assure that I was assisted and looked after in every way. Although I am sure the food must have been very palatable, to me it tasted like chalk; it just would not go down.

If only I had chosen Niamey, but then I shouldn't have been any better off with that boob over Colomb Béchar . . . only just made it as it was . . .

'Monsieur is somewhat apprehensive, n'est ce pas?' said the Commandant, no doubt reading the expression on my face and the struggle I was having with the food. 'Non. Your machine, it is so fast and yet if you become *ensablé* or perhaps maybe you strike the hidden boulder, it is so slow, and to you, mon ami, dangerous.' He raised his hands significantly. 'It would be wiser for you to sleep the night, and then in the morning when you can see, you go to Lagos where you have the information *méteorologique* before you proceed to Libreville. I can tell you the weather it is *mauvais* often near the Bight de Biafra, so bad nothing can fly, nothing. I know because a little time ago, a great friend of mine, he was en route from Lagos to Duala and was caught in the typhoon. It was bad I can tell you, the wind it was so strong and the rain it came down like the sea so that the machine of my friend was forced down on the edge of the jungle and he was lucky to escape with his life. And he is a very good pilot, *je vous assure*.'

Yes, that's all very well. If I had days to spare instead of a few hours then there wouldn't be much to worry about.

Deeming sufficient justice done to the food as not to appear unwarrantably rude I hinted with a gesture that I should like to get a little sleep: I knew there would be no peace from the well-meaning officers as they plied me with ceaseless queries, if I stayed there. The Shell agent came to the rescue with a well-timed question, 'What time exactly do you wish to leave, Monsieur Henshaw?' I replied that I would like to leave at 2315 hrs and would like to be called at 2245 hrs, which only gave me a little over an hour to get some sleep. 'Ah! of course. Monsieur would like to retire immediately.' I rose to shake hands with the officers who had been so helpful, but they laughingly said in chorus that they would all be on the aerodrome to see me leave. A batman then led me away along a narrow wooden corridor to a little room which contained a small iron bedstead with straw mattress, a couple of neatly folded brown blankets and at the head a pillow which was none too clean. The sparse furniture comprised a chair and an iron stand which held a canvas bowl half filled with water, with a grubby white towel neatly balanced on the edge. It was now much cooler so I thought it would be more comfortable and probably a little more hygienic to lie on the bed in my clothes.

If counting sheep is a positive way to induce sleep it certainly failed miserably that night; try as I would, tossing and turning from one side of the bed to the other, my train of thoughts was broken again and again by returning to that morass of loose dry sand: my over-imaginative mind visualised so realistically what would happen when the overburdened machine buried its wheels in the first patch. There was little time, I am thankful to say, to endure many of these morbid thoughts. It was not long before the thud, thud of heavy boots could be heard marching down the corridor, followed by a couple of taps on the bedroom door. It was opened by a uniformed sergeant carrying a hurricane lamp and, after mumbling something I could not understand, he left it on the bedroom floor and marched off again. Leaping out of bed I tore off my leather jerkin, pullover and flannels; these I roughly rolled into a bundle and placed on the foot of the bed, to collect I sincerely hoped—but doubted—on my return journey. This left me clad in tennis shirt and shorts, socks and a pair of old slippers. Glancing down at my bare, thin, knobbly legs and the rolled down tennis socks, the predicament I had got myself into made me think deeply and wonder. I plunged my face into the bowl of tepid water and after a brisk rub down with the rough towel felt much refreshed. 2300 hrs GMT. There was not a great deal of time to spare. I grabbed the lantern and strode to the end of the corridor to find most of my supper friends more or less where I had left them earlier in the evening. I was somewhat embarrassed as their eyes goggled in amazement at my scanty attire, and then murmered exclamations such as

'*Ferai très froid dans le sud ce soir*,' pressingly offered the loan of overcoats, flying suits and gloves, which I had some difficulty in declining.

As we drove towards the aerodrome I glanced anxiously around and up at the sky. It was rather disappointing. A full moon on the desert creates a scene that will live in one's memory for ever, at least that is how it has always impressed me; here, however, the brilliance of the moon and stars was dimmed in a thick heat haze, and visibility, judging by the lighted hangar in the distance, was by no means excellent. As we came into the light of the hangar I was astonished to see so many people: uniforms of the Foreign Legion and L'Armée de L'Air mixed freely with bare-headed blacks and mysteriously hooded and gowned arabs all waiting up for what was to them I guessed an interesting event.

Just discernible a little distance away in the still darkness of the night was another cluster of people, and from its furtive manner and the way in which the silence was now and again broken by a hushed murmur or very occasionally by a high-pitched laugh I assumed it was the native womenfolk timidly venturing as far as they dared. With little effort XF was pushed out of the hangar on to the space selected for the take-off and as there was no time left I decided to start the engine right away and permit it to tick over smoothly for a few minutes whilst I was shaking hands and saying au revoir to my new-found friends. Without any sucking in and on the first swing on contact the engine burst into life, forcing the crowd to disperse hurriedly a little further away, especially those who were unfortunate enough to be near the tail and get the full blast of the desert dust in their eyes and mouths. Content that everything in the machine was in order and that there was five minutes to spare before my ETD I turned to the few Frenchmen close at hand to say 'Cheerio' and also to tell them to light the flares. They did not appear to understand but when the request was repeated one replied 'Ah! but Monsieur the flares they have been alight and waiting for you some time,' pointing as he spoke in the direction the machine was facing.

No, surely not; they never expect me to see with those things!
They're crazy!

Thirty or forty yards ahead was a hurricane lamp, identical to
the one I had been carrying earlier in the evening; beyond this
at approximately the same distance was another similar lamp,
its light faintly gleaming in the haze. In the distance as far as the
eye could see in the poor light was another almost indistinguish-
able glimmer following in line with the other lamps, and still
further beyond this I imagined there would be others; but from
where I stood they certainly could not be seen. This was the last
thing I had expected; they might as well have not put any
lights down at all for what purpose these would serve. It had
been taken for granted when the Commandant had agreed to
put the flares out that paraffin or petrol would be used, and I had
visualised a long streak of the inflammable spirit sprinkled over
the sand which when lit would make it a simple matter, as far as
seeing was concerned, to take off parallel with the line of flame.
As it was, the moment the cockpit hood was clamped down even
the first lamp would not be seen, as the forward view on XF was
practically non-existent. With the Vega it may not have been so
difficult; a reasonable take-off and good forward view might
have permitted the dim line of lights to be kept in sight. With
XF it was ridiculous to contemplate trying; in this thin air the
tail would never lift until well beyond the last discernible lamp
and then providing no soft patches of sand were struck, the full
length of the chosen runway would be needed; probably more
than that. There was no time to argue; the Frenchman obviously
did not understand clearly what I meant and even if he did
there was no time now to wait whilst the flare-path was made. I
thanked goodness I had gone to that little extravagance of fitting
an engine-driven vacuum pump to the blind-flying instruments
rather than relying entirely upon exposed venturis; ice had been
the deciding point in question then and I had never expected
that it would be of so much importance here.

With the aid of one or two of my wellwishers the tail of the
Mew was eased round a few inches so that the nose of the machine
pointed exactly down the chosen path, aiming as far as it was

possible to judge to miss the furthermost lamp in sight by a few yards to the left. The warm glow of the watch needle inside the machine neared the time of departure. Now for it. Stepping into the cockpit, after putting on the parachute and tightening the Sutton safety straps as far as they would go, I carefully set the directional gyro to zero, closed the coupé head securely, switched off the navigation lights to eliminate glare and with a murmured prayer slowly opened the throttle. As expected the moment the engine revved up nothing could be seen for the swirling clouds of dust, which easily found its way into the cockpit filling the inside with choking grit and that strange, inimitable smell as well. The directional gyro quivered slightly at first as the engine picked up and then as the machine slowly rolled forward moved a degree or two over to the right; a little pressure with the left foot on the rudder-bar gradually brought it back to the zero mark. For the first fifty yards or so the machine rolled along quite smoothly, the tail dragging heavily on the ground; then as it was slowly picking up speed we struck one of the dreaded areas of soft sand and but for the control column being snatched hard back and the weight of petrol causing the machine to be very tail-heavy it would certainly have turned over on to its nose. Torturously the small wheels ploughed through the clinging sand and then breaking out on to one of the level rock plateaus accelerated rapidly. A glance at the directional gyro indicated that the machine had swung rather badly and I anxiously eased the rudder over to try and straighten out before too much speed had been gained.

Now the tail was lifting from the ground. In another hundred yards or so the machine was roaring along; in the darkness and not knowing quite where I was going, it felt a terrifying pace. The directional gyro was now quivering gently on the zero mark and the artificial horizon showed a very slight climb. One hand pushed hard on the throttle whilst the other held the control column tensely, feeling for the response on the sensitive elevators that would bring the relief I prayed for. If the stick was eased too far forward to get the tail well up then nothing could prevent the machine from nosing over if another soft patch were struck;

Q

then again if it was held too far back there was the possibility that the machine would not get off the ground at all. A difficult job to compromise, with only the quivering line of the artificial horizon to show just how much; I hoped fervently that flying speed would be reached before the wheels tore into those rocks on the edge of the drome. Another hundred yards and the machine would have been airborne but for the fact that the wheels suddenly ploughed into more soft sand. This time sheer speed and a certain amount of elevator control just saved the situation: as the machine plunged over as if nothing could stop it from tearing into the desert sand with its whirling airscrew, the control column was brought firmly back and held there, and to my intense relief and surprise I felt the whole aircraft pause as if balanced on a tightrope before the tail gently dropped and thumped against the soft ground. The tremendous momentum already gathered forced the machine rapidly out of the soft, loose sand on to another firm stretch; again the directional gyro indicated the machine had swung badly, and this time due to the increased speed and the tail being airborne it was a more precarious task to get straightened out quickly. Now we were surely moving faster than ever before, but I dared not move my eyes from the Sperry panel to glance at the ASI to see what speed we were travelling at. Easing the stick very slightly back I could feel the wheels pattering away in an effort to leave the ground; at the same moment I felt the ominous tug of the treacherous soft sand again but this time a quick, gentle pressure on the control column staggered the machine into the air.

22 ❋ Night of hell

WHEW! As XF climbed steadily in the calm air I was still tense with concentration, my eyes glued to the instrument panel with its almost imperceptible movement in the dull glow of the compass needle creeping steadily but precisely around the large dial on to its correct course. The fact that I was unable to see any of the lights below, that the large river immediately beneath did not reveal its presence and that the moon and the stars were heavily diffused by the thick heat haze would, under normal circumstances, have given me cause for some concern as I peered into a blackness unbroken by any distinguishing features. I could not tear my mind away from those agonising moments as I left Gao. I hoped fervently it would be the last time I ever saw the place. I could not help dwelling upon the consequences of so many unknown dangers that no pilotage of mine could have avoided, perspiring and my mouth going dry and immobile as I did so. How the undercarriage had stood up to the side loads as we swung, heavily loaded, in those soft patches of sand I shall never know; how much room there was to spare as I crossed the airfield boundary was sheer guess-work and had there been Bedouins or stray camels in my path, neither they nor I would have known anything about it. I became so rigid with these morbid thoughts of what might have happened that the sudden appearance of some bushfires stirred me from my mental fixation; I picked up the little torch and examined my map closely, but not before making up my mind that I would break the promise I had made to myself—alter my flight plan and use Niamey instead of Gao on the way back.

Now away from Gao, with sufficient petrol to last until dawn, to be purring along in a peaceful night began to fill me with tremendous confidence; in an almost blasé way I told myself that even if I could not pick out the Niger below, in one hour and twenty minutes I would see the lights of Niamey, visibility permitting. I never did see those lights that should have indicated the town, but sometime later I did observe large fires almost due east of my position. They appeared to be some twenty or thirty miles off my own course and for a brief spell I wondered if they could indeed be the town of Niamey; if so, then I was radically out in my dead-reckoning and would land up in the Atlantic.

What the hell shall I do? I ought to get one good fix before I press on. Shall I turn off and have a look at the fires? What's the good of that? No, trust your compass and keep that needle spot on 160 degrees. You know you've been in the air for nearly two hours, so how can it possibly be Niamey?—that's way back. Don't waste any more time. What was that flash of light ahead? . . . must have been mistaken . . . no I'm not, there it is again— bloody lightning! Still, it's miles away . . . probably move over before I get there.

I was now quite relaxed with the flying in such calm conditions easy, and for a time I felt almost comfortable with my legs resting on the rudder-bar and my fingers lightly holding the control column, with a gentle pressure from time to time as the compass needle moved fractionally to one side or the other of course. I think I must have sensed rather than seen the change in the serenity I was now enjoying. In the haze and completely relying on instruments it was not always possible to tell whether I was in cloud or not, but I could nevertheless always see a dull glint of the polished paintwork on the wings and at times there was some sort of horizon. Now I was suddenly conscious of the intense blackness of the night and at the same time I was stirred from my lethargy by the sight of a deep red glow pulsating beneath the fuselage. For a terrifying moment I thought the machine was on fire. Just as I had concluded that this was the open exhaust flames reflecting on some particularly black and turbulent storm clouds we were about to enter, I puzzled as I peered intently at the wing, which for some reason was no longer visible, and the crash of water hit the machine like so many machine-guns firing at the same time, but in a crescendo so sudden and unexpected that I literally jumped out of my skin with fright. Wham! Wham! The map and flashlamp leapt into the air, struck the side of the cockpit and clattered out of sight somewhere on the floor near my ankles.

Lucky thing I put those harness straps on tight, I think this is going to be a bit rough. Hell, what a deluge! Thank God I've got a metal prop; I hope it doesn't swamp the engine ... I don't know how it can take it; if it floods the air intake I'm going to be in a mess ... I think I'll change over to warm air; at least it will stop a direct flood into the carburettor, even if it does cut down the power. God, that was a rough one. I hope I can hang on ... losing height ... mustn't do that; let's climb as hard as we can, we might get above it.

Wham! Wham! As if kicked by a mule and thrown about by some enormous hand XF shot up and down and bucked in a manner that kept throwing maps, rulers, pencils, flashlamp and slide-rule up and down in front of my face to land on the cockpit floor. There was a momentary lull in the continuous struggle to keep the machine from going over the vertical: what small hope I had would be destroyed if my artificial horizon went out of action; already the gyro compass was useless and spinning like a top, and I now grasped the chance to reset it. How I regretted not being able to fit the reliable turn-and-bank indicator. The torrential blast of water had eased a little and I turned the control back to cold air for the carburettor and hung on to a desperate climb for altitude as I felt the extra surge of power from the engine. I was bracing myself hard against the bulkhead and rudder bar; one violent period of turbulence had caught me unawares: my feet had shot off the rudder-bar, my ankles had hit the bottom of the petrol tank a resounding whack and my head, in spite of the tightness of the Sutton harness, struck the top of the cabin roof, making me grateful that Jack Cross had stressed the frame up adequately.

At 14,000 ft I began to wonder if I should ever break out over the tops of this storm and then I was aware of a noise that I had never before heard in an aircraft in flight, a deep ominous rumble that came over loud and vibrating above the noise of the engine and the rain still beating an hysterical tattoo on the cabin roof—thunder. Seconds after, the sky was rent with a blinding flash of blue and yellow light. We must have been passing between banks of massive cloud because in that flash I glimpsed towering black and grey pinnacles so far above me that I knew there was never any chance of me being able to fly above this storm—those clouds must have been 30,000 ft at least. I was now getting very tired as I braced and struggled to keep the machine on some semblance of a course in the right direction. The gyro continued to spin and the compass was anywhere from twenty or thirty degrees either side of course, I gave up any serious attempt to straighten it out, I was hanging on for my life and all I had in mind at that moment was to survive. Boom! Boom! Wham! It was becoming obvious that I could not hold out much longer. It was now so bad that the throttle had to be continually closed and opened. Sometimes the machine was shuddering and buffeting so badly that it seemed I had no control at all. Sometimes the throttle would remain closed for several minutes as I exerted all the concentration in manipulation of controls I could muster with the machine losing or gaining height as it was thrown about the sky like an autumn leaf in a gale.

The moment of truth has arrived. Clouston was right; he knew I should never have taken XF on a flight like this . . . I must try and think clearly, I must survive what ever happens . . . if that horizon topples I'm finished. God, that was a bad one! Another like that and she'll break up. I've got to get out while there is a chance . . . must try and think clearly and carefully . . . if I release the cockpit top it could hit the tail and I should be in a dive before I had a chance to clamber out . . . I must get out of this Sutton harness and make sure my parachute straps are not tangled. What about the gun? I may need that when I land . . . Damn, I haven't brought anything to cut it free from the back-pack . . . Where am I going to land? Oh hell, we must be past the bush and into jungle, swamp or sea . . . what a hell of

a fix I've got myself into. I don't think much of landing amongst
those bloody crocodiles ... that little automatic won't do you
much good even if you can get to it. Let's try and work out
where we are before saying goodbye ... just under five hours
since take-off ... I reckoned on being at Libreville at 6.30, first
light—why, damn it all, there's over 400 miles of sea crossing the
Gulf of Biafra; I must be over it now if I am anywhere near a
course at all. Oh my God, that means if I don't drown, then the
bloody sharks will get me ... I've got to hang on, I have no
other choice.

Almost as if my prayers had been answered, after a particularly vicious spell that wore me out as I braced in anticipation against every shock that hit us, I was caught holding my
breath as we ran out of the storm. Although still in cloud the
noise of the rain had ceased and the instruments were settling
into a fixed position for the first time in what had felt an age. I
was able to ease the muscles of my legs that were now stiff with
tension and although I still dared not release my harness I
worked my neck around and massaged my shoulder muscles that
had been under a compression strain for so long. What a relief
to lean back and maintain a steady course. Although still in
thick, heavy cloud I was able to let my eyes take a rest by allowing them to roam at will, only occasionally checking upon things
that mattered without having to peer and concentrate until they
watered from fatigue. If I could relax for a while I would then
get down to some calculations as to where I thought I might be
at that moment. I had managed to retrieve my slide-rule and
map by groping for them, but the flashlamp and scale rule were
still somewhere on the floor of the cockpit; fortunately I had
another pencil which was tucked inside the writing pad strapped
to my knee.

It would be too much to hope that I was anywhere near a
dead reckoning position. The wisest plan would be to descend
earlier than originally planned, which would bring me down
over the sea, I hoped; but I must take care not to make it so
early that I struck the Island of Fernando Po. I gave my calculations a lot of thought and analysed as best I could how the

storm might have affected my original flight plan. It was now 0615 hrs, fifteen minutes before my ETA at Libreville.

What do I do? Still damned black, can't see a thing in this stuff . . . Wish I could find that bally torch, it would help if I could see the map . . . Well are you going to circle round in this stuff until daylight or are you going down? I'm getting bloody claustrophobic messing around like this . . . I wish I knew that altimeter setting was correct . . . Right, here goes, better open the trap-window so at least I can see all there is to see . . . Whew, it's that blasted smell coming up from the jungle again; must be over land. Shall I turn west and lose my height or glide straight on course? No, I'll slow right up and keep her headed on track. 1000 ft, I don't like this one little bit . . . better put the flaps down and stick her in fine pitch. Thank God we are on first light and I can see a bit . . . Hope I break out of this cloud soon. 900 ft. What's that below? Hurrah, it's water! Can only be the sea . . .

Peering out of the little side-window, it was with indescribable relief that I saw a filthy green mass of water moving with a gentle swell, and could smell the odour of rotting vegetation that I remembered so well on the survey flight. There was no doubt that I was over the Atlantic, but how far west of course I did not know. I turned the machine exactly ninety degrees to the east carefully, as the light and visibility was by no means good. Hardly had the needle of the compass settled on to the new course when faintly ahead on the starboard side I was sure I could see a thin black and white line on the horizon. I think I must have shouted with joy: there was the surf curled in a thin foaming line swishing up against a debris-strewn beach so narrow that the jungle appeared to come right down to the water's edge.

Turning south down the coast, with the gathering light I was now able to see what the weather was like. Over the water the cloud bases were difficult to distinguish as they seemed to intermingle and form part of the close horizon; on my left, however, the sight was not comforting. I realised more than ever just how lucky I had been; the cloud as a whole was low, about 500 to

700 ft, but over the vast, dense foliage of the jungle large patches of steam or mist rising from the swamps of rotting vegetation met the low cloud in an impenetrable blanket. Fate must have guided the machine: had I come down over land then it might have been another story. The difficulty was now ahead in finding Libreville; and if it was to be found, in landing there, as it was only a narrow clearance cut out of this same steaming jungle.

Suddenly I was startled by a light that blinked ahead; startled is the word as the last thing I expected to see at this moment was a light. Rapidly coming up to it I discovered it was either a small lightship flashing a navigation beacon, or a boat sailing out of a fairly large river. Quick, where was the map? Here was an obvious check. With some difficulty I feverishly sought in the dim light for the map on the floor of the cockpit and eventually found it. Peering with difficulty without the aid of the flashlamp it seemed that the river I had just passed might be one of many, although if I had come down more or less where calculated then it was the River Muni next door to Libreville. No! that would be too good to be true; anyway, I should soon find out, as there should be a large bay only a few miles further south. Yes! Luck was with me once again. A few minutes flying and the coastline turned abruptly to the east.

Here is the bay and the aerodrome should be over there in the midst of those trees . . .

Only a few hours ago all was lost and I was in the depths of despair; now to be flying serenely in heaven-sent daylight with Libreville below, clear of the treacherous mist, put me on top of the world. Nothing could surely stop me now? The worst part of the trip was over and after last night's experience, providing there was no mechanical failure, I was confident that old XF would fly through hell itself.

Quick! Must not lose a second: any delay now would mean a night landing at Mossamedes as well as at Wingfield . . .

When one is keyed up to such a state of haste and excitement it is only with difficulty that one can force oneself to react in a normal manner; my first impulse was to slam the throttle closed and dive in to land irrespective of wind, obstacles or anything else.

I flew in a steady circuit over the long but extremely narrow landing strip. It looked so desolate that a horrible thought flashed across my mind that there would not be anyone there to refuel me. No! there were a few people standing around what looked to be a cart or lorry.

My God, what the Hades have the fools done? . . .

Right across the middle of the landing strip had been dug a large dyke and on either side of this were heaps of rubble, wheelbarrows and I assumed drainage materials and tools. A deluge of water could not have damped my spirits more. Why the devil hadn't I been informed of this?

I suppose they think the place is still serviceable for aircraft; well it may be for some but it certainly isn't for this one . . . Not much petrol left, so I shall have to land whether I like it or not . . .

Circling low there did not seem to be any difference in the length of either side, the drain was cut dead across the middle and both ends looked far too small for my liking. Weighing it up carefully, I reckoned that it might be possible to land with extreme caution but not to take-off. There might be a chance that if I landed safely something could be done about it. Choosing the west side of the strip, the Mew with judicious use of plenty of engine was lowered between the tall surrounding trees and clipping the tops of a few low bushes I dropped it on to the edge of the landing ground. The surface of the aerodrome fortunately was good, being coarse grass on firm sand, and by using the brakes hard I brought the machine to a standstill a few yards from the drain, which at close quarters looked positively menacing.

23 ✳ *Pitfalls*

EAPING OUT OF THE AIRCRAFT I saw that a lorry some hundreds of yards on the other side was racing towards me. I had time to look around and noticed that whilst the drain was really cut right across the landing strip there was a narrow gap on the extreme edge which had not been cut, undoubtedly to permit lorries and wheelbarrows to get over the dyke with draining equipment. Here was salvation; obviously XF could not get off in such a short run with full load, but the machine would be nearly airborne and under a certain amount of control by the time the ditch was reached; I reckoned that if I steered along the extreme edge of the landing ground it would be possible to strike the lorry track and patter the wheels along it until the machine was ready to take off.

With more noise than speed the lorry pulled up nearby and I was amazed to be greeted by two Europeans speaking the first real English since I left Gravesend. Needless to say they were somewhat hurt when I queried their nationality. They had apparently been waiting hours for me, so when I had unscrewed all the various petrol caps they set to work in a businesslike manner to refuel as quickly as they could. I felt sorry that it was not possible to spare a few moments to have a chat with them, but they soon put me at ease: when I started a conversation, in true abrupt British fashion they told me I hadn't time to talk, only to get some food and drink. They would attend to the refuelling, which they aimed to do better and quicker than anyone else en route. I left them to it confidently and started pouring in the oil. As I was doing so I felt my panama hat being lifted from my head, to be replaced by a large sun helmet. Turning round, I was greeted by a charming woman who pushed a sandwich into one of my greasy hands and a glass of lemonade into the other, at the same time admonishing me for not carrying a topee and insisting that I should take hers with me. I explained that I would have carried one if there had been sufficient head-room in XF's cockpit; but surely at the present moment, with the sun so low and the clouds so thick, there was little danger of sunstroke? She said there was every danger and that the more cloud the more likelihood there was of getting sunstroke; she forbade me to take off the helmet until the last moment before leaving.

How I pitied these poor people; what a hole to live in. The sun had scarcely risen, yet my clothes were wet with perspiration and it trickled from my brow and face in a most uncomfortable manner. A steaming mist shimmered up from amongst the trees and it did not need any imagination to visualise a bog of rotting wood and foliage at the foot of them. The air was literally putrid; it stank with an almost indescribable odour and was so thick and heavy that one felt one could grasp and squeeze it through one's fingers. Although I had not by any means exerted myself I could not seem to take a deep enough breath and succeeded with what I was doing in a continuous series of short gasps.

Everything completed in record time, the engine was swung into life again and with a short but sincere word of thanks to my new-found friends I nipped into the cockpit and started to taxi carefully to the extreme corner of the landing ground. On almost touching the overhanging branches of the tall trees which bounded the aerodrome with the whirling blades of the airscrew, I jumped out and eased the tail of XF round so that it was almost hidden in the verge of the jungle. The nose pointed exactly towards the track and with some rubble heaps standing out too clearly and too near for my peace of mind.

Running the engine up to full throttle, the wheel-brakes were released and the machine leapt forward gaining speed rapidly, much to my surprise. The take-off might have been unexpectedly good and without incident, but soon after the tail came up into the flying position the machine swung badly, luckily to the left

away from the trees. This was most unusual for XF; normally
the tailskid dragged for so long with a full load that it auto-
matically kept straight, and as soon as the tailplane was airborne
the speed was such that the airflow over the fin and fuselage—
which had an abnormally good keel surface—was more than
adequate to give positive control. On this occasion something
unusual must have happened: a soft patch in the ground, a
sticking port brake, or maybe the port wheel-fairing fouling
against the tyre, as I could invariably smell burning rubber
when taking off. Whatever it was, the machine swung when
travelling at high speed and after straightening out it was now
impossible to hit off the track without careering into the trees on
the edge.

The wisest course would have been to switch off the engine
and restart, but at the speed already gathered I am convinced
nothing could have prevented the machine from plunging into
the dyke. There was only one chance and I must confess at that
moment it seemed a very remote one: if the machine could not
get off before reaching the drain, with careful timing it might be
made to leap it. So with throttle wide open and the nose held
well down the Mew rocketed towards the heaps of stone and
rubble in a manner that caused a sickening sensation in my
stomach. At that speed it is difficult to judge distance to a
matter of yards, but when it seemed that the machine must
collide with the heaps of rubble, the control column was eased
back and at the same time the landing flaps were lowered. The
machine jumped off the ground three or four feet into the air
with the wheels lightly touching the heaps on both sides of the
dyke—click! click!—and then settled down again for a few yards
on the other side before hanging on to the airscrew and labouring
into the air.

Phew!

I forget how long it took me to regain my breath and normal
heartbeat but it was a long while before I was able to relax and
think of anything else but the click! click! of those wheels
touching the rubble-heaps.

Climbing steadily on course through the clouds, my now

subdued and less violent companions of the night before, it was
amazing how their transformation had taken place in such a
short time. On reaching the correct operating height I was
almost dazzled in spite of dark sun-glasses and literally cooked,
with little relief from the panama hat or green sunblind of the
cockpit. The cloud was now ten-tenths stratus below with a perfect blue sky above; in a way, not being able to see the ground or
sea was not disappointing, as a glance at the map showed that
from Libreville to Mossamedes there is 1200 miles of sea with a
hundred miles from land at the widest point. I had no wish to be
constantly reminded of this.

Everything now going smoothly, I felt decidedly easier and
began to toy with a few range, fuel and navigation problems and
generally to take stock of how my chances stood. I was a few
minutes ahead of schedule, the weather was improving and there
were only two more landings and one more take-off to make.
There was good reason to feel elated, but deeming it wisest not
to count the chickens before they were hatched I forced a mood
of pessimism upon myself. A hundred things could happen before
reaching Cape Town: after all, there was another night trip
ahead, and if the weather happened to be poor I did not fancy
my chances of finding Wingfield amongst those mountains in the
dark. The cloud formation was again changing and soon I was
flying amidst colossal towering cumulus; far higher than I had
ever seen in England and perfectly breathtaking, the enormous
white banks rolled against a background of Reckitts-blue sky.
Flying through many of these mountains of cloud was both
exasperating and tiring; my almost bare shoulders were still sore
from last night's shaking and the jolts of the harness hurt considerably. At the end of four hours flying from Libreville with
only the dubious comfort of an occasional glimpse of the sea
below for company I was heartily reassured to shoot out of a
bank of cloud to find myself in a void of blue; a vast expanse of
rolling sea stretched below and many miles ahead, a little to the
left, very thinly and faintly was a strip of land on the extreme
horizon. Soon it was possible to make out the Portuguese harbour
of Benguela well over to the east, a sight that found me plenty of

work in the few minutes juggling with various routine calculations necessary whenever a good fix was sighted. Whistling over the tops of some barren and desolate-looking mining camps in a fast, shallow dive I peered ahead across that stretch of burning rock and sand to the spot where I knew Mossamedes should be.

Hurrah! Good for the jolly old Portuguese!

Circling low, I was able to pick out an ancient petrol lorry surrounded I should think by at least half the population of the little port. What faith they must have had in the schedules I had sent to them. How strange this cluster of humanity seemed, out there in the barren wilderness: no trees, no buildings of any description and just an occasional cloud of dust in the distance along the poorly marked track, where more onlookers were on the way trudging through the heat. This was a treacherous landing place. Like so many others it was simply a clearer and more level area of desert than the rest, but here the aerodrome was badly undulated and covered with stones. Towards the boundaries, no doubt to serve as markers, were huge boulders; many of these had managed to find their way towards the centre and no one had bothered to remove them.

I intended using the utmost caution: the sun was on the decline and although by no means so powerful was at an angle which reflected badly on the cockpit screen. I removed my sunglasses, but the glare was so intense that it was almost blinding and I quickly replaced them; the lenses had become smeared with dirt and perspiration, causing things to look darker than normal, but a quick rub with a handkerchief soon rectified this.

Although there was little wind it was extremely gusty near the ground, no doubt due to the intense heat of the sun on the sand, as a mirage could be seen all the time rising up in long shimmering waves. It was my practice always when landing XF to open the one and only little side-window and to peer through this, as with any glare or darkness it was impossible to see through the cockpit screen at all. This little window was held back with a steel hook, more or less like a large fishhook with a sharp barb. Closing the throttle, I crossed my left hand over to the right hand side of the cockpit to hook up the window: at that moment the machine struck a bad gust which jerked my arm, causing this steel barb to pierce my index finger. I immediately pulled, expecting the hook to slip out, but it was held by the barb and only worked deeper into the flesh; when I pushed the other way the window just moved back, permitting no pressure to be put on the finger.

It was a silly little predicament to be in; the machine was rapidly gliding towards the ground with the throttle closed and it was clear that it would undershoot the aerodrome unless I opened up again. My left hand was immovable in the hook and my right hand of course was holding the control column. I juggled violently with my finger and the hook but nothing would ease it out. I was in desperation, as it was obvious that unless something was done very quickly the machine would strike the boulders now only a few feet below. I tore my hand away, ripping open the flesh and causing blood to spurt all over the place, but with it I slammed open the throttle.

Having to do another complete circuit to sort things out again, the Mew was brought in this time without further incident. I landed amidst clouds of dust which whirled into the cockpit; there was a blast of air as hot as a furnace which threatened to choke and blind me at the same time. Before there was time to leap out of the machine and almost before the glistening metal blades of the airscrew had come to a standstill, XF was completely swamped by scores of overwilling Portuguese officials and blacks, all shouting, laughing and gesticulating at the same time. Remembering the serious menace of smoking so near to the large drums of petrol, which in this heat gave off a shimmering, explosive vapour at an incredible rate, the moment I stepped out I opened the log-book and to the nearest and most important-looking official I pointed out one of my prepared Portuguese sentences: 'Please ask everyone who is smoking to keep away from the machine as there is imminent danger of fire and explosion.' This had the effect of dispersing the crowd for a short while.

They soon clustered round again, making it most tedious refuelling. I was continually wading through the dense mass of people on my way from the nose of the machine to the cockpit for irritating reasons such as having forgotten a spanner or passport, or to explain something required. An over-helpful official was rummaging through my papers and maps in an endeavour to find and stamp my log-book just when I was perched precariously on top of a petrol drum, and I had to force my way over to him with the required document to save my valuable papers from being lost or disarrayed. There was a hectic spell of attempting to do a dozen things at once at the same time as shouting myself hoarse in an effort to keep off those nitwits who thought my precious machine was a strange animal to be prodded or a nice place for an afternoon siesta.

I felt that all at last was completed when to my utter chagrin someone noticed a streak of blood on the white fuselage: in no time, amidst a hubbub of sympathy and advice, they traced this to a small stream that had seeped through the handkerchief bandage, run down my arm and elbow and was dripping away steadily. More delay. It was only a small, deep cut but I was almost exasperated by the time I had persuaded the kindly people that the bandage they had wrapped round the finger would suffice.

At last satisfying them I made sure everything was finally complete, and then asked the officials with the help of the log-book phrases if they would be good enough to help me with the request: 'Would you please put out landing flares at 0430 hrs on 7th Feb.' As they carefully wrote the request down and assented willingly, I was content.

Taking off from Mossamedes was done with a feeling of absolute tenseness. Having come so far and overcome so much, to have a mishap now would be heart-breaking. I taxied out with the greatest possible care to get the longest run. The Mew was opened up and shot along the hot, rough surface of the desert at a speed and in a manner which must have made the excited crowd's eyes pop out. In a plume of dust we leaped into the air with the acrid smell of burning rubber in my nose from the tyres.

Few people I believe, unless they have experienced it for themselves, realise the awful barrenness and fierce heat of the

R

wilderness known at that time as the Outja Desert. Less formidable in size than the Sahara, it is none the less menacing and forbidding. As I saw it below, having had one uncomfortable experience with it, I did not relish the crossing and was not upset when the sun began to disappear below the horizon and the ground especially towards the sea became covered by the thick low fog that is so prevelant in these parts. Managing to get a navigation fix on Walvis Bay in between the banks of fog, I was fairly hopeful of hitting off Cape Town providing conditions remained as they were and I was able to adhere to the corrected course and exact time. The sight of the white carpet below as the fog filled in, made visible now by the steady twinkle of the stars above, was soothing on the eyes after the glaring heat of but a few hours before.

I suppose by this time I must have been feeling tired and a bit jaded; there was not a bump in the sky and I slumped back relaxed, but I could not fly a straight course. I was flying on the artificial horizon and directional gyro, but the machine would persist in flying one wing low: the more I tried to keep level the more the machine lolled gently and slowly from one side to the other. I think this was brought on by imagination and an over-tired mental state. I am convinced now that the machine in all probability was on an even keel and yet I would somehow sense it was wandering off course and act accordingly. My own reactions at that time were probably so slow that I was really starting up a merry-go-round between myself and the instruments.

The quiet, peaceful conditions also brought on a prolonged mental discussion; like a good argument it made the time slip by, but did nothing to help my flying. The night was dark but crystal clear and the stars twinkled with a clarity rarely seen in our country. Suddenly I saw another light that flashed with the regularity of a lighthouse. I studied it carefully as we drew closer and then with the aid of the little flashlamp I had retrieved ran the scale rule over the map. My calculations confirmed that this was Green Point; I was spot on track and two minutes ahead of schedule. There were lights brilliantly clustered as I sped south, and a wave of deep intense emotion filled my mind and body; I felt that I had given of my best but that something else, call it what you may, had guided my gallant little machine so that victory was now in sight.

I must concentrate on what has to be done when I land. Shall I pull out all the stops and take-off at 2215 hrs instead of the same time tomorrow? That would give me 75 minutes on the ground . . . not enough time for a fifty-hour schedule on the engine and anyway it's a stupid idea: you need a good rest and some food. What's the good of being greedy and probably cracking up on the way back? Besides, there's Niamey to deal with yet . . . Hope there's no damage anywhere, I don't like the smell of those tyres on every take-off; must make sure I check them over carefully. She's a fantastic little aircraft, thank God she's redeemed her reputation . . . incredible to think she's beaten the Comet by six hours: the fastest by any aircraft in the world to Cape Town, and knocked thirty-nine hours off the solo record. What about crowds—Clou said they were the very devil . . . I'm sure George Fisher will look after this angle and keep them clear of my precious XF. Must send a cable to Dad and Jack; I'd love to see their faces . . . My God, isn't that just a fantastic sight, all those lights around the harbour and the coastline and that wonderful beacon flashing on the aerodrome! Had almost forgotten what civilised flying was. Take care now, don't get cocky; you've still got to land and if you boob the whole world will certainly know about it . . . watch those damned hills that Clou spoke about on the final approach.

The lights of Cape Town: a sight that will remain in my mind for as long as I live. Hundreds of cars traced a glowing, snake-like movement over the main autoroutes. I went into a shallow dive towards them with a slight turn to bring me on to the approach for Wingfield airport. For the first time in the air since leaving England I pulled the tiny lever that operated the retractable navigation lights and I could imagine what those below were thinking as they saw the pretty red, green and white light streak across the velvet sky—for a moment I envied them their thrill. As I made my final pass over the aerodrome the whole place became a flood of light as those below prepared for my touch-down. I switched off my own navigation lights to eliminate any risk of dazzle on the instruments and the perspex side-panels and began a cautious engine approach. It was wise that I did so as like a shadow I saw a dark shape float away beneath me and realised I was passing the low hills that had surprised Clouston. The wheels touched down smoothly and we rolled to a standstill with plenty of space to spare in front of the control-tower.

Half my journey completed. Now for the return flight.

24 ✳ Breather half-way

AMIDST THE CROWD that rushed towards me I recognised the beaming face of one of the senior aerodrome mechanics and was considerably reassured. Guiding XF through the darkness with a man on each wingtip and the crowds pressing too near for comfort, a large hangar suddenly loomed up; the engine was switched off to enjoy—that is, if engines do enjoy such things—a warm stable, a short rest and a good grooming. Pushing up the cockpit hood was the signal to be overwhelmed by a flood of humanity: amidst vivid flashes of camera lights I felt myself being lifted and carried away clutching desperately to save the precious maps.

What a figure I must have made; still garbed in what had been white shorts; now covered from head to foot in oil and dirt; my old slippers showing signs of the rough use they had received; my knobbly knees trembling with cold and fatigue; my face trying to smile yes and no to everybody's questions; a growth of beard engrimed with sweat must have made me look more like a hobo than someone who had left England clean and fresh but thirty-nine hours before. My head was swimming round and round and I longed to get away and be quiet. George Fisher, like a real pal, came to the rescue: after I had met Cape Town's jovial Mayor, Mr Foster, and other celebrities and muttered a few unintelligible words into the microphone, he and Pat Murdock forcibly guided me through a cordon of hefty police that the crowd threatened to break through any minute; eventually, to everyone's relief, we reached the sanctuary of his own house, where the police had strict instructions to surround it and admit no one without special permission. Sinking down into a

large sofa in the lounge was like finding dead calm after a
thunderstorm. Unfortunately this was not to last long; a guard
came in and said that there were a lot of press men outside demanding admission and threatening dire results if they did not
get it. I looked hopefully at Fisher and he shrugged his shoulders
and suggested they might come in for a short interview and then
leave immediately: in they rushed shooting questions right and
left, only to be warned by Fisher that we would be as helpful as
possible but any badgering for a spectacular story would only
result in them being kicked out. Actually on the whole they were
a good crowd; I had had worse interviews, and amongst them
were some really decent fellows who asked intelligent questions
and only wanted the facts as they actually happened. I do not
know if they went away satisfied, as I feel my answers must have
been incoherent and vague; none of them got a story first-hand.

Fisher had a nice light supper of cold chicken prepared and
I was attempting to swallow some of this, a difficulty greater
than I had thought, being the first real meal for over forty hours,
when a message came to say that a bosom friend and lifelong
neighbour was waiting outside to see me. I thought at first that
it could have been Sam Bodger, an old friend who with his wife
Margaret was visiting South Africa. My disappointment was
clear when I saw only another crowd of well-meaning enthusiasts
trying to force their way into the room.

I got up, winked at Fisher, and said goodnight. Fisher needed
no prompting and led me up to a cosy little bedroom he had
prepared. His understanding was remarkable, a real friend on
whom I could rely to see that the right thing was done. He said
in his gruff, quiet way:

'I should have a good hot bath and then lie down. I don't
suppose you'll be able to sleep for a while so I've asked a doctor
friend of mine and an osteopath to drop in to see you about that
shoulder. In the morning if you are all right and feel like it, help
yourself to my wardrobe and we'll have a stroll outside and see
how your machine is.'

How on earth had he guessed about my shoulder? It did hurt
like hell at times but I didn't remember saying anything about it.

Relaxing in the hot soapy water with a sigh of contentment was so soothing that everything seemed worthwhile. Staying long enough in the bath for the scum to leave a dirty, greasy water-line all round I nipped under the cold shower and after a brisk rubdown jumped into bed expecting to fall off to sleep right away.

Tossing and turning from side to side, sleep was not to be found; my head ached and buzzed and on attempting to force a state of sleepiness the whole room seemed to be swaying as if in motion. A light tap on the door and in came Fisher followed by his doctor friends. I was very pleased to see them and said I felt more like going for a walk than going to sleep. 'Better tell Doc about your shoulder, Alex; he'll soon fix it for you. You don't want any more aches than you can help on the way back,' said Fisher. I told the osteopath that I had experienced a numbing pain in the fleshy part of the left shoulder for the past twelve hours or so; he expertly examined me all over, commented on my physical condition and said that the shoulder was a little over muscled and the pain was caused by the muscle-fibre rubbing against nerve tissue. He thought he could cure it by massage and I was pleased to feel he soon did. The other doctor said that I must get some sleep and gave me some tablets to take. Having said goodnight, it was not long before I was dead to the world.

The sun pouring in at the window must have awakened me next morning; I leapt out of bed and hung out of the little balcony. What a sight for sore eyes! With the winter of England so fresh in my mind, looking across that brilliant expanse in colour with the attractive red and white buildings and Table Mountain silhouetted against a background of vivid blue sky dotted with tufts of cottonwool clouds, made one glad to be alive. I immediately started flinging on some of Fisher's clothes so that I might go outside and take full advantage of the gorgeous weather before setting off for the cold damp fog that is usually the English winter.

Downstairs Fisher welcomed me to a hearty breakfast which I tucked into and thoroughly enjoyed. We then made our way

over to the large hangar that housed the Mew. The machine had
been wheeled out on to the tarmac and stripped of all her engine
cowlings and was surrounded by a small crowd; Fisher said that
although he had virtually closed the aerodrome to everyone
there were certain people whom he felt duty bound to admit.
Our arrival was again the signal for the bobbing and clicking of
cameras, but that at last over Fisher gently ushered them away
and it was possible to discuss with the engineers working on the
machine what sort of condition she was in.

The head mechanic, a smiling little South African, in a manner which rather overemphasised his anxiety at the responsibility of the job said that the work was almost completed, but
owing to the unusual number of special items of equipment,
which included the first constant-speed De Havilland airscrew
to be seen in the Union, he would be pleased if I could wait a
few minutes and then run up the engine. Running up the engine
gave us all a moment of anxiety as it misfired badly on the starboard magneto switch; new sparking plugs had just been fitted
so it appeared that magneto trouble had developed, but the
misfiring was soon diagnosed as an oiled-up plug and on fitting
another one the engine burst into life with a roar that belied any
weakness. Looking carefully over the machine, except for travel
stains she showed little signs of the strenuous journey.

As I was chatting to the mechanics a police guard came up
escorting Sam Bodger. After an animated greeting he had an
amusing tale to tell about the night before. Apparently he had
heard over the wireless that I was due at Wingfield and had leapt
into a car and rushed down to the aerodrome, to find it completely barricaded by thousands of cars with multitudes of
people forcing their way in, over or between the vehicles. Determined to be there to greet me he had fought his way through
the crowds until he came up against the broad backs of the
South African Police; he pleaded with one, telling him who he
was, how he had arranged this meeting and all the distance he
had travelled just to be there, but the stolid bulwark of the law
never raised an eyebrow. So in desperation poor old Sam decided to dive between the policeman's legs to break the barrier,

only to be caught by the scruff of his neck and turfed back into
the seething mass with a grim retort from the constable: 'I don't
care if you've come from Kingdom Come, you're not coming in
here.' But nothing would deflect Sam. Five months earlier I had
told him facetiously I would be in Cape Town, God willing, at
9 p.m. on February the 6th, 1939. I had arrived two minutes
early for the appointment.

I went into Cape Town that afternoon, as I had been asked
by the Lord Mayor if I would attend a small conference to discuss the possibilities of a big air race from England to the Union
that had recently been proposed. I agreed with pleasure providing they would see I got back in time to get some sleep. The
lunch was delightful. Taffy Drew and George Fisher, no doubt
out of genuine concern, persuaded me all they could to postpone
the return flight, if not altogether then for a few days until I was
thoroughly rested. 'No necessity for it,' said Taffy. 'Your trip
back will take much more out of you if you go now; you've
already set a record that will take some beating and if you stay
here a week you'll still be able to swipe up all the other records.'
If it had not been for the thought of Dad, and I hoped someone
else, waiting for me I think I would have given way and enjoyed
their fine hospitality a little longer. As it was my mind was made
up and the discussion was ended by the head waiter whispering
in Fisher's ear that there was a trunk call for me from London.

Having had an informal chat in the palatial rooms that served
as the Mayoral office with the genial Mr Foster and a few other
dignitaries, we returned to the aerodrome. I carefully checked
things over so that there would be no last minute rush or delay
in getting away that night. There was another pile of telegrams
on the lounge table and I was astonished to note that many
were cabled from countries I had never been to, friends that I
had almost forgotten and organisations or societies that I had
never heard of, certainly not connected with aviation. Amongst
the messages was one saying that Sir Abe Bailey expected to get
down that night to see me off. I thought it was a fine gesture from
a wonderful sportsman; it is no inconvenience for most people to
hang around into the middle of the night to see a small machine

leave the ground, but for a man who had suffered so much personal agony and illness, to put himself out to such an extent was to be admired.

Content that George Fisher would now look after the final details and call me at 2100 hrs GMT I sauntered upstairs to bed. It was again impossible to sleep, either through overstrung nerves or the anticipation and the train of thoughts that resulted about the journey ahead. After my failure to get in touch with Niamey I was compelled to adhere to the original plan. The landing at Gao would prove the greatest obstacle. As the schedule for the return was extremely tight, allowing little margin, the thought of landing there in the dark had caused me considerable reflection and worry, to such an extent that although I had prepared the whole flight plan very carefully not to be altered under any consideration, I had decided to leave that night three-quarters of an hour earlier than originally intended: I would attempt to land at Mossamedes before dawn so as to give an even chance of reaching Gao before sunset. Taffy Drew had kindly sent off a cable to Gao to have flares ready for landing, but this was a small consolation; I very much doubted whether they would receive the message before I arrived. How much fog would there be on the way to Mossamedes? Several hundred miles no doubt but would it stretch as far as the landing ground? I hoped not: if so, I was beaten.

With such thoughts—and there were many of them—I wasted away the hours until footsteps quietly coming up the stairs warned me that the time had come. Jumping out of bed I leapt into the bath of ice-cold water that had been prepared; a smart rub down with a rough towel and again I donned the old shorts and slippers that had raised so many eyebrows on the way down. George had prepared a tasty supper for me but after a poor pretence at eating I said I would like to go along with him to see the machine refuelled. This had purposely been left until the last moment. I had happened to mention quite casually that I always dreaded taxying over rough ground with such a full load and Fisher had said like a flash, 'Don't worry about that here, Alex; we've got plenty of men and they can push your machine over empty to the far end of the drome. We'll send the petrol lorry over there to fill you up just before you leave.'

We walked out to the control and collected my papers and parachute and also had another look at the plan of the landing, boundary and obstruction lights. Going from there on to the aerodrome was a struggle: the whole ground as far as one could see, up to the barriers, was seething with people. Although I had on over my shoulders one of Fisher's thick overcoats which we thought would help to camouflage me, someone shouted, 'Here he is!' Instantly a crescendo of shouts arose and the swaying mob threatened to break down the barriers.

Hastening along a narrow corridor with a mass of hysterical people on either side was like running the gauntlet. The noise was deafening: hands clutched, papers and hats were thrown in the air and everyone appeared mad with enthusiasm. In spite of the time of departure being purposely broadcasted as being later than it actually was, someone must have got hold of the truth and the crowds were not going to be cheated.

As I came to the end of the excited mob a voice shouted in my ear, 'Good luck, Mr Henshaw! Give my love to Father when you see him.' I paused and turning said to a young man whose face looked familiar, 'Where have I seen you before?' He replied, 'Oh, you wouldn't recognise me, but my father works for you.' I remembered one of our area representatives saying that he had a son living in Cape Town, so I heartily shook hands with him and passed on.

With the aid of a score of willing hands, the tail of the Mew was gently lifted from the ground and the machine slowly pushed over the bare grass to the large landing-light at the extreme edge of the drome. The tanks having been filled with meticulous care under the guidance of my good friends, I again went over every detail in the cockpit most thoroughly to satisfy myself that nothing had been overlooked. All completed: a few minutes to say farewell to those who had been so helpful and kind; I felt genuinely sorry that I should not be able to see more of them, and knew that when I left Cape Town behind the memories I took with me would never die.

The night was very dark and clear. Thousands of stars sparkled on the black velvet of sky as yet unspoilt by the light of the moon. There was a strong wind blowing off the sea and in spite of the heavy overcoat I shivered. Fisher noticed this and aware that I intended discarding the coat insisted that I should wear his pullover over my thin open shirt; this I did willingly, and was to be grateful for it during the next few hours. Taffy still showed his concern and said, 'Well, I'd rather anyone be in your slippers tonight than me,' which brought a laugh from everybody who had seen my scanty footwear.

The photographers at last satisfied, I gave the OK to start the engine; in ten minutes time it would be 2215 hrs. With the engine nicely warmed, a wave of goodbye to all and goodwill shouts in return the coupé head was tightly closed and the throttle opened slowly to take off. The machine moved forward and after a very short run compared with those hot sandy airstrips roared into the night, leaving far below a fairyland of coloured lights. I blipped the navigation lights in farewell before retracting them, and turned on to course with the wind on my tail.

25 ✸ *Fever*

WARNED THAT THE strong southerly wind was purely local I was anxious on sighting Hope Town to obtain another accurate fix, as hitting off Mossamedes this time was going to depend upon a very accurate course and time-keeping. After barely 200 miles had been covered instead of the white line of the surf breaking on the beach there spread as far as the eye could see that horrible smooth layer of low fog. This was a nasty blow: although expected, it extended much farther south than I had anticipated.

On and on we sped over the never-ending white carpet, now made more sinister by the light of the moon shining on the surface. Ghostly towering peaks of black desert rock poked up occasionally through the otherwise impenetrable mist. I had given up all hope of picking out anything below and was concentrating on a steady course when a faint beam showed for a split second through the fog on my port side. I pressed the stop-watch button on the chronometer immediately and fumbled for the flashlamp and slide-rule, hoping my assumed position would work out where that beam of light would fit, probably near Walvis Bay or Swakopmund. Although rather slow taking into account the tailwind that should have helped me a short way, there seemed little doubt according to the calculations that I had just passed the small town of Luderitz. In that case the ETA at Mossamedes would be 0512 GMT. More than content, I relaxed keeping an eye on the warm glow of the steady compass needle.

Fog, fog and still more fog; would it never end? For hours nothing had been seen but the white carpet below, broken only occasionally by those huge rocks peeping through and the darker patches to the east where the heat of the barren desert had no doubt fought with the damp, swirling fog and won.

Five a.m. and still no signs of any break. I was out of luck this time: unless it cleared soon things would look grim. Nearly 1200 miles and the only evidence to confirm what I assumed should be below had been that momentary flash of light I had taken to be Luderitz. To make sure of no mistake I checked and rechecked the time and distance and arrived at the same answer by every conceivable method. I decided that in a few minutes, at 0512 hrs precisely, if nothing showed up I'd throttle back and cruise around in wide circles slowly until dawn broke.

Straining to look right and left for a welcome sign, the minutes came and went; there was no alternative as the thin glowing of the chronometer hand ticked its way closer and closer to the point of ETA but to ease down the motor, coarsen the airscrew pitch and keep in the air as economically and as long as possible. It required an effort of will just to remain circling in one spot— maybe I had made a miscalculation: probably I had not reached there yet or, worse still, had overshot. It was a great temptation to chance to luck and strike off at random in a direction I felt Mossamedes most likely to be.

On the second circuit I imagined that there was a slight discoloration of the fog well over to the north east. Feeling nothing would be lost in moving over such a short distance, I headed the Mew in that direction and slowly trickled along to investigate. I thought at first that it might be a bushfire as the discoloration turned out to be a dull red glow, but scorned the idea realising the barrenness of the country I must be over. Coming lower, the red glow appeared to split into four individual fires well spaced apart and with a whoop of joy it dawned on me that the faithful Portuguese had done their part well. The fires were large, and where they had managed to get the fuel to keep them going was a mystery to me; there was no doubt it had required effort on their part and I was truly thankful.

Opening up the engine and flying over the fires as low as I could to let them know their work had not been in vain, the next problem and a serious one was how to land; it was one thing landing in the dark by the light of the fires but out of the question with all this fog below. I decided to keep the fires in sight and to wait for some improvement. After what felt years, the fog condensed itself into thick, rolling banks with fairly clear patches in between. By waiting the right opportunity and manoeuvring for the best approach position I was able to motor the Mew in a steady glide and eventually touch down with considerable apprehension between two of the large bonfires. The enthusiasm of the reception was astounding; almost as many were there as before and I was told by an American negro, a telegraphist for Reuters who spoke good English, that everyone had been up all night waiting for me.

The formalities and refuelling completed in good time, a handshake for those near at hand, a shout of thanks to them all; I turned to step into the cockpit to find it almost filled with parcels tied with string, bunches of bananas, beautiful red apples, luscious looking oranges and large slabs of chocolate. Under ordinary circumstances this would have been most welcome, but here it was nothing but irritating: there was barely room for me to sit in the machine at the best of times and now simply no room at all. With all the diplomacy I could muster, the good fare was handed back with the exception of a small quantity which they insisted I must take with me.

There are a few sights that will remain in one's memory a lifetime and I think the dawn of that morning will be one of them. The sun was just peeping over the tops of the high mountains in the distance as the Mew turned over Mossamedes, and long shadows mingled with the purple haze in the deep gorges sweeping down to the black-brown rock and white sand below. To the west snuggled the little port, sheltered from the barrenness by an emerald border of tidy vegetation; beyond sparkled the ocean with a colour that made me long for a plunge and a swim to absorb some of the exuberance I felt at the moment.

Striking out across the sea, it was not long before the familiar line of cloud appeared on the horizon. Soon it was followed by the torture of the merciless sun aggravated by the reflection of its scorching heat on the snow-white layer below. I sought as much protection as I could from the blinds and crumpled panama hat, but could not help feeling a little worried at the strength of the sun's rays and intensity of the heat.

My exultation and sense of fitness was slowly ebbing away. I was dismayed when somewhere near the mouth of the Congo I had an attack of horrible sickness, which I cursed and blamed on the heat. Kidding myself it would not last, I tried to forget about it by working out the ETA for Libreville.

Shortly before landing at Libreville I realised that things were not going quite right: the sickness was getting worse and a clammy hot and cold perspiration was breaking out all over me, followed by fits of shivering. It did not need a doctor to diagnose the complaint: I was in for a dose of malaria. I fumbled in my small blue bag, found the tiny bottle and swallowed two quinine tablets, hoping they would ward off a bad attack.

The cloud was breaking up with occasionally glimpses of the vast area of steaming, rotting jungle; I could smell the putrid, nauseating odour even as high as 8000 ft. The sight of Libreville in the distance forced a momentary spell of alertness: the fear of what might happen should I relax for one second on taking-off or landing drove off the awful desire to slump back and close my eyes. This time I had been advised to land on the west end of the landing strip as that was considered a little longer.

Circling once again, I could see the ditch which had so nearly caused disaster; from the air there still seemed to be no difference in the lengths of either side of the landing strip, but feeling I could do no worse than last time I decided to take the advice given. There was not a breath of wind and in that humid turkish bath it felt an impossibility to slow the machine up enough to land in such a small space. Clipping the tops of the tall trees, the Mew almost felt its way down the narrow corridor of dense foliage on either side and sank rapidly on to the edge of the landing-ground, to go scuttling along at a pace that threatened once again to put us in the large dyke ahead. Fortunately, the brakes responded well and the machine came to a standstill with its nose actually hanging over the excavations.

26 Preparations for Cape record at Essex Aero Ltd, Gravesend 1938
27 The grimmer side of test-flying: fuel consumption problems

28 Blood, sand and heat at Mossamedes on the way down
29 Landing at Wingfield to break London-Cape record, 1939

I was not feeling so energetic now; by the time I had crawled out of the cockpit my good friends clattered up with the old petrol lorry and, shouting a hearty greeting, without more ado proceeded to get on with the refuelling. Mrs Harvy—for that I found was her name—also hastened up with a generous supply of cold drinks and sandwiches and a large pith helmet which she immediately clamped on my head. Coming towards us was a small party dressed in immaculate tropical whites, and Mr Harvy introduced me to the Governor of Libreville. He must have considered me abrupt and rude as I had neither the time nor inclination for polite conversation; begging his pardon I hurried on with the refuelling and sorting out of necessary papers. All completed at last, with perspiration pouring out of me, I mumbled thanks and farewell and put a letter from Mrs Harvy to her small daughter in London at the back of my knee-pad so that it would be hidden and safe until posted in England. I climbed into the machine with the thought of how I was going to get off again foremost in my mind.

Taxying so close that the wheels would not go a foot nearer without danger of rolling into the dyke, I pointed the nose towards that corridor of high trees; with the engine straining at the leash like a wild dog, the brakes were released and the machine bounded forward. Tearing over the coarse grass with trees flashing by it seemed that XF could never lift in time; only when almost at the end of the landing strip did she leave the ground. She laboured off slowly and it was with bated breath that I was able to snake through the narrow cutting in the trees, gradually coaxing a little more speed and sufficient altitude just before the gap closed in.

Concentration over for the time being, I felt the fever and sickness returning and decided to sacrifice performance some-what; instead of climbing up into the cloud to the best operating height, the Mew was kept below cloudbase and now sped over the sea on a constant-bearing course for Gao. We were heading, I could see, towards some dark shadows on the water which indicated either storms or low cloud. If ever there was a time when I dreaded bad flying conditions it was at this moment: I

s

didn't want to struggle with anything or anyone, my head was throbbing as if to split and every bout of shivering caused me to retch in a futile effort to be sick. When the dark clouds were reached, to be enveloped in heavy rain and mist was a bitter blow. Determined to keep below cloud, I kept the machine skimming the tops of the waves; the rain swept across the cockpit in a deluge which forced its way into every minute crevice, an uncomfortable trickle splashing on my knees and saturating my shorts. How scared I must have been during the night outwards on this sector not even to have noticed the wet that must have been pouring over me.

The stupor I was in was momentarily broken by the sight well to my right of a hill covered in dark green foliage, rising abruptly from the sea to disappear into the low, sweeping cloud above, I had completely forgotten about the Island of Fernando Po and cursed myself for such carelessness: just a little off course to the east and I might have struck it.

With the thought of more high ground ahead the nose of the machine was raised slightly; immediately we entered the wet, swirling mass of cloud and a steady climb to a safe height began. Levelling out at 8000 ft I found the machine bucking about all over the place through turbulence with heavy cloud and rain making small vortices over the wings. Another vomiting fit doubled me up and I fumbled clumsily for the iced orange-juice tube to swill my mouth out.

It is difficult to remember the conditions on this sector, but whatever it may be my misfortune to suffer in the future I sincerely hope I am not tortured mentally and physically to the same degree as during those few but endless hours. Although the cloud was darkened by its thickness the sun's heat was penetrating with such intensity that my left shoulder and side of my face felt as if resting against a radiator; I squirmed lower, seeking the limited protection from that part of the cockpit that shielded its fierceness. My head was swimming with a dizzy sickness, accentuated spasmodically by awful shivering fits.

Whether it was the cooped up position necessitated by the smallness of the modified cockpit or the constant nauseating retching I do not know, but I was suddenly attacked with acute pains of cramp in the stomach. Not knowing if the clouds were on the ground and I believe at that moment caring less, I closed the throttle and allowed the machine to dive at will whilst I struggled to straighten out my body as best I could in an effort to ease the pain. The Mew did not dive for long, it simply shot out of the cloud base a few hundred feet above a country that was rapidly changing from thick jungle to the less dense bush of Upper Nigeria.

It has often been said that one can get used to anything if one has to. There was nothing to relieve the writhing pain of the cramp, as there was no means of extending or stretching my body fully; that would have done so much to ease it. Furthermore there was not the remotest chance of landing anywhere within the next few hours. I bit my lips until the blood ran, to ward off the terrifying feeling when my head pounded and my eyes no longer saw the compass; I realised I was about to faint and forcing myself not to was an effort that I shall never forget. There was no doubt now that I had failed bitterly.

The crowning blow of all was that I suddenly realised I was lost. Before the attack of cramp I had worked a time fix to bring me over a fairly large tributary running off to the west from the River Niger; this would have given me an accurate estimate of ground speed and drift. The ETA for this point was ten minutes overdue and there was not the slightest sign of any river, or of anything else that might have indicated my position on the map.

On and on in an eternity of agony. The pain had reached such proportions and I had become so accustomed to it that it was ceasing to register so crucially in my dulled brain; I flew with a numbness that was easier by comparison. Force myself as I could, as the miles flashed by it was impossible to fix any position; an odd native track winding through the bush would raise a ray of hope and a supreme effort would be made to count up the time and work out the approximate distance covered. Remarkable as it may seem, I would find myself repeating some very simple little calculation for miles and miles beyond the assumed fix, over and over again without getting any nearer the answer.

Failure! It was a bitter pill to swallow. God knows I had tried hard enough. The sun was sinking gradually lower on the horizon, it wouldn't be long now.

Shall I fly on into darkness until the engine cuts through lack of petrol? No, little sense in that as by that time I would be miles in the desert with no hope of finding a landing ground . . . Could I pull off a landing on one of those winding bush tracks before it's too dark? No, that would be futile; this isn't the Vega and she'd break into a thousand pieces on striking a boulder . . . There's only one way if I'm going to save my skin— that's if I've got enough strength left to pull myself over the side . . .

My God, what a state to be in: if only I had spent a little more time at Cape Town this would never have happened . . . Poor old Dad, what a disappointment this will be to him. He'd understand how it happened, but there are thousands that won't.

If I could only think clearly just for five minutes . . . How could I be lost? I may at the worst moments have wandered a bit but most of the time I've managed to keep the needle spot on . . . If I had had just one check and could work out how far I should have come by now.

Sun's going down! Why, I should be at Gao by sunset and before that have run parallel up the Niger for 300 miles or more. That can mean only one thing, I'm either east or west of my true track . . . Let me see: going down, the drift was a little to the right, so if similar conditions have prevailed then I should now have drifted to the left . . . that would mean turning to the east . . . Well, it's no good throwing up the sponge and I can't be worse off; I'll turn 90 degrees to the east for a few minutes and see if anything turns up.

With little hope of picking out a definite fix I turned and flew due east over the endless world of rocks and bush below. The pain and disappointment was such that the disaster that was inevitable made little or no impression on me: it was a bad show and I should have taken the advice of those that knew better. I felt sorry for myself. Yes, I had made so many plans and now they had tumbled down like a pack of cards.

No! Oh no, it just couldn't be; it's too good to be true . . . Yes it is, there's no mistaking that width of water . . . Thank God.

Ahead glinted a slow, winding belt of dirty green water. The hunch had turned out right. Either I had drifted or wandered about thirty miles off course and had been running parallel for hundreds of miles just out of sight of the mighty river. Better still, I picked up an unmistakeable landmark against which on the map I had previously scribbled in an ETA from there to Gao in case I did not arrive before dark; pressing the stopwatch button I felt some relief in the knowledge that there was little distance to go before I should be able to get out of the cockpit that had virtually been a torture rack ever since I left Libreville.

Although my numbed brain was not aware of the fact the Mew was now making excellent time. I vaguely remember seeing dimly below a large cluster of mud dwellings float by, but as the stopwatch hand had not reached the assumed time of arrival I took no notice. In my normal senses I would fully have realised there was no place for scores of miles other than Gao. The time limit up and with nothing below but the snaking Niger and the monotonous sea of sand sparsely dotted with a few scrub bushes, it slowly dawned on me that I had overshot and that the place I had passed a few moments ago was actually Gao. I was too ill and tired to be angry with myself and, turning the machine round, dumbly wondered how I was going to land without damaging the machine.

I cannot remember how many attempts I had at landing, it may have been two, three or even more. I can only remember rushing over the awful aerodrome at a speed that seemed too fast and saying to myself: I must be careful. Plenty of time. If there is the slightest doubt have another shot.

I don't remember whether I taxied up to the hangar or whether the machine plunged to a standstill in the soft sand with the engine switched off and then later was pushed over, but I do remember slumping over the controls and waiting for someone to come along. Then, when no one lifted me out of the cockpit, I levered myself up and fell over the side—to be picked up by willing hands with somebody else forcing a horrid-tasting liquid to my lips.

26 ✵ Home!

SITTING ON a petrol drum surrounded by sympathetic
L'Armée de l'Air officers all offering advice, mostly in French,
made my efforts to concentrate more difficult. The original intention had been to leave immediately after refuelling, cross the
Sahara this time in the dark and land at Oran about midnight.
Obviously this was now out of the question: although I began to
feel somewhat better, especially with relief from the stomach
cramp, another few hours cooped up in the machine would only
bring on a recurrence which might even be worse. Also, in my
present mental state, unless I was lucky enough to hit off Oran
after a long night flight—and that would be too much to hope
for—how on earth did I expect to find that or any other aerodrome in the dark? I had prepared an alternative schedule in
case of just such an eventuality as this, but I felt that under the
present circumstances even that was extremely hazardous. It
would have meant taking off from Gao at midnight and landing
at Oran just before dawn, having the safety-valve of another
hour's supply of petrol should I fail to pick out the aerodrome in
the dark. There would still be this nerve-racking take-off here to
consider, and a long, lonely flight across that forbidding desert.
   I was sickened to death with flying and wished to goodness I
had never thought of such a trip. No! Record or not, I would
have a good night's rest and think about it tomorrow; my head
probably wouldn't ache so much then.
   Stumbling from the petrol drum I made my way towards the
little Citroen that had been so helpful last time. I knew it would
again take me to a place which could give me the only thing I
desired at that moment: perfect quiet, a comfortable bed and a

chance to close and rest these burning eyes. As I did so, I passed an officer who was attempting to take a photograph of the machine in the dim light and he gabbled excitedly in French, pointing to the civil ensign painted on the rudder: 'It is a flag to be proud of, Monsieur; but now the flag will be proud of you.' Pausing, I had almost forgotten the flag was there.

I suppose he's right, it is a flag to be proud of . . . By golly, yes, there's no finer flag in the world than the Union Jack . . . Dad will have one flying over Wings when I get home; yes, of course, he'll be waiting and praying for me right now. There will be many I hope waiting for me, and the longer I stay here the longer they'll wait.

I stumbled on, but instead of getting in the car I asked if they could bring me a bowl of cold water and procure the aid of a doctor: I intended leaving at midnight. A man returned with a large basin of water and a small rough towel, explaining that someone had gone to find a doctor and that he would see me over at the officers' quarters. I buried my face completely in the tepid water, splashing it over my head and shoulders and after a rub-down slowly filled up the machine with petrol and oil.

Fumbling through the work took ages longer than it should have done, but when at last it was completed I crawled into the car and we rushed over to the hut that served as the officers' quarters. I told the doctor how I felt and what I had already taken and after a moment's consideration he replied rapidly so that I did not understand, handing me a large celluloid-looking tablet which I assumed he meant me to swallow. Without much success I tried to eat a few mouthfuls of the food that my French friends had again prepared and then having made certain that they would call me at 11.30, I begged to be excused to go to my room, where I flopped on the bed hoping to get some rest and recuperate a bit.

I suppose I must have dozed but it seemed the very next minute that someone was shaking my shoulder trying to wake me. Stumbling out of bed I clutched at the side to stop falling over and seeing the canvas bowl of water I flung off my shirt and plunged my head into it, splashing the water recklessly over my back and shoulders. I remember chuckling to myself at the thought that here at least was one place that would not worry about soap-water stains on the carpet. There was a feeling of satisfaction in putting on the flannel slacks, polo jumper and leather jerkin again; something comforting and a little different, really the first sign that I was nearing home.

As I stepped from the long corridor to meet the bevy of officers who were waiting to see me off, once more an airman rushed up to the Commandant with a slip of paper; reading it, he turned to me and said, 'I am afraid the weather it is not good; we have report from Bidon 5 of strong wind and sandstorms.'

I spread out my long map on the table and he marked with pencil the area where the storms were reported to be, together with their direction and approximate strength. My practice had been not to allow for drift before flight unless there had been obvious indications of the necessity for it, but to make a mental note of where and when the drift was likely to be expected; then when it was possible to check position on a definite fix I would alter the course accordingly. I found this best for two reasons: I was very rarely in doubt as to whether I was left or right of my true course, as I should have been if I had made certain allowances on doubtful wind forecasts; and more often than not on very long flights in one direction drift would vary considerably and sometimes cancel out. Here however, with no landmark until Oran, I had to fly a good course; if I had to wait for the light of dawn to find myself I should not have sufficient petrol left to find an aerodrome to get down, and I certainly did not relish a forced landing in the Atlas Mountains.

So, carefully considering the belts of high wind on the map I worked out a flight plan, checking it several times. I saw that the pencil-marked course I had worked out ran at an alarming angle away from the true track, but being at last convinced though still apprehensive I folded up the map and hoped for the best.

Take-off from the sands of Gao: the same starlit haze, the tiny glimmer of hurricane lamps and the same awful moments before lurching to safety in the still sky of night.

To my intense relief the desert crossing was easy and might have been even pleasant had I felt in better health. The endless vastness of sand that might prove a land of hell in the heat of the day was now lost in the still, dark shadows, as if to gain what little coolness it could in preparing for the onslaught of another fiery day. A few lights and fires had blinked around Gao and then nothing: the twinkling stars, a waning moon, but below an unfathomable blackness. I had expected violent storms with blinding clouds of sand yet all was still. Although I was truly thankful, I wondered if I had attached too much importance to those French forecasts and had allowed too many degrees to the west for drift, but realising it was ridiculous even to attempt to assess conditions at 8000 ft in the black of night I determined to adhere to my calculated course.

With nothing to see and with but one course to follow my mind rested: I had enough petrol until daylight; my speed did not matter for the time being, as I could not check my position anyway. Hour after hour, occasionally moving the weight of my body from one side to the other to ease the cramped limbs, with the softly glowing chronometer slowly ticking off the miles.

With the time indicating that at least 1200 miles had been covered I began to fly through first wisps and then small banks of cloud, a heartening sight as it signified that the lifeless belt of wilderness was now being left behind. I felt elated, as although the trip had been cool and easy the sight of not a single light or fire for all those miles was disturbing to say the least. A few minutes before the ETA was due, as the night was still clear except for an odd bank of cloud; as I had been flying rather high I started to lose altitude in a fast, shallow dive. Feeling still a bit shaky and tired and also not wishing to deviate from course, as the clouds loomed up the machine was held in the same direction, plunging into the banks of dark grey mist to quickly penetrate them one by one.

I sleepily noticed a dark grey mass ahead, rather larger than most of the other cloudbanks and was about to plunge into it . . . With a start that literally kicked me into life like a flash of lightning and with a vertically banked turn that nearly blacked me out I swung away from that cloud. In the middle of it, saving me by seconds only, had sprung a flickering light: that cloud was part of the Atlas Mountains and the light I imagine was some arab or Berber camp fire.

The fright acted as a tonic; my head was clearer and I was definitely on the alert now as never before. Below was a black background partially covered in grey mist, a thin white line and dullness beyond indicated the Mediterranean and some distance to the west was a small cluster of glimmering lights, which I hastily made towards. Circling the lights several times convinced me that it was not Oran, but left me in a quandary: should I turn east or west? It was still too dark to pick up any roads or railways, and as the storms had not been encountered as was expected it was possible that I had really miscalculated for drift and come out hundreds of miles east of Oran. With this in mind I decided to turn west and fly along the coast.

Dawn began to break after travelling a few minutes along the rocky shore, and a village appeared. Butting up against it near the sea was a small level clearing, which on closer investigation disclosed a tiny white circle marked out on the ground. Somehow the place seemed vaguely familiar: where had I seen that aerodrome before? I had only once been along this part of the African coast and that was with Dad last year. Why! I remember it was on the way to Morocco . . . I quickly dived for the map and shining the torch over it was able to distinguish a small spot marked in pencil and the name Saye scribbled against it. I was going in the wrong direction.

Spinning round, I made off as fast as XF would go to Oran, which I now knew was only a few miles to the east. I had the doubtful satisfaction of knowing that when I had turned over those lights to strike out west I had been only eight miles from Oran; if it had not been for the mist I should most certainly have spotted Lake Negra, which almost adjoined the aerodrome.

The large muddy lake was decorated with flocks of colourful pink and white flamingo, that split into long floating waves like the branches of a cherry tree in full bloom as I swept over them. At the same time, a short distance ahead I saw the small wireless

masts of Oran aerodrome, a sight that instead of filling me with
rejoicing, reminded me of how I had hoodwinked the French
officials into believing that I was landing at Colomb Béchar for
the permits on the outward journey. I had now completed two
crossings of the Sahara and French Sudan and they had not
even seen the vital permits and papers that had taken so many
months to acquire. There was no doubt there would be some very
awkward questions asked: maybe they would detain me as had
happened with the Vega at Khartoum.

No, they can't do that! Once I have managed to get the Mew
filled up then wild horses won't hold me.

The sun was just rising above the horizon as XF came to rest
on the muddy surface of the large aerodrome for the second time
—and I sincerely hoped the last time on foreign soil for many
days to come. Little Boumati was frantically waving his arms as
the machine taxied slowly up to the sunken petrol tanks. Even
now I do not know whether he was waving to me or to the small
crowd that threatened to overwhelm him and his precious petrol.

The knowledge that this was the last time this tiring and
tedious refuelling procedure would have to be carried out, together with the invigoratingly clear air and bright sunshine,
did much to revive me—if I could only get rid of the headache.
With an effort I climbed out and helped Boumati to refuel. I
kept glancing around apprehensively, sure that at any moment
I should be pounced upon and the machine impounded.

I did not have to wait long: in the distance, running down the
control-tower steps so that he almost fell, I recognised my dread
of the moment, the uniformed figure who had asked for my
papers on the way out. I muttered to the already perspiring
Boumati to hurry more: if I could only get filled up and the
engine started he could whistle for his darned permits. I went on
pouring in the oil, cursing to myself at the slowness of the job,
ignoring everyone as if they did not exist; out of the corner of
my eye I saw the dreaded official waiting patiently to one side
with a book and pencil in his hands, as I had seen policemen do
many times when they had a sure case to take down.

The tank filled, caps and fairing tightened up, left no alternative for me than to climb down from the large petrol drums and face the music. To my intense amazement the gendarme sidled up to me almost reverently and apologised humbly for intruding at such a time—but could I possibly spare a moment to sign his autograph book? Not a word about those permits that had been the cause of so much anxiety. I could scarcely believe my own ears and gave an audible sigh of relief; he took it to be exasperation, and when I scribbled across his book he muttered verbose thanks and made a hasty retreat into the crowd.

A kind Moroccan, holding my arm, persuaded me to pause and sip a cup of steaming black coffee. The stimulating comfort of the bitter hot liquid going down my dry throat did much to clear my throbbing head. As I rested against the Shell refuelling steps gaining a brief respite, a man riding a bicycle rushed up to me and jabbered away in French so fast that my numbed brain could only interpret one word—fog. I looked questioningly at the small, sympathetic group gathered around me and in good English someone said, 'This man is from the meteorological office. You must delay your start as the whole of Northern France and Southern England is under thick fog!'

I had foolishly and optimistically thought the flight as good as over if I could only hang on for another six or seven hours. This surely was the cruellest blow of all. I paused as I forced my tired brain to accept this unexpected situation and then, turning, said I was grateful for the information but that I intended leaving immediately. This time as a courteous gesture I was requested to use the one and only tarmac runway at Oran which had been cleared of equipment and other repair materials specially for the occasion.

The Mew seemed to leap over the smooth surface in one of the most comfortable and easy take-offs she had experienced for some time. Striking out across the Mediterranean in the glorious morning sunshine somehow made it seem impossible that fog could exist anywhere. Visibility was perfectly clear, with the Balearic Islands listlessly below in the calm blue water some distance away; it made me wonder whether Franco's fighters were out on a dawn patrol and would collect me as part of the morning bag! Majorca passed safely and I relaxed as the long, wide valley of the Rhône came into view stretching miles away out of sight.

I was just condemning the French for the inaccuracy of their weather reports and congratulating myself for not giving way to the luxury of a short rest at Oran with fog as the excuse, when, as far north as I could see, was an ominous change in the colour of the cloudless sky. In minutes the tranquillity of the scene had changed and I was jogged out of my restful stupor to see cold grey snow cloud ahead sweeping down to ground level in whirling masses that threatened worse to come.

The ground disappeared. I quickly noted an accurate fix on the map and jotted down my time. A nasty kick as I entered the turbulent snowstorm reminded me painfully that I was not home yet. I was surprised and shocked by the violence of the storm and also the amount of ice that was rapidly accumulating.

I was alarmed. I had no chance of flying under the weather. If I was to get above, I must start climbing before I collected too much ice, but I was not at all confident that my physical condition at that moment would permit it. Yet I had made a promise to myself before the Cape attempt had ever started that I would not turn back and with the goal now so close the question of doing anything other than pressing on never entered my head.

I was soon aware that I had no chance of climbing above the weather: the Mew was struggling to stay in the air as snowflakes swirled and streaked over the wings and cockpit. The screen froze solid and disturbing amounts of ice formed on the leading edge of the wings.

Just when I realised I could not climb out of trouble I felt something warm gush over my face and suddenly I was covered in blood. The gory mess splashed on to my flannels, maps and knee-pad. My nose and mouth filled and as I spat it out I looked around for something to stem the flow. I could find nothing, and in my utterly despondent mental and physical condition I weakly rubbed the mess away from my face with a bare hand.

I accepted within myself that I was not going to make it and that the gallant little Mew Gull would come to a final rest on the soil of France—then without warning we seemed to burst out of cloud and turbulence into clear calm air and below as far as the eye could see lay a thick grey layer of fog. The French had been right after all.

Even though I was thousands of feet above I knew enough to realise I could not penetrate the murk below. I looked dully at the large chronometer on the instrument panel and calculated with a bitterness I have rarely felt that there was little over an hour to my destination, Gravesend. Now too tired and completely worn out to worry about the consequences I determinedly made up my mind to continue exactly on the compass course I had previously worked out, until my time showed 1345 hrs. This was my ETA for Gravesend and at that precise moment I would attempt to get down—how, I did not know.

I spotted the Eiffel Tower peeping above the fog and started picking dried blood from my face in a gesture of near resignation . . . Suddenly there unbelievably, as if cut with a knife, was the end of the fog! And beyond it the Channel!

Cold and grey it was, threshing in its winter garb, but no sight to me before or since has ever been more welcome.

Never in my whole life had I been so near complete physical and mental exhaustion as the faint shadow of the coastline came into view. I had clutched at the straw of hope as a matter of survival when my chances had indeed seemed slim, but the adrenalin must have fed my tired nerves and I had been kept alert enough to do my job and work out the navigational problems. Now with the land of my birth in sight the urge to sink back and rest my aching head and body was overwhelming. My emotions surged back and forth and at times came very near the surface as I struggled with what little self-discipline remained to bring them under control. My mouth was parchment dry and caked in blood and I had long ceased picking away at the clots. I am not a religious man but I croaked a few words of prayer to be able to hang on.

We sped across the clean, golden sea-washed shore of England

and habit dictated that I check my time and speed, but as I made the effort I realised it was beyond me. I must remain conscious and hope to God that the compass course I had previously set would take me to Gravesend. I struggled to move and ease my aching thighs and buttocks, numb from hours on the hard floor which the thin rubber mat had done little to alleviate, and tried to regain some circulation in readiness for the landing which must soon take place. As I bent down and at the same time adjusted the petrol-tank control-cock the strain was too much and my eyes went blurred and out of focus. I slumped back and as I did so inadvertently caught the control-column, pitching the aircraft sharply and suddenly so that the movement momentarily blacked me out. I groped to regain control and if there had been anything on which I could have put down immediately below I should have gone in for a landing, whatever the consequences.

Was I going to make it? I thought I was over Kent but was not at all sure; I only knew that I must not cross the large river as I willed myself to keep the compass on a northerly course. I was allowing the machine to lose height at maximum speed in an almost fanatical effort to reach the sanctuary of Gravesend. Suddenly there in front of me were some tall chimneys and white storage tanks along a bold stretch of water—the Thames—and I knew that Gravesend aerodrome must be immediately beneath me.

Take care—this could make or mar the whole flight. A bad landing now in front of my father and all those people!

I gently eased round in a shallow-left-hand turn, conscious as I did so of an unfamiliar sea of faces on the ground below. I made the last circuit to bring me on to a westerly bearing so that I could use the longest part of the airfield nearest to the southern boundary. I had to make it at the first attempt; if I overshot I doubted my ability to go through it all again. The Mew crossed the boundary at just the right height and I gently brought the throttle right back; the little machine sank neatly on to the smooth grass and in my bemused state I was not sure that we had actually landed.

I paused as the aircraft came to a standstill, nearly switching

30 Resetting chronometer before take-off at Wingfield for return
31 Dad displays his usual confidence awaiting XF at Gravesend

32 Jack Cross lifts A.H. from cockpit whilst shocked Courtney, Ricketts and
    Crouch look on
33 Civic reception back home in Lincolnshire, 1939

off the engine there and then, but I became vaguely aware of a crowd waving hands and papers over to my right. I dearly wanted to remain where I was and let them come to me but some instinct or force of habit urged me to move towards them. I opened up the engine slowly and was aware of eager hands grabbing both wingtips and someone clamouring for the coupé top to be unfastened. There seemed to be an abrupt pause in the noisy welcome and then some silence as I failed to move from the cockpit. Suddenly there was lively action: willing hands and arms unbuckled my tight Sutton harness, unclipped the Irvin parachute, and dragged me from the cockpit as I sank into oblivion.

T

27 ✳ Farewell to the Mew

I CAME AWAKE late the following morning. I was in a comfortable bed, the ceiling seemed unfamiliar and light was striking through the thin curtains of a small window. For a moment I thought I was still in Africa but as I looked, drawing back the curtains, there was frost on the ground, the sun was watery and without power and the air felt bitterly cold as I leapt back into the warm bed. I was in the Cross's cottage once again and the realisation of what had passed during the last few days and nights began to crystallise in my mind. I should have been elated but the anticipated exultation was not forthcoming; instead I felt subdued and strangely humble. Of course I was proud of what had been achieved, the return from Cape Town would put the magnificent little Mew Gull in a class of its own. She had broken far more than ordinary class records and the real accolades must surely go to Edgar Percival, the designer and constructor, but with pride of place to Jack Cross whose talents and superb workmanship had lifted the little aircraft to heights in speed and distance not thought possible.

My own contribution? I thought sadly of Stan Halse—he had strived as much as I and with as much competence, he had given of his best but fate had been against him: he of all pilots would know what it was like to fly the little Mew over Africa for days and nights. We had beaten the Comet home by 18 hours, smashed the existing solo record by 57 hours and reduced the Comet's overall time there and back by 31 hours. It was in fact the quickest any man, woman or machine had ever been to the Cape and back. I felt sorry for my old friend Clouston; I rated Clou as amongst the finest half dozen pilots in the world. I knew that notwithstanding his natural disappointment at the loss of his own records, his integrity and clear-minded judgement would in no way impair his expert evaluation of the flight. He like Halse knew Africa and the challenge to any aircraft that trifled with its immense size and changing moods.

What had really been achieved? In one sense not very much, in another probably a very great deal. My flight was not going to convince anyone that passengers or freight could move any faster to the Cape and back. It did not persuade that the western route over Africa was any better than the eastern. Many theorists and enthusiasts would perhaps claim that there were other aircraft that could do as well. I had heard that our fastest and latest fighter the Spitfire with a top speed of 370 mph could do better. I knew that such talk was nonsense: true, the Spitfire on its own terms as a fighter could easily outclass XF but by the same token XF outclassed the Spitfire as a long-distance racer.

As I reflected in the peace and warmth of my bed, no one was more aware than I that this flight should, by all normal circumstances, have failed not once but several times, possibly in disaster. I was stirred from my sombre thoughts by the door opening suddenly and Dad with Jack entering the room in high spirits to throw a batch of national newspapers on to the bed remarking laconically, 'Well, you've arrived.' Glancing at the headlines in bold print I coloured with embarrassment. Here was an awful amount of hair-raising drama connected with the flight, much of it far removed from the truth, particularly the themes of my 'wounded head' and a climb to 18,000 ft in an effort to rise above the storm over France. As I had not spoken to a soul concerning any aspect of the flight—indeed I was in no fit state to do so—I looked at Dad and Jack suspiciously. Jack lowered his head, went red in the face and sheepishly mumbled, 'The reporters pressed me to such an extent I had to tell them something.' They then told me what had happened after my landing, and of much of it I was only vaguely aware.

News of my flight over Africa had been almost negligible; occasional uninformative wireless exchanges passed by Reuters from Mossamedes over ship's radio; and Oran had sent a message in morse that had not proved very helpful. Those waiting at Gravesend had done so in an atmosphere tense with anticipation. My father and a few close friends, knowing my dislike of crowds and guessing I should be exhausted, had had plenty of time to plan a scheme that would get me away rapidly from the press, cameras, microphones and the crowd that had somehow got hold of the news and was pouring on to the aerodrome. It proved to be the main amusement of the day.

Dad said my landing was done in a manner that gave no cause for concern and the official reception committee in front of a boisterous and excited throng were getting all prepared for a rousing welcome. The sight of blood all over the cockpit and the performance as they struggled to lift me out had a very dampening effect upon the crowd and someone shouted for a doctor. Apparently he arrived just as the mayor was endeavouring to get out his carefully prepared speech in front of a battery of cameras and microphones, with other dignitaries and officials in support. When the doctor saw my condition he brushed them aside and carried me with the aid of friends to a large car which in no time at all swept out of the aerodrome gates. The hypnotised crowd, seeing me disappear, suddenly burst into a feverish activity and followed. As they drove their cars in line to go through the narrow gate a friend, who had planned the ruse with my father, suddenly jammed on the brakes of his heavy car to stop, blocking the exit. Pandemonium broke loose: cars piled up behind with irate press-men and photographers clambering out to demand what the hell was going on. My friend, after a comic charade, said more calmly than he felt, 'There's nothing I can do; for some reason my brakes have jammed on.' By this time there were so many surrounding the offending obstacle that with little effort the car was grasped by dozens of forceful hands and literally carried out of the way. By this time the doctor's car was well out of view. I remember being lowered into a deep bath of hot foamy water, someone sponging me down gently to remove the oil and crusted blood, and the doctor probing and checking as he examined me with the diagnosis that there was nothing wrong that a good rest and sleep would not cure.

I felt surprisingly well that morning and after taking my time dressing and enjoying a hearty breakfast I went along with Dad to see how my faithful steed had fared. Ducking through the little trap door into the large hangars revealed XF stripped of all her cowlings and almost hidden by numerous individuals from various editorial staffs, some studying the intricacies of the installation, a few painting, two carefully drawing on upright easels and many taking flashlight photographs. Amongst them was my old friend Bradbrooke, who had been relishing the job of writing up the story in the *Aeroplane*; but the Editor, C. G. Grey, had undertaken the duty himself, so he was here purely to cover the technical side of the flight. I said, 'Would you like to fly the Mew before it is stripped of all the long-distance equipment?' He replied, 'Would I just! I never dreamt you would allow anyone to fly it.' He was the only person other than myself who flew G-AEXF in its full record-breaking configuration.* The moment I was seen to enter the hangar I was literally pounced upon and my head soon began to spin as question after question was fired at me; then the telephone rang and I clutched at this way of retreat. But there was to be no peace. By the time the day had ended I had not had one second to myself; no chance to stop talking and think how to deal with the avalanche of invitations, offers, interviews and propositions that I was not at all happy or sure about.

With this sudden tremendous pressure of publicity and the demands upon me personally, I paused to consider what it was all about, and my conclusions may have been contrary to the thoughts of many of my friends. I would be a hyprocrite if I said the world in which I found myself did not excite, fascinate and flatter me: offer of a suite in one of London's best hotels, promptly turned down; broadcasts on home, British Overseas and foreign; television interviews and programmes; luncheons, dinners, lectures, first nights and sporting events all over the country. It was not long before this way of life began to pall: the constant committal to appointments and engagements revolving around a subject that I was heartily becoming sick of coupled

---

* For Bradbrooke's account, see p. 304.

with the fact that I was rarely able to be myself. In addition telegrams, articles, requests and letters by the sackful continued to pour in—one from remote Alaska addressed in the rough hand of an Eskimo 'Alex Henshaw, Pilot, England'—they all had to be answered and dealt with. Dad could see the effect all this was having, that I was irritable, tired and thoroughly fed up with the whole business, so brushing protests aside he said, 'We're going home.'

I did not realise until we had turned up the drive just how much I had missed it all. I saw Ranger and Spitfire with their heads hanging over the stable door and shouting as I passed; Ranger gave me a whinny of recognition whilst Tony hearing the car came bounding from his kennel barking and whining with uncontrollable excitement. But the phone was ringing as I entered the hall and when I glanced through an open door my breath was taken away by the sight of piles of mail with which I would have to deal. I also was aware that I had little time to spare as in a few hours I was due at the civic reception and banquet for which the local authority had so patiently waited my return. That morning the *Daily Express* had published an article showing that I was now preparing for an attempt on the Australia and New Zealand records with a special machine of new design now under construction, a single-seater of astounding performance and unique in that it would be flown from the prone position. I groaned inwardly; whilst there was some truth in the article very little of the groundwork had yet been covered and I knew it would set in motion a deluge of enquiries that, at that moment, I could have done without.

The next morning I crawled out of bed and after a cup of tea and two aspirins started the daunting task of going through the most important bundles of mail. The night before had been a little more demanding upon my reserves than usual. It was only to be expected that local people would want to show their enthusiasm and this they did without inhibitions. The children had already collected a school holiday from the event and now it was over to the business-men, officials and local and county dignitaries together with any others who had managed to buy, beg or wangle a ticket. The press, cameras and microphones were set up in mass array and between this and the suppressed excitement of the official representatives and the wild enthusiasm outside in the street below I was called constantly through to the open verandah to wave to a swaying sea of faces. I knew so many that, tired as I was, it would have been churlish not to have entered fully into the atmosphere of a small town letting itself rip. I was also not unaware that I was shortly to be presented with a beautiful solid silver bowl of exquisite design, the cost of which had put up the rates.

As I waded through the correspondence I began to realise just how many traps and pitfalls there were. Each day seemed busier than the last so that I was rushing around, bolting my food and at the same time not able to concentrate on the things that mattered. I hoped the pressures and publicity of the Cape flight would die down a little, but if anything it all seemed to get worse. Awaiting me was an invitation to stay with the Earl of Romney; an address to be given to the Civil Air Guard; another to the RAF; an invitation from the Earl of March for the opening of a new aerodrome; a long television series in Oxford Street sponsored by Selfridges, with top sportsmen and artists of the day; lunch with Lord Derby and the West Indies cricket team; BBC programme for Kings of Sport; golf match in aid of charity with top international personalities, etc., etc.

The Mew had been dismantled and re-assembled for display in Littlewoods; there was a large window of maps and photographs in the AA centre; and two flying films in leading cinemas for which I was invited to the premiere. I was never able to sneak away into a quiet corner of London without someone putting a finger on me.

The Australia-New Zealand flight planning was more difficult than I had first imagined. Jack Cross was dealing with the problems related to the construction of a new machine whilst I struggled with the complexities of planning. I was anxious to use the great-circle route which was at that time unknown and passed over some wild country. It had the advantage of reducing the distance by some 500 miles but took one across Russia to a point near Lake Balkhash, flanking the Himalayas and passing through Manchuria near the Gobi desert; it touched the Philipines and would strike Australia at the Gulf of Carpenteria. The whole concept excited me and I was looking forward to the survey flight as soon as the permits could be approved through Russia and Manchuria. Whilst XF, given good fortune, would make light work of the solo records to Australia, I was not too sure how I would stand up to it over the distance competing against the Comet, which had the advantage of two pilots, if I chose to use the normal route via the Persian Gulf and Singapore. Whilst the great-circle route was shorter, the enormous height of some of the mountain ranges and the vast distances over un-mapped terrain had made me realise that I was really asking too much of my faithful little machine and that I must concentrate with Jack and produce something more equal to the task ahead. With so much happening on such a bewildering scale it is per-haps understandable that I gave little thought to the racing calendar.

Jack was bubbling with excitement about his negotiations with an American aluminium organisation to construct the new record-breaking machine. It was of course to be made almost entirely of aluminium, would have four engines and a long thin fuselage in which I was to fly the machine from the prone position. But it was only at the talking stage. As the glorious summer rolled on, the only dark clouds for me were the ominous signs of what might come out of Germany. I had so many friends of long standing over there that I could not really believe they would be crazy enough to listen to the rantings of a politician who would if he persisted plunge the whole of Europe into war.

The largest meeting of the year 1939 for aviators was the official opening of Derby Airport. Bill Courtney had organised the whole affair and had obtained splendid publicity. The airport was packed with private, industrial and service personalities, and aircraft of every sort and size crowded the ground. I was billed in the elaborate gold-leaf programme as 'Young England' and felt more than a little embarrassed waiting near XF for my turn to demonstrate as Bill gave a detailed run-down over the microphone of my entire life in aviation. As I looked around, there seemed to be a subtle change in the normal flying meeting and the gaiety that usually prevailed: there were serious undertones to every lighthearted conversation and, all around, the new military machines which we had not seen before caused more than a casual interest. Just then Mutt Summers was on his approach with the Vickers-Armstrongs Wellington; to our unaccustomed eyes it looked enormous and as it flattened out for the touchdown over the top of the Mew I wondered what it must be like to fly something so large, ten times as powerful as anything I had flown so far. Dick Reynell then burst over the airfield like a clap of thunder in the Hawker Hurricane. It took my breath away as he rocketed up with two-and-a-half perfectly executed vertical rolls and we all ducked involuntarily as he pulled out from the following dive, leaving a plume of orange flame yards long as he rolled away low and out of sight.

This was one aspect of flying I had not at that time yet experienced and which I longed more than anything else to be associated with: the superb artistry I had just seen performed by Dick Reynell. But my real dream was to get my hands on another aircraft, and I had only ever been close to the remarkable machine once. In February I had flown into Waltham, near Grimsby, for a civic ceremony and as I pushed the Mew Gull inside the huge hangar, there in all the beauty of its classic lines was the Mark I Supermarine Spitfire. When Roger Frogley who was helping me said the pilot had got himself lost flying above cloud from Hornchurch, I could not help climbing into the cockpit and absorbing the feel of the machine. It felt as large as a barn after the Mew. I was fascinated with the enormous power, the lethal punch it carried and the thought of flying such an obvious thoroughbred above the clouds over twice as high as I had ever been in my life; I think I would have done almost anything at that moment to have taken it out of the hangar and climb way out into the blue sky. I reluctantly stepped down from the machine and looked back as I slowly walked towards the car. Mechanics were carefully closing one of the large doors in front of the two machines. I had a last glimpse of the diminutive white Mew and by its side the superb lines of that powerful fighting machine.

Little did I know it as I envied Dick Reynell on that bright August day at Derby but in months he was to be killed fighting in the machine he had flown so impressively and my own days with XF were almost done. The chance meeting at Waltham had foretold my future: I was not to go forward with my beloved XF, but for six long years come hail or sunshine with its stable companion of a night, the Supermarine Spitfire, the finest fighting aircraft in the world.

I had got to know XF as well as it is possible to know any aircraft in all its moods and in all conditions; I had come to love that true partnership. If anyone had told me then that I would live, and sometimes almost die, with another machine; that I would climb it, dive it and searchingly test it day after day and that I would come to know it as I had never known XF, I would not have believed them. How was I to know that within a few short weeks those dark clouds way out on the horizon were to burst with a deluge that was to stain the fields of the world?

✳ The Mew Gull today

TODAY it is not difficult to design an aeroplane to exceed 200 mph on 200 hp. Forty years ago it was more difficult but by no means impossible, as has been proved on numerous occasions. The fastest machine that ever I raced against, horsepower for horse-power, was the De Havilland Technical College TK4. It was even smaller than the Percival Mew Gull and the sacrifices that were made to achieve speed no doubt contributed to the death of its pilot in the early stages of its flying.

When the three Mew Gulls failed in the South Africa race of 1936, this established serious doubts on the suitability of such a machine for a contest of this nature, particularly when the race was won by the slower and larger Percival Vega Gull. And remember that the heroic Stan Halse crashed his Mew Gull through fatigue when he still had 1600 miles to go to Cape Town, let alone fly back to England. But my experiences with G-AEXF convinced me that here was a thoroughbred fully capable of competing against any aircraft in the world. Jack Cross had proved his capabilities in preparing racing aircraft, and in particular by the rebuilding of the Comet G-ACSS for long-distance record-breaking; and I formed a partnership with him to develop and draw the utmost from this little machine. The results which I have summarised between pages 294 and 301 speak for themselves.

I now realise the extent to which I abused my willing mount. It is one thing to fly a small, fragile high-performance racer and take off in clear conditions lightly loaded from a smooth firm runway with the engine and airframe meticulously maintained. It is demanding almost the impossible to overload a highly tuned

and intricately modified racing aircraft with so much petrol and
oil on board that the C of G is beyond the normal aft limitations
and then to operate it from rough, unmarked landing strips at
night in temperatures that are unknown in Europe. The Mew
Gull rose to every demand made upon her. And still, over forty
years later, neither the London-Cape-London record nor any of
the solo records have been broken. I would challenge any pilot
to fly any aircraft in the world with no more than 200 hp to the
Cape and back in less time than did XF in 1939.

The true evaluation of an aircraft's qualities or performance
are not always easy to determine and will, inevitably, produce
strong and contentious arguments amongst the knowledgeable.
As I have already said, with 200 hp it is possible to design a
faster racing machine than the Mew Gull and if one were
prepared to lower the priorities of safety, stability, range and
reliability and use only recognised airports then the task was not
too difficult then and is easier now. It is also possible to produce—
and in fact has been done many times—a machine with a better
range and pay-load. It is also comparatively easy to produce an
aeroplane that can fly in adverse weather conditions and do so
at night. The Mew Gull was outstanding in that it had all these
qualities superbly balanced.

Let it never be forgotten that it was Captain Edgar Percival's
brilliant original design that made the Cape Records possible.
Edgar Percival had the foresight, judgement and ability to choose
a particular design of low wing as his base. As I told him, many
times I have been hurtling down a hill in extremely turbulent
conditions racing the Mew to the finishing line when the machine
has trembled from nose to tail and I have been very conscious
that but for the exactitude of stressing, the perfection in design
and the first-class workmanship there might well have been
structural failures.

Jack and I both felt afterwards we could have obtained
greater speeds from XF, but there would have had to be sacrifices
in other directions, and as the King's Cup was first in line this
was a risk and extravagance we could not afford. Even so, few
know that at sea level the tiny Percival Mew Gull was consider-

ably faster than the Hawker Hurricane fighter. Admittedly the Hurricane, like the Spitfire, was a weapon of war carrying a very formidable fire-power and considerable weight to absorb the higher stress loads and other armament, but it also had five times the horse-power of the Mew. The Mew Gull also gave its best power at sea level whereas both the Hurricane and the Spitfire were at their best at an altitude above the Mew's absolute ceiling. In preparation for the King's Cup and on a freezing but calm winter's morning in 1937, XF was flown over a timed stretch of the Thames estuary. Fitted by Jack Cross's team with the superbly tuned DH Gipsy 'R' engine, special high-compression pistons and a glittering Ratier electrical variable-pitch propellor, it flashed across the short course at a speed exceeding 270 mph before overheating thrust-bearings necessitated a quick landing. As I recollect, nearly two years later I was to test my first Spitfire over the choppy waters of the Solent and at full power the maximum indicated speed was 287 mph.

I left G-AEXF at Lyon in the summer of 1939, thinking I would never see it again. Hugh Scrope with determination and not a little courage tracked it down after the war and brought it back to England. The impact upon me when Hugh flew G-AEXF up to Lincolnshire was such that no words could describe my feelings after so many years. During Hugh's ownership it retained the modified shape that has put it in the ranks of famous aircraft. When it passed out of his hands. to my sorrow and shame it suffered the indignity of alterations so crude and disfiguring that I cursed myself for not putting the pressures of my own business commitments to one side and taking it once again into my care. Coupled with the deplorable further modifications was a marked deterioration in its performance and finally when this willing little horse was being flogged to death it crashed and was left to die. I made one attempt to resurrect the remains, but when I saw the rotting debris, with both wings sawn in half and its ownership already subject to a litigation fight, I sadly and reluctantly said farewell forever.

Then by persistent and determined efforts two young men acquired what was left of G-AEXF and started the mammoth task of reconstruction. Tom Storey and Martin Barraclough must be given all the credit for this laudable feat and part of the history of the British light aeroplane will forever be on display as a result of their efforts: they reconstructed the entire machine, and in the summer of 1978 I was able to see it fly once again with the most fitting atmosphere of Old Warden for its debut. For practical and licensing requirements, to say nothing of the increased hazards of flying the Essex Aero version, G-AEXF has been completed in its original form as first produced at Luton, with that grace and smoothness for which credit must always be given to Edgar Percival. But for me as I watch my old friend flying again there is another picture in my mind: the spur-type spats, the low, almost lethal-looking lines of the reduced cockpit, and the beautifully designed and fabricated spinner and air-intake that brought it supremacy in the annals of British light aircraft history.

✳ *Percival Mew Gull G-AEXF*

✳ *Percival Mew Gull G-AEXF*

There were in all only six Mew Gulls ever constructed

Formerly ZS-AHM   Entrant in the 1936 Schlesinger race to Johannesburg
Fitted with Gipsy Six Series II engine
Ratier electrical V/P propeller

Purchased by Alex Henshaw April 1937
Fitted with Gipsy Six Series I engine 200 hp
Fairey Reid metal propeller

Dimensions and performance

Length 20 ft 3 in.   Height 6 ft 10 in.   Span 24 ft 9 in.   Wing area 88 sq. ft.   All-up wt 1850 lb

Maximum speed at sea-level 220 mph   Climb 1400 ft/min.
Cruising speed 200 mph

Note: The side views on the following pages are not works drawings.

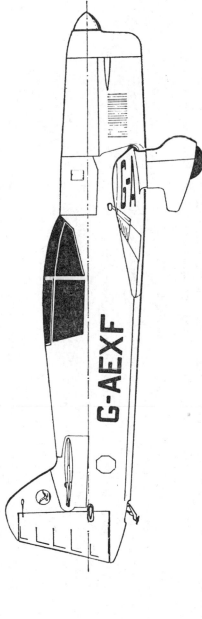

G-AEXF

Competitions and events in 1937

May 15	Winner of arrival competition Cardiff Airport		
29	I.O.M. Race	Fastest time 225·9 mph	
31	Manx Derby	Position 4th	Fastest time 213 mph
July 3	Newcastle race	Position 3rd	Speed 210·5 mph
10	Heston–Cardiff race	Position 2nd	Fastest time 204 mph
24	Plymouth race	Position 6th	Fastest time prize 208 mph
31	Folkestone Aero Trophy	Trophy Winner	Fastest time 210 mph
Aug 21	Isle of Thanet Race	Position 3rd	Speed 207 mph
28	Wakefield International Trophy	Position 4th	Fastest time 208 mph
Sept 11	King's Cup race	Force-landed Stoke-on-Trent engine failure	

Data of G-AEXF with Gipsy Six 'R' engine prepared for King's Cup Race 1938

Length 21 ft. 11 in.   Height 6 ft 6 in.   Span 24 ft 9 in.   Wing area 88 sq. ft.   All-up wt 2125 lb

Maximum speed at sea-level over 270 mph   Initial climb over 1800 ft/min.

Cruising speed 240 mph at 7000 ft

Some of the modifications made during 1937/1938 by Essex Aero Ltd

1   Gipsy Six 'R' engine fitted. Nominal hp 225, compression ratio 6·5:1.
2   Extension to crankshaft. Machined from S.81 steel treated to give 55 tons UTS.
3   Specially spun larger and longer spinner fitted, and cowls adapted.
4   Special air-intake of Essex Aero design, induction manifold partly re-routed.
5   Machine fastest with Ratier airscrew which had to be changed for 2-pitch De Havilland type to comply
    with King's Cup race rules.
6   Pitot-head and control mass-balance weights streamlined.
7   Smaller re-designed wheel-spats fitted.
8   Essex Aero designed spring-steel scale fairings to wheels and spats.
9   Smaller wheels and tyres fitted.
10 All filler caps made with flush lock fittings. 100-octane distilled fuel.
11 One-piece Perspex screen specially moulded.
12 Cabin roof lowered 4 in. to fit pilot's head.
13 Fuselage top-decking lowered to fit pilot.
14 Tail-skid re-designed, and streamlined.
15 Bottom fuselage decking re-shaped.
16 Chassis oleo-legs redesigned and strapped up with high-tensile cable.
17 Blind-flying venturi designed to swivel in and out of cockpit.
18 Seat removed and replaced with sorbo pad to allow further lowering of cabin roof and fuselage top-decking.
19 C of G moved forward with packing at pilot's back.

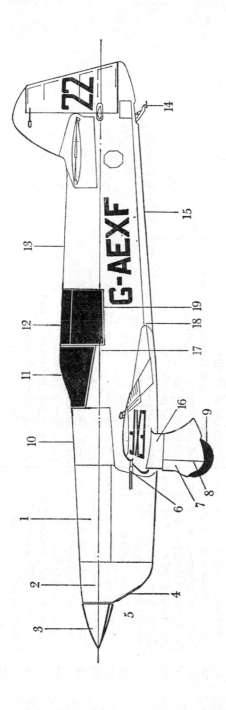

Competitions in 1938

June	24	Hatfield–Speke	Fastest time 250·25 mph	
	25	Speke–Ronaldsway I.O.M. Race	Position 2nd	Fastest time 247 mph
		Manx Air Derby	Fastest time 239 mph	
July	2	King's Cup race	Position 1st	Fastest time 236·25 mph
	3	Folkestone Aero Trophy	Position 6th	Fastest time 231 mph

Data of G-AEXF with Gipsy Six Series II engine prepared for Cape records

Modifications made during 1938/1939 by Essex Aero Ltd

Items 4–15, and 18 listed on p. 296 were retained for the Cape record attempt. In addition the following work was done:

20 Sigmund vacuum pump replaced venturi tube.
21 Gipsy Six Series II engine replaced the 'R'. Nominal hp 205.
22 Oil capacity and cooling increased by special cowling saddle-tank.
23 Special filler funnel which screwed into head of saddle-tank.
24 All petrol tank filler points sealed to prevent over-spill and fumes.
25 Retractable navigation light fitted fuselage top aft of pilot.
26 Airscrew constant speed unit fitted with control welded to cockpit tank.
27 Main fuselage petrol tank enlarged and extended into cockpit.
28 Emergency cockpit petrol tank constructed over pilot's legs.
29 Instrument panel moved as near pilot's face as practicable.
30 Chronometer; ASI; revcounter; sensitive altimeter; oil-pressure gauge; Sperry blind-flying panel.
31 Large Huson P4 compass fitted on special bracket near pilot.
32 Two soup vacuum-flasks fitted with suction tubes.
33 One bag fitted for apples, sweets and milk tablets.
34 Urinating funnel fitted with atmosphere vent.
35 Cockpit air-vent fitted providing warm air to all tanks in ice conditions.
36 Recess built into fuselage to take specially shaped parachute.
37 6·35-mm calibre automatic sewn into parachute harness.
38 Wireless transmitter carried for ground use only in Sahara emergency.
39 Medicine bag fitted containing quinine, benzedrine and aspirin.
40 Locker for logbook, passport, maps and messages.
41 Sun curtains fitted.
42 Flashlamp in lieu of cockpit lighting.
43 British Ensign.
44 Alteration to airscrew blades.

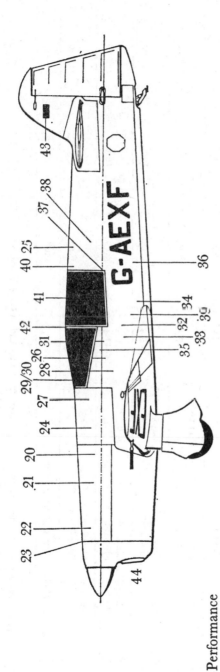

Performance

Maximum speed at sea-level: 247 mph
Cruising speed at 7000 ft: 235 mph
All-up weight increased from 2125 lb to 2350 lb extending C of G beyond aft limits for which a special category certificate was obtained.

Range approximately 2000 statute miles

Competitions in 1939

Feb 5/9   Not only were all Cape Town-and-return records broken but also those for every stage en route. The England–Cape Town–/England is still in 1980 an all-time record for any aircraft. The solo records remain to this day.

May 27   Hatfield–I.O.M. Race   Position 2nd   Speed 247·5 mph

THE CAPE RECORDS

Speeds and times for the flight Gravesend to Cape Town, February 1939

February	Stages	Take-off GMT time	Landing GMT time	Hours in air	Distance stat. miles	Average speed mph
5th 5th	Gravesend Oran	3.35	c. 10.05	6.30	1236	190·15
5th 5th	Oran Gao	c. 11.00	c. 17.15	6.15	1367	218·72
5th 6th	Gao Libreville	23.30	c. 5.45	6.15	1325	212·00
6th 6th	Libreville Mossamedes	c. 6.30	c. 11.45	5.15	1094	208·38
6th 6th	Mossamedes Cape Town	c. 12.45	18.58	6.13	1355	217·96
	Total elapsed time 39 hrs 23 mins.			30.28	6377	209·44

This was the fastest time for any aircraft or crew from England to Cape Town.
It reduced the existing solo record by 39 hours and 3 minutes.

Speeds and times for the flight Cape Town to Gravesend, February 1939

February	Stages	Take-off GMT time	Landing GMT time	Hours in air	Distance stat. miles	Average speed mph
7th 8th	Cape Town Mossamedes	22.15	c. 5.00	6.45	1355	200·74
8th 8th	Mossamedes Libreville	c. 5.45	c. 11.00	5.15	1094	208·38
8th 8th	Libreville Gao	c. 11.30	c. 17.45	6.15	1325	212·00
8th 9th	Gao Oran	23.45	c. 6.30	6.45	1367	200·40
9th 9th	Oran Gravesend	c. 8.00	13.51	5.51	1236	211·28
	Total elapsed time 39 hrs 36 mins.			30.51	6377	206·40

This was in 1939 the fastest time for any aircraft or crew from Cape Town to England.
It reduced the existing solo record by 66 hours and 42 mins.
Not only were all Cape Town-and-return records broken but also for every stage en route and remain so in the solo classification to this day.
The England–Cape Town–England (12,754 miles) is still in 1980 an all-time record.

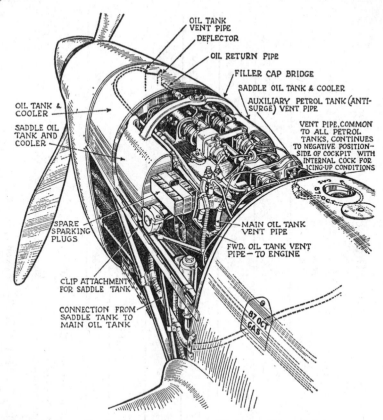

OIL TANK
VENT PIPE
DEFLECTOR

OIL RETURN PIPE

FILLER CAP BRIDGE

SADDLE OIL TANK & COOLER

AUXILIARY PETROL TANK (ANTI-SURGE) VENT PIPE

OIL TANK &
COOLER

SADDLE OIL
TANK AND
COOLER

VENT PIPE, COMMON
TO ALL PETROL
TANKS, CONTINUES
TO NEGATIVE POSITION—
SIDE OF COCKPIT WITH
INTERNAL COCK FOR
ICING-UP CONDITIONS

SPARE
SPARKING
PLUGS

MAIN OIL TANK
VENT PIPE

FWD. OIL TANK VENT
PIPE — TO ENGINE

CLIP ATTACHMENT
FOR SADDLE TANK

CONNECTION FROM
SADDLE TANK TO
MAIN OIL TANK

87 OCT
GAS

A view under the cowling to show the Essex Aero saddle tank, which carried some 4.5 gal. of Castrol well forward of the centre of gravity, and its safety filler-pipe; the store of spare K.L.G. plugs, and the vent for 87 gallons of Shell.

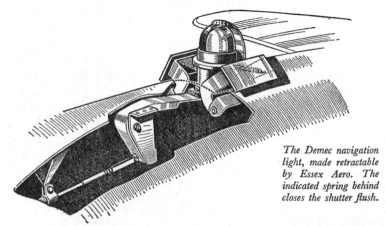

The Demec navigation light, made retractable by Essex Aero. The indicated spring behind closes the shutter flush.

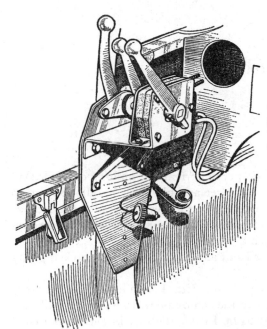

The throttle and twin economiser levers, one per carburettor. The tube below, with cork, is the ventilator.

Vacuum-feed sustenance. The flask is held in a fire-extinguisher clip behind the seat by rubber cords, and the contents drawn through the tube by suction.

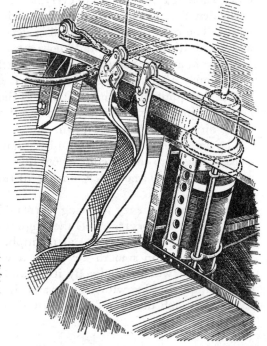

Reproduced from
The Aeroplane
by courtesy of
Aeroplane Monthly.

✳ 'What it feels like'

F. D. BRADBOOKE

ALEX HENSHAW'S personal feat of endurance and skill appears to me still more remarkable since he allowed me to fly the machine. However much one allows for youth, exuberance and perfect tone of eye and hand, his 80-hour ordeal within four days is almost incredible in such a vehicle.

Even darting about over Kent and Essex on a lovely day felt pretty dashing to me.

Getting in was something of a problem. I am a little bigger in every direction than Alex, to whom the aeroplane was very closely tailored. His parachute straps had to be let out slightly, but when battened down I found I could operate everything.

Incidentally that must have been not least of the problems to be solved. The pilot must be strapped in very tightly, as for aerobatics, and yet all the levers, taps and knobs must be within reach.

To avoid any necessity for fiddling with the constant-speed control immediately after the take-off Alex set it to about 2250 rpm. That would give quite an adequate take-off in the light condition, and was not too high for the motor provided one throttled back slightly when in the air to keep the boost down.

The aerodrome and the leeward sky have to be prospected when at right angles to the take-off before turning into wind. There is no real forward view and I defy anyone to turn and look behind once strapped in.

There is no tendency to swing when taking off. At 70 to 80 mph the undercarriage begins to feel the roughnesses and then the machine comes off and climbs very fast at 140 mph.

Merely to fly in smooth air this is a very normal and pleasant aeroplane. It will not quite fly itself, and the elevators are rather light. Pump-handling with a finger and thumb is quite enough alternately to stretch the shoulder straps and put a lot of G on the seat.

Neither is pleasant, because the seat is a thin piece of sorbo-rubber on the floor of the fuselage.

The rudder is light and lively, but is hardly needed, as directional steadiness is perfect. In fact the Mew Gull would fly feet-off very nicely if there were any other possible place to put one's feet. The ailerons are stiffer but very pleasant, and turns on the stick alone work perfectly.

All this I found at 6000 ft above the broken clouds where the air was perfectly smooth. Lower down there were some bumps, in and among the clouds, and although they were quite gentle they gave a taste of what rough-weather flying must be. They kick like mules.

So small an aeroplane must necessarily be tipped about in turbulent air, and after a mild few minutes of it I cannot imagine how Henshaw managed to endure five hours of continuous blind flying in tropical storms. All the same the general steadiness of the Mew Gull is much better than I expected. I apologise to Mr Edgar Percival.

Up in the smooth air again I found the stall to be about 76 mph with the flaps open. I admit I was in no mood for dropping into a spin so it may be slightly less. Without flaps the nose gets so high and outlook so poor that I did not pursue that line of research.

The top and cruising speeds are a mystery to all but Alex Henshaw. The needle goes a quadrant beyond the last mark on the dial, which is 200 mph, and a large position error is admitted. Alex has his private speed course.

In the course of cruising about over the countryside the Mew Gull overtook a cruising Henley and flying southwards came within sight of the sea in a few minutes. The stop-clock showed just 10 minutes from Marden to Gravesend; 270 mph, but there was a tail-wind.

Mr Henshaw must have perfected his own technique for picking up landmarks. The high speed and limited outlook must make Bradshawing almost impossible in anything but perfect weather. No one suggests that he stoops to such pseudo-navigation, but it is sometimes necessary at the end of a voyage.

The limited outlook is most trying when approaching to land. The flaps are put on at about 100 mph and the normal glide is 90 mph, at which there is no outlook forward. Alex lands 'right', which means looking out to the right, and his little window is on that side. I land 'left'.

The touch-down is about 80 mph, tail-skid first, and the first part of the run is fairly rough.

One feature of the Mew Gull which deserves special mention is its directional steadiness; nice in the air but invaluable on the ground. Any tendency to swing would be very unpleasant indeed, but it just does not exist.

All the same, how Alex Henshaw handled that machine in and out of inferior aerodromes, particularly in the dark, will always be a mystery to me. His blood was still all over everything, doubtless to remind me that Life is Real and Life is Earnest.—F.D.B.

The above account was published in *The Aeroplane* of 15 February 1939. F. D. Bradbooke was born in 1895 and became the finest aviator-journalist of his time. He joined the staff of *The Aeroplane* in 1930 and from then on flew everything that came his way in civil flying until the outbreak of World War II, racing in the King's Cup of 1935. He was one of the founder members of Air Transport Auxiliary and was killed with others of ATA in a Liberator crash in 1941. There is a splendid obituary in *The Aeroplane* of 22 August 1941.

NOTE FOR MODELLERS

A metal 1/48th-scale model kit of G-AEXF which makes up into any one of the three configurations shown between pages 295 and 299 is available from Lawrence Designs and Models, 194 Stoneleigh Avenue, Worcester Park, Surrey.

✷ Index